FINAL JUDGMENTS

Final Judgments: The Death Penalty in American Law and Culture explores the significance and meaning of finality in capital cases. Questions addressed in this book include: How are concerns about finality reflected in the motivations and behavior of participants in the death penalty system? How does an awareness of finality shape the experience of the death penalty for those condemned to die as well as for capital punishment's public audience? What is the meaning of time in capital cases? What are the relative weights accorded to finality versus the need for error correction in legal and political debates? And, how does the meaning of finality differ in capital and non-capital (LWOP) cases? Each chapter examines the idea of finality as a legal, political, and cultural fact. *Final Judgments* deploys various theories and perspectives to explore the death penalty's finality.

AUSTIN SARAT is William Nelson Cromwell Professor of Jurisprudence and Political Science and Associate Dean of the Faculty at Amherst College and Justice Hugo L. Black Senior Faculty Scholar at the University of Alabama School of Law. He is the author or editor of numerous books, including the recent *A World without Privacy* (2014), *Civility, Legality, and the Limits of Justice* (2014), and *Reimagining* To Kill a Mockingbird: *Family, Community, and the Possibility of Equal Justice under Law* (2013). His book *When Government Breaks the Law: Prosecuting the Bush Administration* was named one of the best books of 2010 by *The Huffington Post*.

Final Judgments

THE DEATH PENALTY IN AMERICAN LAW AND CULTURE

Edited by

AUSTIN SARAT

Amherst College

CAMBRIDGE
UNIVERSITY PRESS

CAMBRIDGE
UNIVERSITY PRESS

University Printing House, Cambridge CB2 8BS, United Kingdom

One Liberty Plaza, 20th Floor, New York, NY 10006, USA

477 Williamstown Road, Port Melbourne, VIC 3207, Australia

314-321, 3rd Floor, Plot 3, Splendor Forum, Jasola District Centre, New Delhi - 110025, India

79 Anson Road, #06-04/06, Singapore 079906

Cambridge University Press is part of the University of Cambridge.

It furthers the University's mission by disseminating knowledge in the pursuit of education, learning and research at the highest international levels of excellence.

www.cambridge.org
Information on this title: www.cambridge.org/9781316609019
DOI: 10.1017/9781316658765

First published 2017
First paperback edition 2018

A catalogue record for this publication is available from the British Library

Library of Congress Cataloging in Publication data
NAMES: Sarat, Austin, editor.
TITLE: Final judgments : the death penalty in American law and culture / edited by Austin Sarat, Amherst College.
DESCRIPTION: Cambridge, United Kingdom ; New York, NY, USA : Cambridge University Press, 2017. | "This volume is the product of a symposium held at the University of Alabama, School of Law on April 8, 2016." | Includes bibliographical references and index.
IDENTIFIERS: LCCN 2016050851 | ISBN 9781107155480 (Hardback : alk. paper)
SUBJECTS: LCSH: Capital punishment–United States–Congresses.
CLASSIFICATION: LCC KF9227.C2 F548 2017 | DDC 345.73/0773–dc23
LC record available at https://lccn.loc.gov/2016050851

ISBN 978-1-107-15548-0 Hardback
ISBN 978-1-316-60901-9 Paperback

To Ben, with love

Contents

Contributors

Jenny Carroll is Associate Professor of Law at the School of Law at the University of Alabama

Jennifer L. Culbert is Associate Professor of Political Science at the Johns Hopkins University

Daniel LaChance is Assistant Professor of History at Emory University

Corinna Barrett Lain is Professor of Law and Associate Dean for Faculty Development at the University of Richmond School of Law

Carissa Byrne Hessick is Anne Shea Ransdell and William Garland "Buck" Ransdell, Jr. Distinguished Professor of Law at the School of Law at the University of North Carolina

Daniel S. Medwed is Professor of Law and Faculty Director of Professional Development at Northeastern University School of Law

Austin Sarat is Associate Dean of the Faculty and William Nelson Cromwell Professor of Jurisprudence and Political Science at Amherst College and Justice Hugo L. Black Senior Scholar at the School of Law at the University of Alabama

Acknowledgments

This volume is the product of a symposium held at the University of Alabama School of Law on April 8, 2016. I want to thank the colleagues, students, and staff who helped make it such a successful event. I am grateful for the financial support of the University of Alabama Law School Foundation and for the able research assistance of John Malague.

Introduction

Starting to Think about Finality in Capital Cases

Austin Sarat

"We now recognize the important interest in finality served by state procedural rules and the significant harm to the States that results from the failure of federal courts to respect them."

Justice Sandra Day O'Connor, *Coleman v. Thompson*

"The continued pursuit of that punishment could bring years of appeals and prolong reliving the most painful day of our lives... We believe that now is the time to turn the page, end the anguish, and look toward a better future – for us, for Boston, and for the country.

Bill and Denise Richard, "To End the Anguish, Drop the Death Penalty."

Today America is in a period of national reconsideration of capital punishment.[1] Signs of change are all around us. Public support for the death penalty is at a 40-year low.[2] A Pew Research Center survey released recently found only 56 percent of the American public saying that they favor capital punishment. Pew noted that, since 2011, support for capital punishment has declined from 62 percent to its current level. In addition, over the last two decades, the number of people being sentenced to death in the United States declined by more than two-thirds.[3] In 1996, 315 people were given death sentences across all death penalty jurisdictions. In 2014, there were

---

[1]   Charles Ogletree and Austin Sarat, eds., *The Road to Abolition? The Future of Capital Punishment* (New York: NYU Press, 2009).

[2]   "Support for the death penalty in the United States dropped by two percentage points over the last year and opposition rose to its highest levels since before the Supreme Court declared existing death penalty statutes unconstitutional in 1972, according to the 2015 annual Gallup Poll on the death penalty. Gallup reports that 61% of Americans say they favor the death penalty, down from 63% last year and near the 40-year low of 60% support recorded in 2013." Death Penalty Information Center, www.deathpenaltyinfo.org/node/6275. Accessed June 1, 2106. See also Andrew Dugan, "Solid Majority Continue to Support Death Penalty," www.gallup.com/poll/186218/solid-majority-continue-support-death-penalty.aspx, Accessed June 1, 2016.

[3]   "Less Support for Death Penalty, Especially among Democrats," Pew Research Center, www.people-press.org/2015/04/16/less-support-for-death-penalty-especially-among-democrats/, Accessed June 1, 2016.

just 73 new death sentences.[4] This is the lowest number since the death penalty was reinstated by the United States Supreme Court in 1976.

America also is following through on fewer executions. In 1999, 98 people were executed in the United States. In 2014, that number was 35.[5] And, of the 19 states that do not have capital punishment on the books, six abolished it since 2007. Another 13 states that still retain capital punishment have either formal or de facto moratoria.

What explains these changes? Declines in violent crime and the widespread embrace of life imprisonment without parole surely have played a part. So, too, have growing concerns about the economic cost of the death penalty system, with its lengthy and very expensive legal process.[6]

However, among the most important factors explaining this change are growing concerns about the prospect of error in capital cases and the risk of executing the innocent. More and more, Americans believe that the administration of the death penalty is deeply flawed and broken in important respects. Many of those who fervently support capital punishment nonetheless worry about the risk of executing the innocent. The Pew survey found that 71 percent of the public think there is some risk of an innocent person being executed, while only 26 percent say that there are adequate safeguards in place to prevent that from happening.[7]

It is perhaps too obvious to say that the concerns about making an irreversible error in death cases are largely a function of one of the most genuinely distinctive features of the death penalty as a punishment, namely its finality. Indeed since the last part of the twentieth century the jurisprudence of capital punishment has been built around the idea that, because of its finality, "death is different." As former Supreme Court Justice Potter Stewart put it, "The penalty of death differs from all other forms of capital punishment, not in degree but in kind. It is unique in its total irrevocability. It is unique in its rejection of rehabilitation of the convict as a basic purpose of criminal justice. And it is unique, finally, in its absolute renunciation of all that is embodied in our concept of humanity."[8] As a result, those who are accused of capital crimes are entitled to enhanced legal and procedural protections.

In addition to its jurisprudential significance, debates about the significance of finality have animated death penalty politics for several decades. Abolitionists have put it at the center on a new abolitionist politics that shifts attention from the abstract morality associated with arguments against the death penalty. Opponents of capital

[4] Death Penalty Information Center, www.deathpenaltyinfo.org/death-penalty-sentencing-infor mation, Accessed June 1, 2016.
[5] Death Penalty Information Center, www.deathpenaltyinfo.org/executions-united-states, Accessed June 1, 2016.
[6] See Ogletree and Sarat, *The Road to Abolition*.
[7] "Less Support for Death Penalty, Especially among Democrats," Pew Research Center.
[8] *Furman* v. *Georgia*, 408 U.S. 238 (1972) (Stewart, J., concurring), https://en.wikisource.org/wiki/ Furman_v._Georgia/Concurrence_Stewart, Accessed June 1, 2016.

punishment take finality to be a reason in itself to oppose its use.[9] They cite the risk of executing the innocent as an especially telling reason to end the death penalty. They point to the fact that since 1976, 1,406 executions have been carried out in America and that in that same time period, 152 people who received death sentences were exonerated and freed from death row.[10] For every nine people we execute, one person is falsely convicted and sentenced to death.[11] For abolitionists this is an unacceptable error rate.

Death penalty supporters also focus on finality, taking it to be a kind of broken promise associated with capital punishment. As evidence they cite the fact that inmates in the United States typically spend over a decade awaiting execution and that. Some prisoners have been on death row for well over 20 years.[12] As Jamie Orenstein, a former Justice Department official, put it, "Society has a real and legitimate need for finality in answering the question of whether someone is guilty of a crime."[13] This sentiment was reflected in the Supreme Court's 1993 decision in *Herrera* v. *Collins*, which held that the threshold of proof in claims of actual innocence made in late stage habeas would "necessarily be extraordinarily high because of the very disruptive effect that entertaining such claims would have on the need for finality in capital cases."[14]

In the mid-1990s concerns about the absence of finality led to the enactment of the Anti-Terrorism and Effective Death Penalty Act, which sought to limit the reach of federal habeas corpus protections for those on death row, and the de-funding of Post-Conviction Defender Organizations, which provided legal representation for many of those contesting their death sentences. But neither of these actions have substantially sped up the path from death sentences to executions or resolved the dispute about finality.[15]

---

[9] See Michael Admirand and G. Ben Cohen, "The Fallibility of Finality," *Harvard Law and Policy Review* (February 5, 2016), http://harvardlpr.com/wp-content/uploads/2013/11/10.2_Admir and-and-Cohen_Glossip.pdf, Accessed June 1, 2016.

[10] See Amnesty International, "Death Penalty and Innocence," www.amnestyusa.org/our-work/issues/death-penalty/us-death-penalty-facts/death-penalty-and-innocence, Accessed June 1, 2016.

[11] Samuel Gross, Barbara O'Brien, and Edward Kennedy, "Rate of False Conviction of Criminal Defendants Who Are Sentenced to Death," *Proceedings of the National Academy of Sciences of the United States of America*, www.pnas.org/content/111/20/7230.full.pdf, Accessed June 1, 2016.

[12] See "Death Row Inmates, 1953–2013," http://deathpenalty.procon.org/view.resource.php?resourceID=004433, Accessed June 1, 2016.

[13] Adam Liptak, "Prosecutors See Limits to Doubt in Capital Cases," *The New York Times* (February 24, 2003), www.nytimes.com/2003/02/24/us/prosecutors-see-limits-to-doubt-in-cap ital-cases.html?pagewanted=all.

[14] *Herrera* v. *Collins*, 506 U.S 390 (1993), www.law.cornell.edu/supct/html/91-7328.ZO.html, Accessed June 1, 2016.

[15] See Lincoln Caplan, "The Destruction of Defendants' Rights," *The New Yorker*, June 21, 2015, www.newyorker.com/news/news-desk/the-destruction-of-defendants-rights, Accessed June 1, 2016.

As a subject of scholarship, there has been some empirical work on the length of time from death sentence to execution[16] and some normative scholarship weighing the competing values of finality and fairness.[17] But, other than Jennifer Culbert's 2007 book, *Dead Certainty: The Death Penalty and the Problem of Judgment*,[18] there is not a lot of scholarship on the significance and meaning of finality as a factor in the legal, political, or social world of the death penalty.

Final Judgments: The Death Penalty in American Law and Culture offers a book-length treatment of the significance and meaning of finality in capital cases. Questions addressed in this book will include: How are concerns about finality reflected in the motivations and behavior of participants in the death penalty system? How does an awareness of finality shape the experience of the death penalty for those condemned to die as well as for capital punishment's public audience? What is the meaning of time in capital cases? What are the relative weights accorded to finality versus the need for error correction in legal and political debates? And how does the meaning of finality differ in capital and non-capital (LWOP) cases? Each chapter takes up the challenge of understanding finality as a legal, political, and cultural fact. They deploy various theories and perspectives to explore the death penalty's finality.

This book's first chapter takes up the meaning of finality by comparing death sentences and non-capital sentences. It questions the well-known idea that "death is different" and asks whether the way we think about finality in non-capital cases has anything to teach us about finality where death is a punishment. This chapter then is a kind of argument with those who, like Justice Brennan in his *Furman* v. *Georgia* concurrence, claim that unlike a defendant who has been wrongfully convicted and sentenced to prison, the wrongfully convicted capital defendant cannot be released or compensated after his sentence has been carried out. "[T]he finality of death precludes relief."

Since the mid-1970s, Cynthia Hessick reminds us, the Supreme Court has embraced the idea that "death is different" and, as a result, placed many distinctive procedural and substantive limits on capital punishment. Because of the finality that seems to separate capital punishment from mere incarceration, the Court has required capital procedures to be more rigorous than others. As a result, what Hessick calls "judgment-based finality," the point at which the verdict and sentence are final and cannot be changed, often comes later in capital cases. Capital

[16] "Why So Many Death Row Inmates Will Die of Old Age," *The Economist*, February 3, 2014, www.economist.com/blogs/economist-explains/2014/02/economist-explains-0, Accessed June 1, 2016.

[17] Ron Tabak, "Finality without Fairness: Why We Are Moving toward Moratoria on Executions and the Potential Abolition of Capital Punishment," 33 *Connecticut Law Review* (2001), 733, http://heinonline.org/HOL/Page?handle=hein.journals/conlr33&div=27&g_sent=1&collection =journals#, Accessed June 1, 2016.

[18] Jennifer Culbert, *Dead Certainty: The Death Penalty and the Problem of Judgment* (Palo Alto, CA: Stanford University Press, 1998).

defendants have access to many more resources than do other defendants to have their verdicts reversed or sentences vacated. Of course, the most obvious difference in finality is, as Brennan noted, the inability for courts to revisit past cases once the condemned is executed. This is what Hessick labels "outcome-based finality."

Hessick calls our attention to a rare exception to death is different jurisprudence, namely the Supreme Court's decision in *Graham* v. *Florida*. In *Graham*, the Court held that a state could not impose life without parole (LWOP) on juveniles for non-homicide offences. *Graham* rejected LWOP for juveniles because of its "irrevoc-ability," which Hessick takes as a synonym for outcome-based finality. As with death sentences, children given LWOP are permanently denied an opportunity to rejoin society, based on a determination that they are completely incorrigible. The Court found that determination to be unreasonable.

Instead, states were required to offer juveniles post-sentencing assessments to determine whether or not they could be rehabilitated. This is a special case in which a distinctive procedural protection is made available outside the realm of capital punishment. Hessick's chapter questions whether "outcome-based finality" makes capital punishment really different from other forms of punishment. As she notes, a person released after being wrongfully convicted cannot have back the years spent in prison. She concludes by focusing on how non-capital finality concerns – specifically, the perceived need for post-sentencing assessment – could inform the ongoing debate over the death penalty in the United States.

In Chapter 2, Corinna Barrett Lain returns to the distinctive death is different jurisprudence that Hessick describes. Lain suggests that this jurisprudence has produced a series of "cascading effects," the most important of which has been the extraordinary length of time it takes to carry out death sentences. In her view, awareness of the irrevocability of an execution has had the effect of making the death penalty less final.

The commitment to super due process opened up the death penalty to lots of appellate and post-conviction litigation, much of which was initially handled by incompetent attorneys. This led to a 68 percent reversal rate for death sentences. Congress, unhappy with the high reversal rates, passed the Anti-Terrorism and Effective Death Penalty Act (AEDPA), which restricted federal habeas review. Yet, because the AEDPA was poorly drafted, it spawned new avenues of litigation. In addition, Congress attempted to defund death penalty resource centers, but the lawyers that worked there still found ways to involve themselves in litigation. All of this created a fleet of capital defense lawyers who were able to slow the death penalty process considerably.

Once the death penalty process was slowed down, exonerations of those on death row became more common. The increase in time to make the case for actual innocence, advances in DNA technology, and the newly specialized capital defense bar all helped make these exonerations much more common. Lain suggests that the modern death penalty has run into trouble because of both the risk of executing the innocent and the failure to execute the guilty. The increasing duration between crime and punishment diminishes the retributive satisfaction that the death penalty can offer. In the end, the finality of capital punishment is what makes it so rarely final, and so cumbersome, costly, and slow that it no longer makes sense. Following finality reveals the cumulative nature of its heavy burden and helps explain why capital punishment is collapsing under its own weight.

The observation that law is constrained, if not compromised, by its relation to a time-table, Jennifer Culbert contends in Chapter 3, is commonplace. But this limitation is never more salient than in discussions of criminal law and, in particular, the death penalty. Like Lain, Culbert notes that defendants sentenced to death, however, face more than just the possibility of execution. A long delay has been implicitly built into the sentence. Culbert argues that the time it now takes to die unsettles both the capital punishment and criminal justice systems, while scuttling the understanding of the "life" that is alternative to death.

In the mid-1970s the death penalty was reinstated on the grounds that it was accepted by the Framers and that it served the social principles of deterrence and retribution. The Framers, however, could not imagine waiting more than a decade to execute a criminal. Judge Cormac Carney has called the death sentence "life…with the remote possibility of death." Moreover, agreeing with Lain, Culbert suggests that delay complicates the effort to achieve retribution. Deterrence is minimized by the disconnection between crime and punishment. Moreover, life "in the shadow of death" cruelly gives defendants a substantial period of time to anticipate it.

Culbert goes on to question, given the time involved, how death is different at all. Recalling Hessick's discussion in Chapter 1, Culbert contends that it is only our "culture of death" that makes capital punishment seem so special. This obsession has led the Supreme Court to institute expensive protections to solve procedural problems that are no more present in the death penalty than anywhere else in criminal justice. The death penalty, which rarely brings about death, distracts the Court from addressing serious problems in other areas. Nor from the prisoner's perspective is death all that different. Extended time on death row renders the prisoner "socially dead," long before he is executed.

Culbert finishes by exploring the meaning of death in relation to our conception of time. Viewing time as "duration," an amorphous sliding entity rather than a series of moments, death, although still a final barrier, can be viewed as a change rather than an endpoint. Interacting with finitude gives people a chance to be transformed. This interaction that occurs in confronting an end happens slowly with death row prisoners, calling into question the concept of death as a definite, final moment.

Chapter 4 moves from examining the structural features of finality discussed in the first three chapters to examine the significance of finality in the work of one group of participants in the death penalty system, assistant prosecutors assigned to handle the post-conviction phase of capital cases. Daniel Medwed seeks to understand the zealous efforts of prosecutors assigned to post-conviction proceedings and why they often refuse to join defense requests for evidentiary hearings or new trials, even when they have misgivings about the conditions of the original conviction.

Medwed begins by exploring why prosecutors seek the death penalty in the first place. Although the Supreme Court has required legislatures to delineate which crimes are "death eligible," the criteria for eligibility are often amorphous, giving prosecutors considerable latitude. Their charging decisions are largely unregulated as is their decision making in appellate and post-conviction proceedings.

Despite frequent and well-documented problems in the capital trial process, prosecutors, Medwed argues, fight to uphold even the most problematic death sentences. He suggests that this behavior is inconsistent with the prosecutor's obligation to act as a "minister of justice." Professionally, many prosecutors assigned to argue cases fear the consequences of not doing so in a zealous way. Additionally, because conviction rates are used as measures of job performance, there is a false duality, where convictions are wins and reversals are losses. Funding and pay is often tied to conviction rates, creating pecuniary incentives to preserve the trial result. Political variables also come into play, especially with elected prosecutors.

Prosecutors are also driven to seek finality by psychological factors. These include confirmation bias and belief perseverance, status quo bias, top-down processing, self-righteous conformity effects, deference to those with more information, diffusion of responsibility, groupthink, cognitive dissonance, the determination to avoid sunk costs, and implicit racial bias.

Some see the search for finality as a necessary part of the criminal justice system, seemingly offering cost savings and factual accuracy. Trials are costly, evidence goes stale, and final verdicts reinforce procedural legitimacy. Yet, in Medwed's view, there is no value to finality in itself. As he sees it, justice would be served by reducing prosecutors' desire for finality.

Chapter 5, by Daniel LaChance, broadens the focus of inquiry to consider the way the finality of death itself gives capital punishment its cultural meaning. To do so he locates the contemporary situation of capital punishment within a broad cultural frame. Executions long have served as opportunities for ordinary Americans to contemplate what a good death – a different kind of "finality" – entails and what role pain and fortitude play in achieving it. Yet executions today have been transformed from expiating and cleansing acts of torture to empathy-inviting events. LaChance shows how portrayals of executions have reflected this pivot, with a greater focus on the inner world of the condemned and his approach to death.

Before the Enlightenment, execution was a means of restoring the legal, moral, and divine order. Executions gave evidence of the brutal force that "underlay divinely-given law." Since the enlightenment, observers of executions no longer have seen the condemned "solely as an expiator of sin or the vindication of the divine order, but as a discrete individual with an identity that could be valued and understood outside of a reference to God." The body, too, was considered more self-possessed, and could not be seen simply through the lens of sacrifice.

The growing recognition of the condemned person's inner world has given onlookers the chance to grapple with the finality of death and their own mortality. Diminishing the pain involved in execution allows for greater access to the consciousness of the person facing death. Since, according to Elaine Scarry, a torturous execution robs the victim of language, it denies observers the chance to "contemplate what a good death entailed and what role pain and fortitude played in achieving it." The empathetic selfhood described by LaChance is what Michelle Brown calls "dark empathy." The empathy-inviting narratives of execution are arenas of voyeurism, allowing the public to get closer to seeing the other side of the life's ultimate mystery.

Empathetic selfhood, LaChance claims, propelled the search for more humane methods of execution, which have in turn made the retributive quality of capital punishment much murkier. As the execution process has become more medical, moving from hanging (while standing) to electrocution (while sitting) to lethal injection (while lying down), the condemned has come to be seen as a patient or a specimen, not a moral agent facing the consequences of actions. Lethal injection amplifies the presence of the condemned person in his final moments. The condemned's last acts are volitional attempts to leave an impression on the world, preserving the image of dignity that allows for the expression of the meaning found in death. Yet the growing uncertainty of death sentences and the illegibility of executions in the contemporary period have made it increasingly difficult for Americans to imagine the moment of execution as "an opportunity for a final *self*-judgment: a moment of apprehending, evaluating, and making sense of one's life that makes the leaving of it bearable."

Taken together the work collected in this book shows the complexity of finality as it plays out in capital cases. The awareness of the finality of execution has helped make death sentences less final. This has consequences for our understanding of, and attachment to, capital punishment. Yet for those responsible for administering death as well as for those who seek to find meaning when death is imposed as a punishment, finality is both necessary to, and an unnerving part of, the capital punishment process.

1

Finality and the Capital/Non-Capital Punishment Divide

Carissa Byrne Hessick

The death penalty occupies a unique space in American criminal law. Because "death is different" from other modern punishments, death penalty sentences are subject to limitations that are not imposed on sentences that consist only of incarceration.[1] Those limitations are both substantive and procedural. Substantive limits on the death penalty include limitations on groups of offenders who can be subject to the penalty and limitations on crimes that may trigger the punishment. Procedural limits include requirements about how death penalty statutes may be written, how the capital punishment decision is made, and who makes the decision.

One reason the Justices have offered for their different treatment of capital and non-capital punishment is the finality that accompanies the death penalty. As Justice Brennan stated in his *Furman* v. *Georgia* concurrence: "Death is today an unusually severe punishment, unusual in its pain, in its finality, and in its enormity."[2] Unlike a defendant who has been wrongfully convicted and sentenced to prison, the wrongfully convicted capital defendant cannot be released or compensated after his sentence has been carried out. "[T]he finality of death precludes relief."[3] This "qualitative difference" between death and other punishments "requires a correspondingly greater degree of scrutiny of the capital sentencing determination," the Supreme Court tells us.[4]

Nevertheless, in a series of recent cases, the Supreme Court has begun to import some of its unique capital punishment jurisprudence into non-capital cases.

---

[1] *See generally* Note, "The Rhetoric of Difference and the Legitimacy of Capital Punishment," *Harvard Law Review* 114 (2001): 1559. The substantive and procedural protections for death penalty cases are so different than for non-death penalty cases, that one prominent scholar characterized the relevant doctrines as having originated with two different Courts – a Court of Life and a Court of Death. Rachel Barkow, "The Court of Life and Death," *Michigan Law Review* 107 (2009): 1145.

[2] *Furman* v. *Georgia*, 408 U.S. 238, 287 (1972) (Brennan, J., concurring).

[3] *Id.* at 290.

[4] *California* v. *Ramos*, 463 U.S. 992, 998–99 (1983).

Specifically, in cases involving life-without-parole sentences for juveniles, the Supreme Court has imposed limitations on non-capital sentences using a doctrinal approach that it had previously reserved for cases involving the death penalty. A major justification that the Court offered for extending its death penalty jurisprudence is the finality of life-without-parole sentences. The Court expressed concern that the life-without-parole regime offers juvenile offenders no chance to demonstrate rehabilitation. Because juveniles have not yet completed their cognitive and emotional development, a juvenile who engages in illegal behavior may be more likely to mature and avoid such behavior in the future than a non-juvenile who engages in similar behavior. Consequently, the Court decided that states must give juvenile defendants who committed a non-homicide crime "some meaningful opportunity to obtain release based on demonstrated maturity and rehabilitation."[5] Interestingly, the decision to forbid life-without-parole sentences for juveniles was not a decision that defendants must be released from prison. But rather, it was a decision that the states must give defendants the opportunity, after the imposition of the original sentence, to demonstrate that they should not remain in prison for the full duration of the sentence. In other words, in the non-capital context, the Supreme Court has held that the finality of a sentence may require a post-sentencing assessment – that is, the original sentence must be revisited at a later date.

Although defendants ordinarily receive more procedural protections in death penalty cases, the Supreme Court has not extended its post-sentencing assessment requirement to capital cases. The Supreme Court does not currently require states to revisit death sentences in a manner that allows for post-sentencing assessments of a defendant's conduct and character. Unless a capital defendant's conviction or sentence is reversed on appeal, she does not have an opportunity to argue that she should receive a different sentence after the initial sentence has been announced.

This chapter examines the role that concerns about finality have played in both capital cases and juvenile life-without-parole sentencing cases. It will describe how finality has shaped the Supreme Court's death penalty cases, as well as the role it has played in recent juvenile life-without-parole cases. It will then offer some tentative thoughts on whether the non-capital finality concerns – specifically, the perceived need for post-sentencing assessments – should be extended to capital defendants and how post-sentencing assessments might inform the ongoing debate over the death penalty abolition in the United States.

FINALITY AND THE DEATH PENALTY

When we speak about finality and the death penalty, the term finality may refer to two related but distinct concepts. Some discussions of finality revolve around how often a defendant ought to be permitted to challenge a judgment before it becomes

---

[5]   Ibid.

final and sentence is carried out. This judgment-based finality is a major concern in debates about habeas corpus and other collateral attacks by defendants facing the death penalty.[6]

Judgment-based finality is, of course, not limited to the death penalty. Any defendant who has been convicted may wish to repeatedly challenge that conviction. But concerns about the judgment-based finality of a sentence (as opposed to a conviction) are more often discussed in the death penalty context rather than the non-capital context.[7] There are several reasons that judgment-based finality is more often discussed in the death penalty context. As a practical matter, defendants who are sentenced to death have more time and resources to challenge their convictions and sentences than many non-capital defendants. A defendant who is sentenced to three years in prison, for example, may be released before doing much more than filing a direct appeal from conviction.[8] Defendants who are sentenced to death are far more likely to have attorneys volunteer to represent them,[9] and much of that *pro bono* assistance is offered only once the case is at the collateral review stage.[10] As a result, it is more likely that a capital defendant will litigate a claim in which judgment-based finality is a concern.

In addition, the question of expense associated with resentencing is more likely to arise in the capital context. As Sarah French Russell has noted, "[v]acating a death sentence raises resource issues not at play in noncapital cases – as capital sentencing proceedings are much more time consuming and must be held before

---

[6] *See, e.g.,* Paul M. Bator, "Finality in Criminal Law and Federal Habeas Corpus for State Prisoners," *Harvard Law Review* 76 (1963): 441. Meghan Ryan has described this type of finality as "the notion that a legal judgment – whether that be a judgment of conviction or of sentencing – should be considered the last word on a matter once the courts have completed direct review of the case, and the judgment then should not be revisited by a court at any future time." Meghan J. Ryan, "Finality and Rehabilitation," *Wake Forest Journal of Law and Policy* 4 (2014): 121, 123.

[7] Sarah French Russell, "Reluctance to Resentence: Courts, Congress, and Collateral Review," *North Carolina Law Review* 91 (2012): 79, 145 ("[O]utside the context of capital cases, the Court has rarely noted the different finality interests at stake with respect to sentencing claims as compared to conviction-based claims.").

[8] As Eve Brensike Primus has noted, "most defendants have served their full sentences by the time they reach the collateral review stage. Under the current system, only defendants sentenced to more than four or five years in prison have an incentive to challenge their convictions on collateral review, because it takes that long to exhaust the appellate process in many jurisdictions." Eve Brensike Primus, "Structural Reform in Criminal Defense: Relocating Ineffective Assistance of Counsel Claims," *Cornell Law Review* 92 (2007): 679, 693.

[9] *Cf.* James S. Liebman, "The Overproduction of Death," *Columbia Law Review* 100 (2000): 2030, 2131 (noting that the anti–death penalty bar has "deployed extensive defense resources into post-trial proceedings").

[10] Liebman, "The Overproduction of Death," 2074–75 (explaining that "most death penalty lawyers have targeted their efforts" at cases "in which all potentially available state relief has been denied and in which only United States Supreme Court review on certiorari or, thereafter, federal habeas review remains to be tried" and at cases "in which the Supreme Court has granted review").

a jury."[11] Conservation of resources is one of the major reasons not to revisit final judgments.[12] In light of the expense associated with a new capital sentencing, the parties and the courts may be more likely to discuss finality in capital cases.

What is more, as a rhetorical matter, judgment-based finality may be more contested in the context of the death penalty. Those who seek to push back against judgment-based finality are more likely to do so in the context of the death penalty. They argue that the state's interest in insulating judgments from review is outweighed by the defendant's interest in avoiding death.[13]

But finality concerns extend beyond judgment-based finality. Finality concerns in the death penalty context have also included the finality of the sentence itself, that is to say, the concern that death, once imposed, cannot be reversed. This outcome-based finality has played a significant role in the Supreme Court's death penalty cases. For example, in Justice Brennan's *Furman* concurrence, he noted "that the punishment of death must inevitably be inflicted upon innocent men" and that death "may have been unconstitutionally inflicted, yet the finality of death precludes relief."[14] Put differently, the finality of the death penalty prevents the criminal justice system from correcting errors in capital cases: legally deficient cases cannot be retried and factually innocent defendants cannot be released.

For Justice Brennan, the finality of the death penalty and the possibility that factually or legally innocent defendants might be executed was a reason to abolish the death penalty. In more recent years the Court has cited this finality concern, not as a reason to abolish the death penalty, but as a reason to impose various procedural limitations on capital punishment.[15] Those limitations are meant to ensure reliability. For example, in *Turner* v. *Murray*,[16] the Court cited "the complete finality of the death sentence" as a reason to take additional procedural precautions against juror racial bias in capital cases.[17] The Court explained that those precautions were necessary to ensure the reliability of the defendant's conviction – that is, to ensure that his conviction was based on his factual guilt rather than the racial bias of a juror.

The outcome-based finality of the death penalty has been cited not only as a reason to require reliability regarding the guilt of the defendant, but also to require reliability in the determination that an individual defendant deserves capital punishment. For example, in *Woodson* v. *North Carolina*,[18] which declared mandatory imposition of the death penalty unconstitutional, the Supreme Court stated:

---

[11] Russell, "Reluctance to Resentence," 146.
[12] Bator, "Finality in Criminal Law," 451.
[13] *See, e.g.*, Dean A. Strang, "The Rhetoric of Death," *Wisconsin Law Review* (1998): 841, 848.
[14] 408 U.S. 238, 290 (1972) (Brennan, J., concurring).
[15] *See, e.g.*, Jeffrey Levinson, Note, "Don't Let Sleeping Lawyers Lie: Raising the Standard for Effective Assistance of Counsel," *American Criminal Law Review* 38 (2001): 147, 161–62.
[16] *Turner* v. *Murray*, 476 U.S. 28 (1986).
[17] *Id.* at 35.
[18] *Woodson* v. *North Carolina*, 428 U.S. 280 (1976).

Death, in its finality, differs more from life imprisonment than a 100-year prison term differs from one of only a year or two. Because of that qualitative difference, there is a corresponding difference in the need for reliability in the determination that death is the appropriate punishment in a specific case.[19]

In other words, the *Woodson* Court said that the outcome-based finality of the death penalty required individualized sentencing in order to ensure that only those who truly deserve the penalty receive it. That the finality of the death penalty requires individualized sentencing is also reflected in *Gregg v. Georgia*, which states that "the reluctance of juries in many cases to impose the sentence may well reflect the humane feeling that this most irrevocable of sanctions should be reserved for a small number of extreme cases."[20]

FINALITY AND JUVENILE LIFE-WITHOUT-PAROLE SENTENCES

In *Graham v. Florida*, the Supreme Court held that imposing life-without-parole sentences on juveniles who committed non-homicide crimes violates the Eighth Amendment. *Graham* is a noteworthy decision for a number of reasons: It used the constitutional framework ordinarily reserved for the death penalty to invalidate a non-capital sentence;[21] it indicated that the subjective perceptions of an individual may be a relevant measure of punishment severity;[22] and it reaffirmed the desirability of parole, which had been abolished or curtailed in many jurisdictions.[23]

The *Graham* decision relied, in large part, on the "irrevocability" of life-without-parole sentences. The Court appears to have used the term irrevocability as a synonym for outcome-based finality. *Graham* described life without parole as "a forfeiture that is irrevocable" because the sentence does not contemplate an end to the punishment.[24] In that respect, according to the *Graham* Court, the outcome-based finality of life-without-parole sentence is comparable to the outcome-based finality of capital sentences. Specifically, the Court stated:

It is true that a death sentence is "unique in its severity and irrevocability," yet life without parole sentences share some characteristics with death sentences that are

---

[19] *Id.* at 305.

[20] *Gregg v. Georgia*, 428 U.S. 153, 182 (1976).

[21] As Justice Thomas said in his dissenting opinion: "'Death is different' no longer." *Graham v. Florida*, 408 U.S. 238, 102 (Thomas, J., dissenting). For more on this point, see Alison Siegler & Barry Sullivan, "'Death Is Different No Longer': Graham v. Florida and the Future of Eighth Amendment Challenges to Noncapital Sentences," *Supreme Court Review* (2010): 327.

[22] Alice Ristroph, "Hope, Imprisonment, and the Constitution," *Federal Sentencing Reporter* 23 (2010): 75, 77.

[23] As Rick Bierschbach notes "[p]arole fell from favor as sentencing discretion came under attack in the 1970s" yet *Graham* "put parole's significance to the constitutional regulation of punishment at center stage." Richard A. Bierschbach, "Proportionality and Parole," *University of Pennsylvania Law Review* 160 (2012): 1745, 1751, 1753.

[24] *Graham v. Florida*, 560 U.S. 48, 69–70.

shared by no other sentences. The State does not execute the offender sentenced to life without parole, but the sentence alters the offender's life by a forfeiture that is irrevocable. It deprives the convict of the most basic liberties without giving hope of restoration, except perhaps by executive clemency – the remote possibility of which does not mitigate the harshness of the sentence.[25]

The Court further bolstered its comparison of the outcome-based finality of life without-parole sentences to the finality of capital sentences by direct reference to *Roper* v. *Simmons*.[26] *Roper* held that the death penalty was an unconstitutional punishment for juvenile offenders.

> The juvenile should not be deprived of the opportunity to achieve maturity of judgment and self-recognition of human worth and potential. In *Roper*, that deprivation resulted from an execution that brought life to its end. Here, though by a different dynamic, the same concerns apply. Life in prison without the possibility of parole gives no chance for fulfillment outside prison walls, no chance for reconciliation with society, no hope.[27]

Just as outcome-based finality resulted in concerns about reliability in the death penalty context, so too did reliability concerns play a significant role in the *Graham* opinion. As noted earlier, the Court has cited the finality of the death penalty as a reason to require procedures that ensure reliability in capital cases. In the context of the death penalty, reliability concerns include both concerns about a defendant's legal or factual innocence and concerns that only the truly deserving receive the punishment. In *Graham*, the concern about reliability was framed as a concern about the accuracy of relative sentencing judgments. In particular, the Court focused on whether a judge would be able to "make a judgment that a defendant is incorrigible" despite the fact that the "characteristics of juveniles make that judgment questionable."[28] And the Court also noted that juveniles "are less likely than adults to work effectively with their lawyers to aid in their defense." As a result, it will be more difficult for counsel to represent a juvenile, which increases the risk that "a judge or jury will erroneously conclude that a particular juvenile is sufficiently culpable to deserve life without parole for a nonhomicide."[29] Put simply, the Court believed that judges are not able to make a reliable determination at the initial sentencing about whether a juvenile defendant is likely to rehabilitate.

Importantly, the *Graham* Court relied on outcome-based finality as a reason to disregard judgment-based finality. That is to say, because a sentence of life without parole offers a defendant no chance to rehabilitate and rejoin society, the Court

---

[25] *Id.* at 69–70 (quoting *Gregg* v. *Georgia*, 428 U.S. 153, 187 [1976] [joint opinion of Stewart, Powell, and Stevens, JJ.]).

[26] 543 U.S. 551 (2005).

[27] 560 U.S. at 79.

[28] *Id.* at 72–73.

[29] *Id.* at 78–79.

insisted that the judgment be revisited from time to time. Sacrificing judgment-based finality because of outcome-based finality is remarkable because, as Meghan Ryan has explained, it breaks with previous notions of the role that finality plays in rehabilitation.

> Finality has historically been thought to promote offender rehabilitation. It allows an offender the chance to set aside his battle with the criminal justice system and instead focus inward, on his own potential for change. Paradoxically, though, this movement away from finality is now considered to *further* rehabilitative goals. Indeed, rehabilitation is now commonly thought to be at complete odds with the doctrine of finality: If there is no hope that a court will revisit an offender's conviction or sentence, ... what incentive does the offender have to work on rehabilitating himself?[30]

Graham also diverged from previous cases in which the Supreme Court Justices suggested that life without parole was not incompatible with rehabilitation. In their *Furman* v. *Georgia* opinions, Justices Stewart and Marshall both stated that the death penalty was unique in its rejection of rehabilitation as a basic purpose of punishment.[31] Justice Marshall went so far as to state that the death penalty "makes rehabilitation impossible" but "life imprisonment does not."[32]

In short, over time, the Court has made inconsistent claims about the effect of judgment-based finality on the rehabilitation prospects of offenders. *Graham* claims that rehabilitation is more likely if the defendant believes her sentence might be changed; previous opinions assumed that rehabilitation would occur only if the sentence was fixed. And *Graham* assumes that life without parole makes rehabilitation impossible, while previous opinions said the opposite.

We should not be surprised that the Court has taken inconsistent views on what will further rehabilitation. What is likely to rehabilitate an offender is an empirical question. But it has hardly been treated as such in the criminal justice system. In the heyday of rehabilitation – that is, the period in which rehabilitation was the driving force in the United States criminal justice system – sentencing decisions depended almost entirely on the personal judgments of judges (for front-end sentencing decisions) and parole boards (for back-end sentencing decisions).[33] While parole board officials may have had the relevant backgrounds to make informed clinical judgments,[34] judges almost certainly did not. Nonetheless, judges routinely based

---

[30] Ryan, "Finality and Rehabilitation," 144.

[31] *See* 408 U.S. 238, 306 (1972) (opinion of Stewart, J.); *id.* at 346 (opinion of Marshall, J.).

[32] *Id.* at 346 (opinion of Marshall, J.).

[33] *See* Carissa Byrne Hessick & Douglas A. Berman, "A Theory of Mitigation," *Boston University Law Review* 96 (2016): 161, 167–69.

[34] As Stefan Bing has documented, statutory requirements for parole board membership differs significantly across jurisdictions. Some jurisdictions have requirements that arguably enhance the ability to make clinical judgments. Stefan J. Bing, "Reconsidering State Parole Board Membership Requirements in Light of Model Penal Code Sentencing Revisions," *Kentucky Law Journal* 100 (2012): 871.

their sentencing decisions on factors that they believed indicated a defendant's likelihood of rehabilitation. For example, judges routinely imposed harsher sentences on defendants who displayed a lack of remorse. Yet there is no empirical support for the conclusion that remorseful defendants are less likely to reoffend.[35] Judges simply relied on their own intuition about a defendant's rehabilitative prospects. That same appeal to intuition (rather than empirical support) appears to be the cause for the inconsistent approach to finality's role in rehabilitation.[36]

This inconsistency about finality's effect on rehabilitation is not a minor point. The *Graham* opinion relies heavily on rehabilitation. That juveniles are more susceptible to rehabilitation, that their propensity for rehabilitation cannot be judged at the time of sentencing, and that incentives are necessary for a defendant to undertake rehabilitation all played significant roles in the logic and analysis of the Supreme Court's decision to require the state to afford "a meaningful opportunity for release." And this remedy – affording a defendant an opportunity for release – is particularly noteworthy.

But before turning to the remarkable remedy that the *Graham* Court adopted, it is worth noting that there are reasons to doubt the *Graham* Court's statement that, like death and unlike other sentences, life without parole "alters the offender's life by a forfeiture that is irrevocable."[37] (Previous opinions had claimed that irrevocability was unique to the death penalty.[38]) As others have astutely observed, irrevocability does not actually distinguish life without parole (or death) from other sentences. "There is no way to revoke any portion of a sentence, be it a death sentence or a term of years, once it has already been served."[39] The wrongfully convicted person who is subsequently released following exoneration is hardly restored to her previous state. The exonerated prisoner who is released may be entitled to money damages for the time that she was wrongfully incarcerated. But money damages cannot restore to her the time she spent in prison, just as money paid to a family in a wrongful death

---

[35] Lack of remorse is a traditional sentencing factor thought to indicate that a defendant is unlikely to rehabilitate. *See* Carissa Byrne Hessick & F. Andrew Hessick, "Recognizing Constitutional Rights at Sentencing," *California Law Review* 99 (2011): 47, 67–69. But the social science evidence on offending does not appear to bear out the assumption that remorseful defendants are less likely to reoffend than unremorseful ones. *See* J. C. Oleson, "Risk in Sentencing: Constitutionally Suspect Variables and Evidence-Based Sentencing," *SMU Law Review* 64 (2011): 1329 (providing a summary of those variables that predict recidivism; the summary does not include remorse).

[36] Of course, the courts' reliance on intuition, rather than data, to decide empirical questions is hardly limited to the sentencing context. *See, e.g.,* Shima Baradaran, "Rebalancing the Fourth Amendment," *Georgetown Law Journal* 102 (2013): 1 (discussing this issue in the context of the Fourth Amendment).

[37] 560 U.S. 48, 69 (2010).

[38] *E.g., Coleman v. Balkcom,* 451 U.S. 949, 953 (1981) ("[D]eath cases are indeed different in kind from all other litigation. The penalty, once imposed, is irrevocable."); *Woodson v. North Carolina,* 428 U.S. 280, 323 (1976) ("One of the principal reasons why death is different is because it is irreversible; an executed defendant cannot be brought back to life.").

[39] Note, "The Rhetoric of Difference and the Legitimacy of Capital Punishment," 1621.

suit does not restore to them their loved one. That is why no one suggests that money damages paid to the family of a wrongfully executed capital defendant are a sufficient remedy for the erroneous imposition of the death penalty.[40]

Of course, an individual who has been executed cannot be released from prison if she is later exonerated. So long as a capital defendant is awaiting execution, she – like any other defendant – could be released if she were exonerated. But once the death sentence has been carried out, release is no longer an option. This is an obvious difference between capital punishment and non-capital punishment. But it is hard to explain what, precisely, the difference is. Is it the ability to avoid the full amount of punishment imposed? Because that does not necessarily distinguish capital sentences from non-capital sentences. A wrongfully convicted defendant who serves her full sentence and who is released before she is exonerated seems, in some respects, to resemble the capital defendant who is exonerated after her execution is carried out. Neither defendant was able to prevent the state from carrying out the full extent of her sentence.

Putting this in remedial terms may help to drive the point home: Once their sentences have been carried out, neither the wrongfully incarcerated nor the wrongfully executed can obtain equitable relief – that is, "relief that specifically avoids threatened harm."[41] Both can obtain only legal relief, that is, money damages.

Nonetheless, intuition tells us that there is a significant difference between the wrongfully incarcerated and the wrongfully executed. Unfortunately, the Supreme Court has failed to adequately explain what that difference is. Perhaps the most important difference between the death penalty, life without parole, and other sentences is the severity of punishment. Capital punishment is widely believed to be the most severe sentence currently imposed in the United States. Life without parole is the second most severe.[42] And severity of consequences often play a determinative role in the procedural protections that an individual receives. This is true both in the criminal justice system[43] and in the legal system more generally.[44]

In any event, neither irrevocability nor the opportunity to prevent the full extent of one's punishment appears to be the relevant point of distinction. What is more, neither of those differences distinguishes between defendants sentenced to life

---

[40] As Alice Ristroph has put this point: "We cannot revive the dead, but nor can we turn back time." Ristroph, "Hope, Imprisonment, and the Constitution," 75.

[41] Douglas Laycock, "The Death of the Irreparable Injury Rule," *Harvard Law Review* 103 (1990): 687, 689.

[42] *See* 560 U.S. at 69 (quoting *Harmelin v. Michigan*, 501 U.S. 957, 1001 (1991) (opinion of Kennedy, J.).

[43] *See, e.g., Scott v. Illinois*, 440 U.S. 367 (1979) (holding that whether a defendant is subjected to actual imprisonment determines whether she is entitled to the appointment of counsel under the Sixth Amendment).

[44] *See, e.g., Mathews v. Eldridge*, 424 U.S. 319, 341 (1976) (identifying "the degree of potential deprivation that may be created by a particular decision" as one of three considerations in determining the proper amount of due process).

without parole and defendants sentenced to other terms of imprisonment. Indeed, a defendants serving a life sentence is *more* likely to prevent the state from carrying out the full extent of punishment if she is exonerated – after all, there is no risk that she will either be executed or released prior to her exoneration because her sentence requires her to spend her natural life in prison.

Whatever one's view of the broad questions surrounding irrevocability, the remedy for the Eighth Amendment violation that the *Graham* Court adopted does not appear to necessarily solve the problem. The Court stated that a life-without-parole sentence deprived a defendant of the "chance for reconciliation with society."[45] Yet the Court did not hold that juvenile offenders need ever actually be released from prison. According to the Court, the Constitution does not require release; some juveniles may be imprisoned for their entire lives. So long as a defendant is given "some meaningful opportunity to obtain release based on demonstrated maturity and rehabilitation" at some point in time after the initial sentencing, the "Eighth Amendment does not foreclose the possibility that persons convicted of nonhomicide crimes committed before adulthood will remain behind bars for life."[46]

Because the Court did not forbid juveniles from *serving* life sentences, *Graham* may be best understood as a procedural ruling rather than a substantive ruling.[47] It does not forbid life sentences. It simply forbids states "from making the judgment at the outset that those offenders never will be fit to reenter society."[48] In other words, it is a decision about the timing of sentencing decisions.

As a procedural decision, *Graham* leaves much to be desired. The Court tells us that defendants must be given "a meaningful opportunity to obtain release," but it does not tell us much about what that opportunity must look like. Instead, the Court left it to the states "in the first instance, to explore the means and mechanisms for compliance."[49] Conceivably, states could comply with the decision by sentencing defendants only to life *with* parole. If states respond to *Graham* by imposing life-*with*-parole sentences on juveniles, then they need not address the uncertainty left by the *Graham* remedy. Parole systems provide both procedural structure and substantive considerations for release decisions. For example, a typical parole system specifies when a defendant becomes eligible for parole, the notice to which a defendant is entitled, and an opportunity for the defendant to be heard regarding whether she ought to be released.[50] A defendant who is denied release on parole receives a new hearing at a future date, and relevant statutes or regulations ensure

---

[45] 560 U.S. at 79.
[46] *Id.* at 75.
[47] Rick Bierschbach articulated this important insight in his thoughtful article on *Graham*. Bierschbach, "Proportionality and Parole."
[48] 560 U.S. at 75.
[49] *Id.*
[50] *See, e.g.,* California Penal Code §3041.5.

that parole hearings occur at regular intervals for prison inmates.[51] The parole system provides not only procedures for early release, but also the substantive considerations for those decisions. Parole boards ordinarily enjoy broad discretion regarding whether to release an inmate on parole. But statutes, regulations, and board practice indicate that those decisions ought to be based on particular considerations, such as the defendant's rehabilitative prospects, the likelihood of a successful reentry into society, and the crime the defendant committed.[52]

But the *Graham* decision did not direct states to impose life-with-parole sentences on juvenile defendants. Instead, it required only that the decision to keep a juvenile offender in prison for her entire life not be made "at the outset"[53] – that is, at the initial sentencing hearing. Because a number of states and the federal government have abolished parole or limited its application through the adoption of truth in sentencing laws,[54] those states may look to address these juvenile life-without-parole sentences without creating a new parole bureaucracy. Because *Graham* says so little about what is required, a state could arguably comply with *Graham* simply by reviewing a defendant's sentence only once, such as after a certain period of time has elapsed or when the defendant reaches a particular age. And those states could place significant restrictions on the substantive considerations that could result in an early release. It is implicit in *Graham* that the defendant be afforded the opportunity to show that she has rehabilitated herself since the initial sentencing. But it is not clear that the defendant be permitted to raise any other arguments in favor of early release.

In sum, while some states may ultimately provide more, the *Graham* opinion appears to require that a juvenile defendant must receive at least one opportunity to have her sentence reassessed after she reaches the age of eighteen. And that assessment must allow the defendant to argue for early release based on post-sentencing rehabilitation.

REVISITING SENTENCES OUTSIDE THE JUVENILE LIFE-WITHOUT-PAROLE CONTEXT

As noted earlier, a defendant facing a capital sentence ordinarily enjoys more substantive and procedural protections than a defendant facing a non-capital sentence. Since *Graham*, however, some non-capital defendants have enjoyed a

---

[51] To be clear, parole means different things in different jurisdictions. In some jurisdictions, prisoners are automatically released on parole after having served a certain fraction of their sentences. The term parole as used in *Graham*, as ordinarily used in the academic literature, and as I use it in this chapter, refers to discretionary parole releases – namely when a prisoner may be released upon the decision of the parole board, and the board retains discretion over that decision. *See* John F. Pfaff, *Sentencing Law and Policy* 771 n.12. (Foundation Press, 2016).

[52] *See, e.g.,* Georgia Code Annotated § 42-9-40(a).

[53] *Graham,* 560 U.S. at 75.

[54] *See* John F. Pfaff, "The Continuing Vitality of Structured Sentencing Following *Blakely*: The Effectiveness of Voluntary Guidelines," *UCLA Law Review* 54 (2006): 235, 245–46.

protection not afforded to capital defendants. Specifically, juveniles facing life sentences for non-homicide crimes must be given "some meaningful opportunity to obtain release based on demonstrated maturity and rehabilitation."[55] In other words, it is not enough for an assessment to be made at sentencing that the juvenile defendant ought to receive a sentence of life in prison; that initial determination must be revisited at a later date to determine whether it remains an appropriate sentence.

Although the *Graham* decision is explicitly limited to juveniles serving life-without-parole sentences for non-homicide crimes, the idea that original sentencing determinations ought to be revisited has appeared in other non-capital contexts.[56] Most visibly, the American Law Institute (ALI) has recommended the adoption of post-sentencing assessments for non-capital offenders – a recommendation that it calls "second-look sentencing."[57] Second-look sentencing provides for the routine reconsideration of sentences after a substantial period of incarceration for those inmates who are serving lengthy prison sentences. Although the ALI did not recommend specific legislation for jurisdictions to adopt,[58] it did indicate that assessments should occur after a defendant has served fifteen years in prison, that defendants should be permitted to apply for sentence modification at regular intervals, and that sentencing modification can occur for any reason that would have been an appropriate consideration at an initial sentencing.

Given the new-found enthusiasm for revisiting sentencing determinations in the non-capital context, one might ask whether post-sentencing assessments ought to be available to capital defendants as well. After all, we ordinarily accord capital defendants more procedural protections than non-capital defendants, not fewer. There are reasons both for and against extending post-sentencing assessments to capital defendants. The following paragraphs articulate some of those reasons.

Before turning to those reasons, however, it is worth noting that, as a practical matter, a high percentage of capital defendants already receive post-sentencing assessments. That is not because there is a formal, legal mechanism for ensuring that a capital sentence is revisited. It is instead because most capital defendants have their convictions or sentences reversed on appeal. One study found that more than two-thirds of capital judgments are reversed either on direct appeal, during state

[55] 560 U.S. 48, 74 (2010)
[56] *See, e.g.*, Cecelia Klingele, "Changing the Sentence without Hiding the Truth: Judicial Sentence Modification as a Promising Method of Early Release," *William & Mary Law Review* 52 (2010): 465.
[57] Model Penal Code: Sentencing § 305.6 (Tentative Draft No. 2, 2011).
[58] "The Institute does not recommend a specific legislative scheme for carrying out the sentence-modification authority recommended in this provision, nor is the provision drafted in the form of model legislation. Instead, the language below sets out principles that a legislature should seek to effectuate through enactment of such a provision." *Id.*

collateral review, or in federal habeas corpus proceedings.[59] If the state elects to retry such a defendant, then the sentencing stage of the retrial may allow the defendant to introduce evidence of rehabilitation that occurred after the original sentencing. On average, the reversal of capital judgments occurs five to eleven years after the initial trial,[60] which is not dissimilar to the time period associated with parole in some jurisdictions.[61]

But there are significant differences between the resentencing that capital defendants receive following a reversal and the "meaningful opportunity to obtain release" contemplated by *Graham*. For one thing, not all capital defendants have their convictions or sentences reversed, and so not all capital defendants receive resentencing. For another, the sentencing determination at a resentencing following reversal is still likely to place primary importance on the defendant's crime, rather than her "demonstrated maturity and rehabilitation" following the offense. That is because any resentencing following reversal will use the same enumerated aggravating and mitigating factors from the relevant capital sentencing statute. Defense counsel is, of course, free to introduce evidence of how the capital defendant has matured and otherwise rehabilitated herself since her initial sentencing. But counsel may not wish to draw attention to the fact that the defendant had previously been convicted out of fear that it might prejudice the jury against the defendant.

REASONS TO EXTEND POST-SENTENCING ASSESSMENTS TO CAPITAL SENTENCES

One reason to extend post-sentencing assessments to capital defendants is that they may encourage defendants to rehabilitate and mature. Without the possibility of post-sentencing assessments, capital defendants have no hope, making "good behavior and character improvement immaterial."[62] Just as the "denial of hope" was a reason to require "some meaningful opportunity to obtain release" for the juvenile defendants in *Graham*,[63] so too could post-sentencing assessments instill hope in capital offenders, giving them a reason to work toward self-improvement.

[59] Liebman, "The Overproduction of Death," 2053–54 (reporting the results of a study of capital cases from 1973–1995, which found that state and federal courts reversed 68 percent "of the capital judgments that were fully reviewed").

[60] Liebman, "The Overproduction of Death," 2019 (citing data from James S. Liebman et al., *A Broken System: Error Rates in Capital Cases, 1973–1995* [Columbia University 2000]).

[61] To be clear, the five to eleven year period is not inconsistent with the time periods associated with parole hearings following a denial. E.g., California Penal Code §3041.5(3) (requiring that parole hearings be scheduled at three, five, seven, ten, or fifteen year intervals); Nevada Revised Statutes §213.142 (requiring subsequent parole hearings to be scheduled within three or five years). The date when a defendant is *initially* eligible for parole is ordinarily linked to the length of her initial sentence. E.g., Nevada Revised Statutes §213.120; Tennessee Code Annotated §40-28-115.

[62] 560 U.S. 48, 70 (2010).

[63] *Id.*

Another reason to extend post-sentencing assessments to capital defendants is that they are consistent with the Supreme Court's broadly inclusive approach to consideration of mitigating evidence at sentencing. In *Lockett v. Ohio*, for example, the Court said that a sentencer must "not be precluded from considering, as a mitigating factor, any aspect of the defendant's character or record and any of the circumstances of the offense that the defendant proffers as a basis for a sentence less than death."[64] Some have suggested that this language requires a defendant be permitted to introduce any evidence that might possibly be considered mitigating[65] (though there is language from the Court suggesting otherwise[66]). In any event, it is clear that evidence of a defendant's post-sentencing rehabilitation falls within the holding from *Lockett*. It is evidence of a defendant's "character." Indeed, the Supreme Court's recent non-capital decision, *Pepper v. United States*, confirms that a defendant's post-sentencing rehabilitation constitutes "information concerning the background, character and conduct of the defendant" that is appropriately considered at sentencing.[67]

Of course, post-sentencing assessments are not required by *Lockett*. *Lockett* involved limitations on mitigating evidence at the initial sentencing. The very logic of post-sentencing assessments is that some potentially mitigating evidence does not *exist* at the time of the initial sentencing. Adopting post-sentencing assessments in capital cases would not simply prevent the state from limiting the mitigating evidence a defendant may introduce; it would require the state to create new sentencing procedures that occur after the initial sentencing.

A third reason to extend post-sentencing assessments to capital defendants is that they may help to ensure that the death penalty is reserved for only the worst

---

[64] *Lockett* v. *Ohio*, 438 U.S. 586, 604 (1978) (emphasis omitted).

[65] E.g., Carol S. Steiker & Jordan M. Steiker, "Let God Sort Them Out? Refining the Individualization Requirement in Capital Sentencing," *Yale Law Journal* 102 (1992): 835, 839, 844 (stating that the Court appears to have concluded "that individualized sentencing necessarily entails uncircumscribed consideration of mitigation evidence" and that the Court "regards consideration of *all* aspects of an individual as constitutionally indispensable") (emphasis in original).

[66] See *Franklin* v. *Lynaugh*, 487 U.S. 164, 188 (1988) (O'Connor, J., concurring in the judgment) ("'[R]esidual doubt' about guilt is not a mitigating circumstance. We have defined mitigating circumstances as facts about the defendant's character or background, or the circumstances of the particular offense, that may call for a penalty less than death. 'Residual doubt' is not a fact about the defendant or the circumstances of the crime. It is instead a lingering uncertainty about facts, a state of mind that exists somewhere between 'beyond a reasonable doubt' and 'absolute certainty.'") (internal citations omitted); *Lockett*, 438 U.S. 586, 605 n.12 ("Nothing in this opinion limits the traditional authority of a court to exclude, as irrelevant, evidence not bearing on the defendant's character, prior record, or the circumstances of his offense."); *see also Skipper* v. *South Carolina*, 476 U.S. 1, 11–14 (1986) (Powell, J., concurring).

[67] *Pepper* v. *United States*, 562 U.S. 476, 490–91 (2011) (concluding that a "categorical bar on the consideration of postsentencing rehabilitation evidence would directly contravene" 18 U.S.C. §3661, which directs that "No limitation shall be placed on the information concerning the background, character, and conduct of a person convicted of an offense which a court of the United States may receive and consider for the purpose of imposing an appropriate sentence.").

offenders.[68] Post-sentencing assessments help ensure this in at least two ways. First, those assessments allow a sentencing decision to be made at a point in time when cooler heads may prevail. Sometimes the publicity and anger surrounding a particular murder will make a defendant's crime appear more heinous and deserving of punishment. In those cases, a sentencer will be able to dispassionately assess the seriousness of a defendant's crime only after the passage of time. One wonders, for example, if Dzhokhar Tsarnaev would have been sentenced to death if more time had passed between the bombing at the Boston Marathon and the decision to impose capital punishment.

Post-sentencing assessments also help to distinguish between offenders because the passage of time gives us more information about a defendant as a person. As Meghan Ryan has explained: "One might argue that revisiting an offender's sentence can lead to more just punishment because the government, at this later point in time, has greater information about whether the offender has been working toward rehabilitation and whether he has been successful in that respect."[69] Although the *Graham* Court suggested that the rehabilitative prospects of juvenile defendants were especially unclear at the time of initial sentencing, it seems equally improbable that we are able to predict accurately the personal development of offenders in their twenties. There is little doubt that people continue to change and grow as they leave adolescence and enter adulthood. But equally significant changes occur as individuals approach middle age. Indeed, the data on lifetime offending patterns suggest that many persistent offenders "age out" of their criminal behavior as they enter middle age.[70]

Finally, depending on what states elect to include as appropriate considerations, post-sentencing assessments could help ensure that capital punishment is not imposed on factually innocent defendants. States that did not restrict a defendant's post-sentencing assessment to questions of rehabilitation would doubtlessly modify a capital sentence if presented with credible evidence of innocence. Of course, states may elect to limit post-sentencing assessments to questions of a defendant's post-sentencing rehabilitation. But one suspects that a credible claim of factual innocence might affect rehabilitation decisions – after all, a defendant who did not actually commit a murder need not be rehabilitated.

---

[68] "Death Penalty statutes and sentencing procedures must ensure that juries give death sentences only to 'the worst of the worst' – these defendants who deserve this particularly severe punishment." Note, "The Rhetoric of Difference and the Legitimacy of Capital Punishment," 1604–05.

[69] Ryan, "Finality and Rehabilitation," 144–45.

[70] A study by the United States Sentencing Commission found that the recidivism rate for offenders under the age of 21 was 35.5 percent, while the recidivism rate for offenders over 50 was only 9.5 percent. These were, respectively, the highest and lowest recidivism across age groups. Recidivism rates for offenders age 26–35 was approximately 24 percent. *U.S. Sentencing Commission, Measuring Recidivism: The Criminal History Computation of the Federal Guidelines* 28 ex.9 (2004), www.ussc.gov/sites/default/files/pdf/research-and-publications/research-publications/2004/200405_Recidivism_Criminal_History.pdf.

REASONS AGAINST EXTENDING POST-SENTENCING
ASSESSMENTS TO CAPITAL SENTENCES

One reason not to adopt post-sentencing assessments for capital defendants is that the procedure may lessen the responsibility that the jury feels when imposing the initial sentence. The Supreme Court has repeatedly stated how important it is that those imposing the death sentence "view their task as the serious one of determining whether a specific human being should die at the hands of the State."[71] If jurors believe that the ultimate sentencing responsibility lies elsewhere – particularly if they believe that it lies with one or more judges – then they may fail to internalize the "awesome responsibility" that they are ending another person's life. And if they do not internalize that responsibility, then they may be more likely to return a death sentence than if they had. Jurors likely perceive themselves as far less familiar with the law generally, and capital punishment in particular, than judges. And so they may rely on judges in post-sentencing assessments to correct any errors that they may have committed. And if the jurors happen to know that the sentence they impose is reviewable only if it is death, then "in a case in which the jury is divided on the proper sentence," the prospect of a post-sentencing assessment "could effectively be used as an argument for why those jurors who are reluctant to invoke the death sentence should nevertheless give in."[72] After all, post-sentencing assessments would allow the possibility of a death sentence being reduced to life, but they would not permit a life sentence to be increased to death.

Relatedly, post-sentencing assessments might confuse the jury about their role in the capital process. They might not simply *feel* less responsibility; they also might *misunderstand* the scope of their responsibility. For example, capital jurors might mistakenly believe that decisions about a defendant's prospects for rehabilitation are meant to be decided at post-sentencing assessments rather than at the initial sentencing. This misunderstanding might persist no matter how clear the instructions that a jury receives. Indeed, even without post-sentencing assessments there appears to be significant confusion by capital jurors about their role. The Capital Jury Project's extensive interviews with capital jurors reveal that "many jurors report that they arrived at a death sentence because the law required it, or that the responsibility for the sentence in some other way rested elsewhere."[73] In other words, many capital jurors understand neither that they are the individuals entrusted with the ultimate decision in capital sentencing nor that they can decline to impose that punishment for any reason.

---

[71] *Caldwell* v. *Mississippi*, 472 U.S. 320, 329 (1985); *see also McGautha* v. *California*, 402 U.S. 183, 208 (1971) (stating "that jurors confronted with the truly awesome responsibility of decreeing death for a fellow human will act with due regard for the consequences of their decision").

[72] *Caldwell*, 472 U.S. at 333.

[73] Ursula Bentele & William J. Bowers, "How Jurors Decide on Death: Guilt Is Overwhelming; Aggravation Requires Death; and Mitigation Is No Excuse," *Brooklyn Law Review* 66 (2001): 1011, 1041.

Another reason not to adopt post-sentencing assessments for capital defendants is that the assessment might convince judges that the enhanced procedural protections that have been afforded to capital defendants are unnecessary. As noted earlier, the Supreme Court has cited the finality of the death penalty when creating additional procedural protections for capital defendants. Indeed, in *Lockett* v. *Ohio*, the Supreme Court explicitly tied the need for procedural protections at sentencing to the fact that there was no mechanism available to modify an initial sentence of death:

> A variety of flexible techniques-probation, parole, work furloughs, to name a few-and various postconviction remedies may be available to modify an initial sentence of confinement in noncapital cases. The nonavailability of corrective or modifying mechanisms with respect to an executed capital sentence underscores the need for individualized consideration as a constitutional requirement in imposing the death sentence.[74]

A post-sentencing assessment is clearly a "corrective or modifying mechanism," as it is similar to (and in some jurisdictions, possibly interchangeable with) parole. If all capital defendants were going to receive an additional chance for sentence modification, then the Court may either fail to adopt new procedural protections or begin chipping away at existing protections.

Finally – and most importantly – post-sentencing assessments may not be practically or theoretically compatible with a system of capital punishment. For one thing, post-sentencing assessments could raise difficult timing issues in capital cases. Right now, most capital defendants are not executed until long after their initial convictions. But the time between conviction and execution is usually filled with appeals and petitions for collateral review. Of course, the post-sentencing assessment process could occur at the same time as those appeals and collateral reviews. But this would prove problematic for defendants who continue to challenge their factual guilt on appeal and during the habeas process. The decision-maker in a post-sentencing assessment is not likely to think that such a defendant has been rehabilitated. Conventional wisdom dictates that a person must first accept responsibility for her crime before she can rehabilitate; a defendant who continues to insist on her innocence has not, by definition, accepted responsibility.

Post-sentencing assessments may also not be conceptually compatible with the death penalty. In the non-capital context, post-sentencing assessments offer an opportunity for a defendant to shorten her incarceration period once she has demonstrated personal growth and maturity. Until and unless that growth and maturity occur, the defendant remains incarcerated. But in the capital context, the defendant is incarcerated only until it is time for her execution. If she is able to demonstrate personal growth and maturity before the date of her execution, then

---

[74] 438 U.S. 586, 605 (1978).

a post-sentencing assessment would give the defendant an opportunity for a modi-fied sentence, such as life in prison. But if a defendant does not demonstrate growth and maturity before the date of her execution, the execution would be carried out, despite the fact that the defendant might have demonstrated growth and maturity at a later date.

Of course, one might argue that the logic of post-sentencing assessments indicates that the executions of capital defendants ought to be deferred for many years in order to allow rehabilitation. But that argument is likely to be perceived as little more than obstruction. That is because the modern American death penalty is premised on the notion that those sentenced to death are not going to rehabilitate. Indeed, in some jurisdictions, jurors are told to impose the death penalty if they are convinced that the defendant poses a risk of future dangerousness. What is more, capital punish-ment decisions are not just about rehabilitation. They are also decisions about a defendant's crime. Death penalty laws suggest that some crimes are serious enough that rehabilitation is irrelevant to the capital sentencing question. Adopting a system of post-sentencing assessments arguably comes at the expense of the role of that crime in the punishment decision. Put simply, the premise of post-sentencing assessments – that people change and that those changes ought to be considered after initial sentencing – is incompatible with the premise of capital punishment – that we can sort the redeemable from the irredeemable and impose the death penalty only on the latter group.

POST-SENTENCING ASSESSMENTS AND DEATH PENALTY ABOLITION

As noted earlier, the idea that the finality of death renders capital punishment qualitatively different from all other criminal punishments was originally offered as an argument in favor of abolishing the death penalty. Indeed, Justice Brennan's famous opinion in *Furman* was an argument that capital punishment violates the Eighth Amendment. Since then, the finality of death has been used as a reason to enforce limitations on the imposition on the death penalty – namely, limitations to ensure the reliability of capital punishment decisions and to limit the imposition of the penalty to the "worst of the worst."[75]

The abolition question has become salient again in recent years. Justice Breyer's dissenting opinion in *Glossip v. Gross*, which was joined by Justice Ginsburg, raised the question whether it is time to revisit the constitutionality of the death penalty as a punishment.[76] Thus there is a possibility that the Supreme Court will take up that question in the near future.

---

[75] Note, "The Rhetoric of Difference and the Legitimacy of Capital Punishment," 1601–06.
[76] *Glossip v. Gross*, 135 S. Ct. 2726, 2755 (2015) (Breyer, J., dissenting) ("[R]ather than try to patch up the death penalty's wounds one at a time, I would ask for full briefing on a more basic question: whether the death penalty violates the Constitution.").

So how do post-sentencing assessments fit into the abolition debate? It depends on how, precisely, groups are seeking to end the death penalty. One approach is to reduce the imposition of capital punishment incrementally. Such an approach includes seeking court decisions further narrowing the class of defendants or offenses that are death-eligible. It also includes limiting the imposition of the death penalty as a practical matter. Those practical limitations include creating procedural hurdles for the imposition of the death penalty, such as requiring jury unanimity. They also include creating pragmatic hurdles, such as making it more difficult to obtain medication necessary for lethal injection. Both procedural and pragmatic hurdles make the death penalty more time-consuming and costly for the state to impose. To the extent that the abolition movement wishes to continue this incremental approach to reducing the imposition of the death penalty, post-sentencing assessments may be a good policy to pursue. After all, post-sentencing assessments may result in the modification of at least some capital sentences. Assuming that those sentence modifications are not offset by jurors imposing more capital sentences or judges refusing to adopt other procedural limitations, post-sentencing assessments may result in a net decrease in the number of executions.

But incremental reduction may not be the best approach to abolition. To the contrary, it may actually buttress public support for capital punishment. That is because it may limit the imposition of capital punishment in a fashion that brings it more in line with public support for the death penalty.

The public has long supported the availability of capital punishment.[77] Indeed, even in Western European countries that have abolished the death penalty, public opinion polls show majority support for capital punishment, support that existed at the time of abolition as well.[78] But public opinion for the death penalty may be best conceived of as support for availability of capital punishment in extreme cases, rather than support for the penalty as it is currently implemented.[79] When I speak with my students, for example, many who support the death penalty say that they support the penalty because it is appropriate for serial killers or terrorists who perpetrate mass killings. They do not support its use in cases involving a single murder. National polls on capital punishment ordinarily do not ask whether the

---

[77] Andrew Dugan, "Solid Majority Continue to Support Death Penalty," Gallup, Oct. 15, 2015, www.gallup.com/poll/186218/solid-majority-continue-support-death-penalty.aspx?g_source=posi tion2&g_medium=related&g_campaign=tiles (reporting that 61 percent of U.S. adults favor use of the death penalty).

[78] *See* Sara Sun Beale, "Public Opinion and the Abolition or Retention of the Death Penalty: Why Is the United States Different," paper presented at the International Society for Reform of Criminal Law, June 23, 2014, http://scholarship.law.duke.edu/cgi/viewcontent.cgi?article= 6043&context=faculty_scholarship.

[79] For example, see this statement by President Obama: "Statement from Obama," www.latimes .com/nation/la-oe-temkin-death-penalty-20140527-story.html.

death penalty ought to be limited in this fashion.[80] A 2001 *Newsweek* poll, however, did. That poll asked respondents the following:

> Which of the following four choices comes closest to your opinion about who should be subject to the death penalty? Should it be used for: [a] all those convicted of murder, other especially violent crimes, and major drug dealing, [b] limited to those convicted of murder, [c] further limited to cases of the most brutal murders, mass murders and serial killing, or [d] do you oppose the death penalty in all cases?[81]

By far the most popular response was limiting the death penalty to "cases of the most brutal murders, mass murders and serial killing." Forty-three percent of respondents chose that option. Fourteen percent of respondents said they would subject everyone convicted of murder, other violent crimes, and major drug dealing to the death penalty; 13 percent would limit the death penalty to those convicted of murder; 25 percent said that they were opposed to the death penalty; and 5 percent declined to answer.

Post-sentencing assessments might result in the imposition of the death penalty in only those cases that most resemble the extreme cases that my students mention. Ted Bundy and Timothy McVeigh are two examples of mass killers who appeared to remain unrepentant for their actions up through their executions. As a result, they almost certainly would not have been given non-capital sentences under post-sentencing assessments. Their crimes were also shocking and outrageous, making them appear to be the proverbial "worst of the worst" that the death penalty is intended to be reserved for. The horror and anger their crimes inspired did not appear to dissipate in the years following their convictions.[82]

Karla Faye Tucker, on the other hand, might have been given a non-capital sentence in a post-sentencing assessment. Tucker's widely publicized conversion to Christianity led many to argue that she should not receive the death penalty. And Tucker remains an example for abolitionists of the excesses of capital punishment.

Of course, the nature of a defendant's crime is not necessarily linked to her rehabilitation potential. And, as noted earlier, some states may wish to limit post-sentencing assessments to questions of rehabilitation. Thus, it is possible that post-sentencing assessments will not necessarily result in the death penalty being imposed only in those cases where public opinion would appear most strongly to

---

[80] *See* Frank R. Baumgartner & Emily Williams, "Constructing an Index of Public Opinion on the Death Penalty," Nov. 30, 2015, www.unc.edu/~fbaum/Innocence/Baumgartner-PublicOpinionIndex.pdf (collecting the questions from national surveys on capital punishment conducted from 1976 through October 2015).

[81] The survey, which had a sample size of 1,056, was conducted via telephone on May 10–11, 2001. The poll results can be found at http://ropercenter.cornell.edu/ipoll-database/.

[82] For example, the execution of serial killer Ted Bundy by the state of Florida was reportedly "seen by many around the country as a cause for celebration" when it occurred. Jack Levin, "The Death Penalty and Mass Murder," *Bridgewater Review* 7(1) (1989): 3.

support it. But assuming that post-sentencing assessments did tend to eliminate all but the most egregious crimes and despised defendants from death row, abolitionists may ultimately undermine their own agenda. They would no longer be able to point to sympathetic defendants, like Karla Faye Tucker, as a reason why the death penalty ought to be abolished. The death penalty might be imposed on fewer people, but the imposition of the punishment would have more public support.

Post-sentencing assessments could also reduce public anxieties about executing innocent defendants. As noted earlier, even if states limited post-sentencing assessments to questions of rehabilitation, credible evidence of factual innocence would still likely result in a sentence modification. Thus, post-sentencing assessments might reduce the likelihood that an innocent defendant will face execution. Or they might create the *perception* that an innocent defendant is less likely to be executed.

Concerns about wrongful convictions appear to have a negative impact on public support for the death penalty.[83] Those who oppose the death penalty are more likely to perceive a risk that an innocent person will be executed.[84] Thus, one might conclude that some opposition to the death penalty is premised on concerns that it will be used to execute the factually innocent. Indeed, it was this concern with the factual innocence that led Illinois Governor George Ryan, who otherwise supported capital punishment, to institute a moratorium on the death penalty in his state. If the public is less worried that a factually innocent defendant will face execution, then opposition to the death penalty may wane.

*   *   *

I do not pretend to know whether the abolitionist community should support post-sentencing assessments or not. I do not consider myself part of that community. Until today, I have written about the death penalty only to observe (and at times complain about) how much more developed death penalty doctrine is than the doctrine surrounding non-capital punishment.[85] In any event, it does not strike me as a foregone conclusion that abolitionists ought to seek post-sentencing assessments in capital cases. Rather it is a question that the abolitionist community should consider quite carefully.

[83] Drew DeSilver, "Lower Support for Death Penalty Tracks with Falling Crime Rates, More Exonerations," Pew Research Center, March 28, 2014, www.pewresearch.org/fact-tank/2014/03/28/lower-support-for-death-penalty-tracks-with-falling-crime-rates-more-exonerations/.

[84] "Less Support for Death Penalty Especially among Democrats," Pew Research Center, April 16, 2015, www.people-press.org/2015/04/16/less-support-for-death-penalty-especially-among-democrats/ (reporting that 84 percent of those who oppose the death penalty say there is a risk that an innocent person will be put to death as compared to 63 percent of death penalty supporters).

[85] E.g., Carissa Byrne Hessick, "Ineffective Assistance at Sentencing," *Boston College Law Review* 50 (2009): 1069, 1070–71.

Following Finality

Why Capital Punishment Is Collapsing under Its Own Weight

*Corinna Barrett Lain**

Death is different, the adage goes – different in its severity and different in its finality.[1] Death, in its finality, is more than just a punishment. Death is the end of our existence as we know it. It is final in an existential way.

Because death is final in an existential way, the Supreme Court has held that special care is due when the penalty is imposed.[2] We need to get it right. My claim in this chapter is that the constitutional regulation designed to implement that care has led to a series of cascading effects that threaten the continued viability of the death penalty itself. Getting death right leads to things going wrong, and things going wrong lead to states letting go.

I am not the first to see how the Supreme Court's regulation of the death penalty has led to its destabilization over time. Others have written about it.[3] And several judges have now brought the conversation full circle, recognizing

* Special thanks to Ron Bacigal, Jim Gibson, and Mary Kelly Tate for comments on an earlier draft, and to Holly Wilson and Zack MacDonald for their excellent research assistance.

[1] Beck v. Alabama, 447 U.S. 625, 637 (1980) ("As we have often stated, there is a significant constitutional difference between the death penalty and lesser punishments. 'Death is a different kind of punishment from any other which may be imposed in this country. . . . From the point of view of the defendant, it is different in both its severity and its finality.'").

[2] Woodson v. North Carolina, 428 U.S. 280, 305 (1976). For the Supreme Court's declarations to this effect, see text accompanying notes 5–7.

[3] Carol and Jordan Steiker's work is particularly noteworthy in this regard. Carol S. Steiker and Jordan M. Steiker, "Entrenchment and/or Destabilization? Reflections on (Another) Two Decades of Constitutional Regulation of Capital Punishment," *Law & Inequality* (2012): 211; Carol S. Steiker and Jordan M. Steiker, "Cost and Capital Punishment: A New Consideration Transforms an Old Debate," *University of Chicago Legal Forum* (2010): 144; Jordan Steiker, "The American Death Penalty from a Consequentialist Perspective," *Texas Tech Law Review* 47 (1995): 214; Jordan Steiker, "Restructuring Post-Conviction Review of Federal Constitutional Claims Raised by State Prisoners: Confronting the New Face of Excessive Proceduralism," *University of Chicago Legal Forum* (1998): 320.

the constitutional implications of this phenomenon.[4] But thus far, the role of finality has received little attention in the discourse. This chapter aims to give it its due.

To make my point, I first discuss the role of finality in the earliest developments of the modern death penalty era – constitutional regulation, habeas litigation, and the rise of a specialized capital defense bar to navigate those complicated structures. *Because death is final, we need to get it right.* Next I turn to the effects of those developments – a massive time lag between death sentence and execution, and with it, the discovery of innocents among the condemned, skyrocketing costs, and concerns about the conditions of long-term solitary confinement on death row. *Getting death right leads to things going wrong.* Finally, I examine the cascading effects of those developments – falling death sentences and executions, penological justifications that no longer make sense, and a growing number of states concluding that capital punishment is more trouble than it is worth. *Things going wrong lead to states letting go.* In the end, the finality of capital punishment is what makes it so rarely final, and so costly, cumbersome, and slow that it threatens to collapse under its own weight.

Before getting started, a few caveats merit mention. First, we do not know how the story ends. We can see the trajectory we are on now, but predicting the future is risky business – anything can happen. Second, even if our current trajectory continues, some states will cling to the death penalty no matter how little sense it makes or what the rest of the country does. In short, Texas will go down swinging. Third, the accumulated weight of finality is not the only factor threatening the death penalty's long-term feasibility. Other factors, like declining homicide rates and problems procuring lethal injection drugs, are also having an impact, but they are not what got the ball rolling and are not my focus here. Fourth and finally, history is a bit messier than the linear story I tell. Some developments I mention later were beginning to percolate earlier, some I mention earlier became stronger later, and many were interdependent with other developments also in play. I deal with this complexity by discussing each development where I believe it to have had the biggest impact, recognizing the nuances as best I can along the way.

Caveats aside, my point is simply this: Following finality allows us to see the cumulative nature of its heavy burden, and the weight of that burden on the death penalty today. Death is indeed different in the nature of its finality. But what makes it different may be what leads to its demise.

---

[4]   Glossip v. Gross, 576 U.S. ____, ____, 135 S. Ct. 2726, 2755–80 (2015) (Breyer, J., dissenting); Baze v. Rees, 553 U.S. 35, 78–87 (2008) (Stevens, J., concurring); Jones v. Chappell, 31 F. Supp. 3d 1050 (2014). *Jones* is discussed at text accompanying notes 181–82.

BECAUSE DEATH IS FINAL, WE NEED TO GET IT RIGHT

In the beginning, there was regulation. When the Supreme Court revived the death penalty in 1976, it did so on the premise that the death penalty would not be imposed unless "every safeguard is ensured."[5] "This conclusion rests squarely on the predicate that the penalty of death is qualitatively different from a sentence of imprisonment, however long," the Court explained.[6] "Because of that qualitative difference, there is a corresponding difference in the need for reliability in the determination that death is the appropriate punishment in a specific case."[7] *Death is final, so we need to get it right.*

In *Gregg v. Georgia* and its companion cases in 1976, getting death right meant requiring guided discretion statutes that told sentencers to consider certain aggravating and mitigating circumstances in the imposition of death.[8] "No longer can a jury wantonly and freakishly impose the death sentence," the Supreme Court declared. "It is always circumscribed by the legislative guidelines."[9]

But the turn to legislative guidelines raised more questions than it answered. What aggravating factors were permissible? And what happened when the sentencer relied on both permissible and impermissible aggravators? What mitigating factors warranted consideration? And what could states do to cabin the consideration of mitigating evidence? What if the sentencer found that aggravating and mitigating factors were in equipoise? And what guidance did states owe to the juries that were making life-or-death decisions under this system? These questions and more made their way to the Supreme Court for resolution.[10]

And that was just ground zero. Because the whole point of the guided discretion statutes was to identify the "worst of the worst" for whom death was appropriate, the Supreme Court's regulatory project also invited a number of categorial challenges to the death penalty's application. Sometimes the Court's resolution of these challenges had staying power. Those who raped without killing could not be executed.[11] Nor could those who were mentally incompetent at the time of execution.[12] Other times the Court changed its mind. Executing juvenile offenders and the

---

[5] Gregg v. Georgia, 428 U.S. 153, 187 (1976). Gregg revived the death penalty after the Supreme Court had ruled it was unconstitutional as then administered in *Furman v. Georgia*, 408 U.S. 238 (1972).

[6] Woodson v. North Carolina, 428 U.S. 280, 305 (1976).

[7] Ibid.

[8] Gregg v. Georgia, 195–207.

[9] Ibid., 206–07.

[10] See, for example, Arave v. Creech, 507 U.S. 463 (1993); Zant v. Stephens, 462 U.S. 862 (1983); Clemons v. Mississippi, 494 U.S. 738 (1990); Lockett v. Ohio 438 U.S. 586 (1978); Hitchcock v. Dugger, 481 U.S. 393 (1987); Kansas v. Marsh, 548 U.S. 163 (2006); Caldwell v. Mississippi, 472 U.S. 320 (1985).

[11] Coker v. Georgia, 433 U.S. 584, 597–98 (1977); Kennedy v. Louisiana, 554 U.S. 407, 421 (2008).

[12] Ford v. Wainwright, 477 U.S. 399, 409–10 (1986).

intellectually disabled was constitutional, until it was not.[13] And executing offenders who committed felony murder but did not themselves kill or intend to kill was not constitutional, until it was.[14]

Other issues added to the heap. Questions regarding the permissible bounds of jury selection in capital cases,[15] the necessity of proportionality review,[16] the admissibility of victim impact statements,[17] the minimal responsibilities of counsel in capital cases,[18] and the constitutional significance of racial bias in the imposition of death[19] are called for clarification, crowding the Supreme Court's docket. By one unofficial count, the Court had issued over 80 opinions in capital cases between 1976 and 1995 – roughly four per year in the first two decades of the modern death penalty era.[20]

In terms of the sheer number of capital cases decided, the Supreme Court's claim to "an especially vigilant concern for procedural fairness"[21] in the death penalty context made sense. But as others have shown, the Court's regulatory project was largely a façade – over 90 percent of those sentenced to death before the Court's 1976 rulings were just as death-eligible afterwards.[22] What slowed executions was not so much the Court's rulings, but the fact of litigation itself.

And litigation required lawyers – lawyers to litigate the law of capital punishment, and lawyers to litigate claims of lawyers litigating it wrong. In the first two decades of the modern death penalty era, there was plenty of work for both. While some of the legal wrangling centered around clarifying the death penalty's contours, much focused on the basic representation that capital defendants received at trial, which was bad – breathtakingly bad.

---

[13] Roper v. Simmons, 543 U.S. 551 (2005) (overruling Stanford v. Kentucky, 492 U.S. 361 (1989)); Atkins v. Virginia, 536 U.S. 304 (2002) (overruling Penry v. Lynaugh, 492 U.S. 302 (1989)).

[14] Tison v. Arizona, 481 U.S. 137 (1987) (overruling Enmund v. Florida, 458 U.S. 782 (1982)).

[15] Witherspoon v. Illinois, 391 U.S. 510 (1968); Morgan v. Illinois, 504 U.S. 719 (1992); Uttecht v. Brown 551 U.S. 1 (2007).

[16] Pulley v. Harris, 465 U.S. 37 (1984).

[17] Payne v. Tennessee, 501 U.S. 808 (1991) (overruling Booth v. Maryland, 482 U.S. 496 (1987)).

[18] Strickland v Washington, 466 U.S. 668 (1984).

[19] McCleskey v. Kemp, 481 U.S. 279 (1987).

[20] Alex Kozinski and Sean Gallagher, "Death: The Ultimate Run-On Sentence," *Case Western Reserve Law Review* 46, no. 1 (1995): 3, n.10. Jordan and Carol Steiker describe the Supreme Court's constitutional regulation of the death penalty as "the defining feature of the 'modern era' of the American death penalty." Carol S. Steiker and Jordan M. Steiker, "Capital Punishment: A Century of Discontinuous Debate," *Journal of Criminal Law & Criminology* 101, no. 3 (2010): 668.

[21] Strickland v. Washington, 466 U.S. 668, 704 (1984) (Brennan, J., concurring).

[22] David C. Baldus, George Woodworth and Charles Pulaski, *Equal Justice and the Death Penalty: A Legal and Empirical Analysis* (Boston: Northeastern University, 1990): 102. For excellent comparisons of the death penalty before and after the Supreme Court began regulating its administration, see Charles L. Black, Jr., *Capital Punishment: The Inevitability of Caprice and Mistake* (W. W. Norton & Co., 1982); Carol S. Steiker and Jordan M. Steiker, "Sober Second Thoughts: Reflections on Two Decades of Constitutional Regulation of Capital Punishment," *Harvard Law Review* 109, no. 2 (1995): 357.

In the early years especially, capital representation was provided by inexperienced, underpaid, and unsympathetic generalists.[23] Compensation averaging $5–15 per hour was not uncommon,[24] and states got what they paid for. Stories of shockingly poor capital defense representation were legion, and the litigation to set it right played out largely on the field of habeas corpus.[25] From 1976 to 1995, death sentences suffered a whopping 68 percent reversal rate – and the number one reason was grossly ineffective assistance of counsel.[26]

Something had to give; the question was what. One possible response to the high reversal rates in capital cases was to fix the problems that caused them (ineffective assistance of counsel was the number one reason for reversal, prosecutorial miscon-duct was number two).[27] Another possible response was to make reversals harder, and in 1996 that is exactly what Congress did. The Supreme Court had been tightening the availability of federal habeas corpus review for years,[28] and in the 1996 Anti-Terrorism and Effective Death Penalty Act (AEDPA), Congress codified those restrictions and added new ones of its own.

Responding to concerns about "delay and the lack of finality in capital cases,"[29] the AEDPA instituted an unprecedented array of procedural hurdles to federal habeas corpus review. To obtain relief, petitioners had to get past newly imposed statutes of limitations, restrictions on successive petitions, limits on evidentiary hearings, state exhaustion requirements, nonretroactivity doctrine, and a standard of review that required federal courts to find that the state court's ruling was not just wrong, but patently unreasonable.[30] A number of these hurdles came with excep-tions – some with exceptions to the exceptions – and every single one raised questions of its own. Further complicating matters was the AEDPA's poor drafting,

---

[23] Roscoe C. Howard, Jr., "The Defunding of the Post-Conviction Defense Organizations as a Denial of the Right to Counsel," *West Virginia Law Review* 98 (1996): 879, 881–82, 889; Steiker and Steiker, "Sober Second Thoughts," 399.

[24] Howard, "The Defunding of the Post-Conviction Defense Organizations," 892.

[25] Stephen B. Bright, "Counsel for the Poor: The Death Sentence Not for the Worst Crime but for the Worst Lawyer," *Yale Law Journal* 103 (1994): 1835; Carol S. Steiker and Jordan M. Steiker, "No More Tinkering: The American Law Institute and the Death Penalty Provisions of the Model Penal Code," *Texas Law Review* 89 (2010): 387.

[26] James S. Liebman, Jeffrey Fagan, Valerie West, and Jonathan Loyd, "Capital Attrition: Error Rates in Capital Cases, 1973–1995," *Texas Law Review* 78 (2000): 1846–56.

[27] Ibid.

[28] Wainright v. Sykes, 433 U.S. 72, (1977): 87–91 (adopting the "cause" and "prejudice" standard rescinding deliberate bypass); Teague v. Lane, 489 U.S. 288, 300–07 (1989) (adopting nonre-troactivity doctrine).

[29] Ad Hoc Committee on Federal Habeas Corpus in Capital Cases Committee Report (Powell Committee Report), printed in 135 Cong. Rec. 24694 (1989). The Powell Committee was charged with investigating "the necessity and desirability of legislation directed toward avoiding delay and the lack of finality in capital cases in which the prisoner had or had been offered counsel."

[30] Antiterrorism and Effective Death Penalty Act of 1996, P.L. 104–32, 110 Stat. 1214 (1996); Steiker, "Confronting the New Face of Excessive Proceduralism," 320.

which made navigating the statute's provisions all the more difficult.[31] The only thing clear about the AEDPA was its purpose: to frustrate federal review of state convictions and move the locus of litigation to state habeas corpus, an edifice that was itself designed to frustrate federal review of state convictions.[32]

The AEDPA was a success, at least by way of lower reversal rates,[33] but in the process of curbing federal habeas review, it fed the monster it tried to tame. However arcane and elaborate federal habeas corpus was before the AEDPA, it was many times more afterwards. Federal habeas litigation continued unabated; indeed, it grew more prodigious over time.[34] What changed was its focus. Rather than ruling on the merits of claims, federal courts were mired in ruling on procedural rules.[35] Looking back on the dense procedural thicket that federal habeas corpus had become, Jordan Steiker had it right: what Congress meant was to prune the forest, but what it did was add more trees.[36]

Once again, the complexities of capital litigation called for lawyers. At first that was a problem. In a separate (but related) move in 1996, Congress defunded the death penalty resource centers that had been providing counsel in federal habeas cases.[37] "We should not be spending federal money to subsidize think tanks run by people whose sole purpose is to concoct theories to frustrate the implementation of the death penalty," read an open letter to Congress.[38] In the AEDPA, Congress did its best to shut down federal habeas claims. In defunding the death penalty resource centers, it shut down the lawyers who filed them too.

But those lawyers did not just pack up and go home. They found private funding, took positions in the system elsewhere, submitted reimbursements, and sometimes worked for free.[39] Then came 2000, with its high-profile death row exonerations and revelations of lawyers falling asleep during capital trials.[40] Over the next several

---

[31] Lindh v. Murphy, 521 U.S. 320, 336 (1997) ("[I]n a world of silk purses and pigs' ears, the [AEDPA] is not a silk purse in the art of statutory drafting.").

[32] Steiker, "Confronting the New Face of Excessive Proceduralism," 342–44.

[33] Steiker and Steiker, "No More Tinkering," 387, n.70 (citing studies showing a 40 percent federal habeas reversal rate in capital cases before the AEDPA and 12.5 percent reversal rate afterwards).

[34] See infra discussion at notes 49–51.

[35] Steiker, "Confronting the New Face of Excessive Proceduralism," 317 (exploring causes of "emerging procedural fetishism" of federal habeas corpus in the wake of the AEDPA).

[36] Ibid. 320.

[37] Compare Judiciary Appropriations Act, 1995, Pub. L. No. 103–317, 108 Stat. 1724, 1750–51 (allocating up to $19.8 million for Death Penalty Resource Centers) with Judiciary Appropriations Act, 1996, Pub. L. No. 104–34, 110 Stat. 1321 (providing that "none of the funds provided in this Act shall be available for Death Penalty Resource Center or Post-Conviction Defender Organizations after April 1, 1996").

[38] Howard, "The Defunding of the Post-Conviction Defense Organizations," 915 (quoting Representative Inglis, R., South Carolina).

[39] Mark Hansen, "From Death's Door: With Federally Funded Appeals from Capital Punishment on the Way Out, Lawyers Are Wrestling with Questions About Who Will Pursue the Arguments to Keep Condemned Inmates," *ABA Journal* 82, no. 6 (1996): 58–59.

[40] Corinna Barrett Lain, "Deciding Death," *Duke Law Journal* 57, no. 1 (2007): 43–45.

years, quality capital defense became vogue. The Supreme Court started enforcing its competency standards.[41] The American Bar Association issued new guidelines for defense attorneys in capital cases.[42] And the 2004 Innocence Protection Act gave states grants to improve the quality of representation in state capital cases.[43] A new era of capital defense was born.

Inadvertently, the Supreme Court played a part in creating it. Decades of constitutional regulation added complexity to capital litigation, and that gave rise to a specialized capital defense bar skilled in harnessing that complexity and making it work for them.[44] From investigation, to mitigation, to voir dire, to pre- and post-trial motions and collateral review, these lawyers left no stone unturned and no legal argument overlooked.[45] They mounted a vigorous defense, negotiated the case when they could, fought tooth and nail at sentencing, and sought reversal of death sentences every step of the way. They held conferences, conducted training, and shared notes, all with a single objective: keeping their clients alive.

This is not to say that the world of capital defense had become a bed of roses. States with the most executions still did the least to provide capital defendants with the level of representation one would expect when the stakes were life and death.[46] And states without fully staffed, specialized units dedicated to litigating capital cases on collateral review still faced a massive shortage of lawyers willing and able to do the work.[47] But both had the unintended effect of further slowing executions. Poor capital defense at trial left more to litigate on collateral review, and the dearth of lawyers to do it created waitlists – long ones. California today presents a prime example: its wait from death sentence to the appointment of counsel for state habeas review is an incredible 8–10 years, and that's just the beginning of the long and drawn-out process of collateral review.[48]

In sum, the death penalty's finality gave rise to voluminous constitutional regulation and habeas litigation, which gave rise to complaints about the lack of finality in litigating capital cases, which then gave rise to habeas reform legislation and yet more litigation. Over time, what emerged was a specialized capital defense bar well versed in both structures, which slowed the "machinery of death"[49] even more. And that gave rise to cascading effects of its own.

---

[41] Wiggins v. Smith, 537 U.S. 1231 (2003).
[42] ABA, "Guidelines for the Appointment and Performance of Defense Counsel in Death Penalty Cases (rev. ed. 2003)," *Hofstra Law Review* 31 (2003): 913.
[43] The Innocence Protection Act of 2004, Public Law No. 108–405.
[44] Steiker and Steiker, "Entrenchment and/or Destabilization," 232.
[45] Ibid.
[46] Sean D. O'Brien, "Capital Defense Lawyers: The Good, the Bad, and the Ugly," *Michigan Law Review* 105 (2007): 1069–70.
[47] Kozinski and Gallagher, "Death: The Ultimate Run-On Sentence" 19.
[48] Jones v. Chappell, 1058.
[49] Callins v. Collins, 510 U.S. 1141, 1130 (1994) (Blackmun, J., dissenting).

GETTING DEATH RIGHT LEADS TO THINGS GOING WRONG

Having discussed how the death penalty's finality added complexity to capital litigation, I focus here on how that complexity fundamentally changed the death penalty's contours along another dimension – time. In the mid-1980s, the first years for which data are available, the average time lag between death sentence and execution was six years.[50] In 1995, when Congress was considering the AEDPA, the average time lag was eleven years.[51] In 2016, it was eighteen and a half years.[52]

One consequence of the massive time lag between death sentence and execution is a pile-up on death row. Today, just under 3,000 condemned await their fate, a backlog that would take one execution per day for the next eight years to clear, assuming no new death sentences in the meantime.[53] The time it takes to get death right, and the pile-up it has produced, have in turn led to yet more disruptive developments: the discovery of innocents among the condemned, concerns about the inhumane conditions of long-term solitary confinement on death row, and skyrocketing costs. *Getting death right leads to things going wrong.*

Concerns about actual innocence came first. The problem wasn't new; DNA had been quietly exonerating the condemned since 1993.[54] But by the late 1990s, advances in DNA had made the technology more available,[55] and two other developments occurred that were needed to put it to use: lawyers and time.

The lawyers that made a difference were not just any lawyers. They were the new-fangled variety, the professional capital defenders who had emerged from decades of constitutional regulation and habeas litigation. These lawyers were committed to canvassing the record for errors and conducting the factual investigations necessary to make their claims stick, and in the process, they provided an unprecedented level of scrutiny to capital convictions.[56] And because habeas claims come with a statutory right to counsel in capital cases,[57] these lawyers were in the right place, at the right time, to put advances in forensic technology to use.

---

[50] Tracy L. Snell, "Capital Punishment, 2012 – Statistical Tables," *U.S. Department of Justice,* (NCJ 245789, May 2014), 14, www.bjs.gov/content/pub/pdf/cp12st.pdf.

[51] Ibid.

[52] Death Penalty Information Center, "Execution List 2016," Death Penalty Information Center, www.deathpenaltyinfo.org/execution-list-2016.

[53] Death Penalty Information Center, "Death Row Inmates by State and Size of Death Row by Year," Death Penalty Information Center, www.deathpenaltyinfo.org/death-row-inmates-state-and-size-death-row-year?scid=9&did=188#year.

[54] Lain, "Deciding Death," 47.

[55] Death Penalty Information Center, "Innocence and the Crisis in the American Death Penalty: Executive Summary," Death Penalty Information Center, 2004, www.deathpenaltyinfo.org/innocence-and-crisis-american-death-penalty (discussing emergence of more sophisticated technologies for evaluating DNA evidence).

[56] Steiker and Steiker, "Entrenchment and/or Destabilization," 238–39.

[57] Steiker, "The American Death Penalty from a Consequentialist Perspective," 213–15.

But a cadre of committed lawyers would have made no difference if the innocents languishing on death row had not been around to be exonerated. Time, as it turns out, is a necessary (but not sufficient) condition for vindicating claims of innocence. On average, exonerations take just over eleven years, and many take substantially longer.[58] In 2015, for example, five death row inmates were exonerated on a finding of actual innocence.[59] One had been on death row just ten years; the others had been there between nineteen and thirty.[60] Exonerations take time, and the death penalty's finality has played a critical role in providing it.

By the year 2000, the convergence of these three developments – time, advances in DNA, and the rise of a specialized capital defense bar – led to a number of high profile exonerations, catapulting the issue of innocents on death row into the national spotlight.[61] Illinois Governor George Ryan declared a moratorium on executions in his state.[62] The book *Actual Innocence* hit the shelves, chronicling the sagas of the wrongfully convicted and the reasons the system had failed them.[63] And media investigations confirmed the public's worst fears; the problem was even worse than it looked.[64] Wrongful convictions became the topic du jour of the national news, and a slew of exonerations over the next several years would keep it that way.[65]

These events brought a dramatic shift in the script of the death penalty debate. In 1995, when Congress was considering the AEDPA, Ninth Circuit Judge Alex Kozinski epitomized prevailing sentiment in writing:

> [E]rrors that go to guilt or innocence are exceedingly rare in criminal cases, and even more rare in death cases. Even if an error occurs, it is most likely to turn up sooner rather than later. Cases where the defendant is exonerated years after his conviction because the one-armed man is found and made to confess are seen only on television.[66]

By 2000, it was clear that none of that was true. No one was even claiming it was anymore. What marked the death penalty discourse were not claims of competence, but confessions of doubt about the reliability of capital convictions.[67] It was the

---

[58] Death Penalty Information Center, "Innocence: List of Those Freed from Death Row," Death Penalty Information Center, January 10, 2016, www.deathpenaltyinfo.org/innocence-list-those-freed-death-row.

[59] Ibid.

[60] Ibid. For those wondering if 2015 was an anomaly, the year 2014 saw six death row inmates exonerated on a finding of actual innocence. Each one of them had been on death row for more than thirty years – one, almost forty. Ibid.

[61] Lain, "Deciding Death," 43–44.

[62] Ibid. 44.

[63] Ibid. 44–45.

[64] Ibid. 44.

[65] Ibid. 44–45; Death Penalty Information Center, "Innocence and the Crisis in the American Death Penalty: Executive Summary."

[66] Kozinski and Gallagher, "Death: The Ultimate Run-On Sentence," 21–22.

[67] Illinois Governor George Ryan stated when announcing a moratorium on executions in his state, "Our capital system is haunted by the demon of error, error in determining guilt and error

nation's first crisis of confidence in the death penalty (at least in the modern era) and it was a doozy. A moratorium movement took hold,[68] conservatives weighed in against the death penalty for the first time,[69] and calls for more executions, faster, quietly faded away.

Sixteen years later, the death penalty still has not recovered. The number of death row exonerations now stands at a whopping 156, and a recent study has shown that an estimated 4 percent of those sentenced to death are innocent.[70] This unusually high wrongful conviction rate reflects a number of dangers unique to capital cases: community outrage, tremendous pressure on police to solve the crime and on prosecutors to get a conviction, death qualification of jurors, and strategic decisions by defense counsel to make concessions at trial in hopes of gaining credibility at sentencing.[71] The sheer number of exonerations has in turn led courts to scrutinize capital cases more closely, and the public to view the death penalty more warily.[72] *USA Today*'s 2015 exposé on the death penalty captured the prevailing view: "Of all the arguments against capital punishment, none is as powerful as the risk of executing the innocent."[73]

If executing the innocent is a problem at one end of the death penalty spectrum, the problem at the other end is not executing the guilty. Here again, time has played a key role. Most of the condemned will spend more than a decade awaiting their execution.[74] In the half-dozen states with an official or de facto moratorium, that day will likely never come.[75] In the meantime, however, the condemned are subject to the exceptionally harsh conditions of solitary confinement on death row, and that has emerged as a problem in and of itself.

It all started with *Lackey v. Texas*, a case the Supreme Court decided not to decide in 1995.[76] Justice Stevens had no problem passing it by, but he wrote separately to

---

in determining who among the guilty deserves to die." Kevin Davis, "Faith and Fiscal Responsibility Cause Many Conservatives to Change Their View of the Death Penalty," *American Bar Journal*, June 1, 2015, www.abajournal.com/magazine/article/faith_and_fiscal_responsibility_cause_many_conservatives_to_change_their_vi.

[68] Jeffrey L. Kirchmeier, "Another Place Beyond Here: The Death Penalty Moratorium Movement in the United States," *University of Colorado Law Review* 73 (2002): 1.

[69] Davis, "Faith and Fiscal Responsibility Cause Many Conservatives."

[70] Death Penalty Information Center, "Innocence: List of Those Freed from Death Row"; Samuel R. Gross, et al., "Rate of False Conviction of Criminal Defendants Who Are Sentenced to Death," *Proceedings Nat'l Acad. Sci. U. S. A.* 111, no. 20 (2014): 7230–35.

[71] Steiker and Steiker, "No More Tinkering," 408; Glossip v. Gross, 2757.

[72] Jordan Steiker, "The American Death Penalty from a Consequentialist Perspective," 213; Death Penalty Information Center, "Innocence and the Crisis in the American Death Penalty."

[73] Richard Wolf and Kevin Johnson, "Courts, States put Death Penalty on Life Support," *USA Today*, September 14, 2015, www.usatoday.com/story/news/nation/2015/09/14/death-penalty-execution-supreme-court-lethal-injection/32425015/.

[74] See discussion at supra note 52.

[75] Death Penalty Information Center, "Jurisdictions With No Recent Executions," Death Penalty Information Center, www.deathpenaltyinfo.org/jurisdictions-no-recent-executions.

[76] Lackey v. Texas, 514 U.S. 1045 (1995).

credit the strength of the petitioner's claim – that seventeen years on death row was itself cruel and unusual punishment.[77] Two decades later, the Court has yet to consider a so-called *Lackey* claim on the merits, although Justices Breyer and Kennedy have now joined in the calls to do so.[78]

Internationally, however, a number of tribunals have considered similar claims, consistently holding that prolonged incarceration under a sentence of death constitutes cruel, inhuman, and degrading treatment in violation of basic human rights.[79] These rulings have brought increased scholarly and media attention to the conditions of death row in the United States, and that, in turn, has led to a growing public awareness of how we house our condemned. The facts are sobering.

In virtually every state, the condemned are physically separated from the rest of the prison population and housed on death row, an isolated unit removed from the day-to-day activities of the mainstream institution.[80] On death row, each condemned prisoner spends at least 22 hours a day, typically 23, within the confines of a windowless cell the size of a standard parking lot space.[81] They are fed through slots in doors, monitored by cameras, and spoken to through intercoms.[82] Most are not allowed contact visits from family or friends.[83] Death row inmates are typically allowed an hour or less of exercise each day, and typically that takes place in caged exercise pens akin to dog runs.[84] These are the conditions of long-term solitary confinement on death row, and the condemned are subject to its hallmarks – extreme isolation and forced idleness – for agonizingly long periods of time.

The result is what has now been named "death row syndrome," a condition more generally known as "isolation sickness."[85] As it turns out, the absence of significant human interaction for extended periods of time is bad for humans. Even a few days of solitary confinement will cause a shift in EEG patterns indicative of cerebral dysfunction,[86] and over time, the effects are debilitating. Studies show that

---

[77] Ibid.
[78] Davis v. Ayala, 576 U.S. ___, ___, 135 S. Ct. 2187, 2208–09 (2015) (Kennedy, J., concurring); Smith v. Arizona, 552 U.S. 985 (2007) (Breyer, J., dissenting from the denial of certiorari); Foster v. Florida, 537 U.S. 990 (1999) (Breyer, J., dissenting from the denial of certiorari).
[79] Glossip v. Gross, 2765.
[80] Craig Haney, "Mental Health Issues in Long-Term Solitary and 'Supermax' Confinement," *Crime & Delinquency* 49 (2003): 125; Marah Stith McLeod, "Does the Death Penalty Require Death Row? The Harm of Legislative Silence," *Ohio State Law Journal* 77 (2016), 523.
[81] Haney, "Mental Health," 127, 146; Davis v. Ayala, 2208–09.
[82] American Civil Liberties Union, "A Death before Dying: Solitary Confinement on Death Row," ACLU, 4, July 2013, www.aclu.org/sites/default/files/field_document/deathbeforedying-report.pdf (accessed January 10, 2016); Haney, "Mental Health," 126.
[83] American Civil Liberties Union, "A Death before Dying," 5.
[84] Ibid.; Haney, "Mental Health," 126.
[85] American Civil Liberties Union, "A Death before Dying," 5; Haney, "Mental Health," 134–37.
[86] Stuart Grassian, "Psychiatric Effects of Solitary Confinement," *Washington University Journal of Law & Policy* 22 (2006): 331.

prolonged solitary confinement causes severe anxiety, hypersensitivity to stimuli, perceptual distortions and hallucinations, paranoia, insomnia, difficulty with concentration and memory, confused thought processes, and suicidal ideations and behavior.[87] The impact is similar to that suffered by victims of severe sensory deprivation torture techniques[88] and is exacerbated by the stress of not knowing when execution will come, if it ever does. Execution dates that come and go, and death warrants that are signed and then stayed, and then signed and then stayed again, are an innate part of living on death row.[89]

For many condemned inmates, the conditions are too much to bear. Some go insane.[90] Some commit suicide.[91] And some drop their appeals and volunteer to be executed.[92] Just over 10 percent of the executed are "volunteers".[93]

Granted, concerns about the conditions of death row are controversial. Some say the condemned deserve what they get.[94] Others say the condemned forfeit their right to complain when their own appeals are the reason their executions are delayed.[95] But whatever one's view as a normative matter, the torturous conditions of long-term confinement on death row as a descriptive matter are difficult to deny.

For those not concerned about long-term solitary confinement on death row for humane reasons, another reason may have more sway – cost. Early in the modern death penalty era, cost was a reason to support the death penalty; surely it cost less to execute murderers than to feed and house them for the rest of their lives.[96] Today the opposite is true. Cost has become one of the most potent arguments against the death penalty, and the reason is this: capital punishment costs substantially more than life imprisonment at every turn.[97]

Start with trial. Constitutional regulation has fundamentally changed the nature of capital trials, and with it, capital defense. Today, competent capital representation at trial is marked by extensive investigation, a focus on mitigation, the pervasive use of experts, and motions – lots of them.[98] Jury selection imposes additional costs too.

[87] Haney, "Mental Health," 125, 130–31, 137.
[88] Ibid. 132.
[89] Glossip v. Gross, 2765; American Civil Liberties Union, "A Death before Dying," 9.
[90] Haney, "Mental Health," 144; American Civil Liberties Union, "A Death before Dying," 6–7.
[91] Steiker, "The American Death Penalty from a Consequentialist Perspective," 215; Glossip v. Gross, 2766.
[92] Glossip v. Gross, 2766.
[93] Ibid.; American Civil Liberties Union, "A Death before Dying," 8.
[94] Davis v. Ayala, 2210 (Thomas, J., concurring).
[95] Thompson v. McNeil, 129 S. Ct. 1299, 1301 (Thomas, J., concurring).
[96] Steiker and Steiker, "Entrenchment and/or Destabilization," 231; "Capital Punishment in America: Revenge Begins to Seem Less Sweet," *The Economist*, August 30, 2007, www.economist.com/node/9719806.
[97] Steiker and Steiker, "Cost and Capital Punishment," 118, 139; Steiker and Steiker, "Entrenchment and/or Destabilization," 231; "Capital Punishment in America: Revenge Begins to Seem Less Sweet."
[98] Steiker and Steiker, "Entrenchment and/or Destabilization," 231; Steiker and Steiker, "Cost and Capital Punishment," 139–40.

Voir dire in capital cases takes around five times longer than in non-capital cases, in part so the prosecution can "death qualify" the jury, and in part so the defense can ensure it is open to the consideration of mitigating evidence.[99] Then there is the trial itself. Capital cases take over three times longer to try than non-capital cases because they are more complex and consist of essentially two trials – one to decide guilt or innocence, and one to decide life or death.[100] Every step of the trial process takes additional time and money, and with lawyers doing the work, the additional time is money too.

Although the bulk of extra expense in capital cases is trial-related,[101] appellate and collateral review of death sentences costs substantially more as well. Capital cases enjoy a statutory right to counsel on state and federal habeas review that other cases typically do not, and with trial records in capital cases running into the tens of thousands of pages, just reviewing the record for error imposes sizable costs.[102] Add that to the hours of investigation that go into building a case for non-record claims, the hundreds of pages of briefs that get filed, and the sheer number of issues that capital cases present – on average, three times that of non-capital cases – and one can begin to see how post-trial expenses can easily rack up to hundreds of thousands of dollars.[103]

And then there is the cost of long-term confinement on death row. Solitary confinement is incredibly expensive. In California, for example, a recent study estimated that it cost an additional $90,000 per inmate per year to house the condemned on death row, adding a hefty $63 million per year to the state's total incarceration spending.[104]

Put it all together and the cost of capital punishment is staggering. The California study, for example, estimated that the total cost of the death penalty in that state was $137 million annually, compared to the $11.5 million annually that it would cost to maintain a criminal justice system with a maximum punishment of life without parole (LWOP).[105] An additional $125 million per year – that is the cost of capital punishment in California, and other states estimate the additional cost per year in multi-million dollar figures as well.[106]

But nowadays, the cost of capital punishment is not just what it takes to maintain the system. Part of the cost calculus is what the states get in return, and with the

---

[99] Steiker and Steiker, "Cost and Capital Punishment," 141.
[100] Kozinski and Gallagher, "Death: The Ultimate Run-On Sentence," 12–13.
[101] Steiker and Steiker, "No More Tinkering," 404–05; Steiker and Steiker, "Cost and Capital Punishment," 143–44.
[102] Steiker and Steiker, "Cost and Capital Punishment," 143–44.
[103] Kozinski and Gallagher, "Death: The Ultimate Run-On Sentence," 12–16.
[104] Gerald Uelmen, ed., "California Commission on the Fair Administration of Justice Final Report" (2008), 141, http://digitalcommons.law.scu.edu/cgi/viewcontent.cgi?article=1000&content=ncippubs.
[105] Ibid.
[106] Bill Mears, "Study: States Can't Afford Death Penalty," CNN, October 20, 2009, www.cnn.com/2009/CRIME/10/20/death.penalty/index.html?eref=rss_us.

massive time lag between death sentences and executions, the answer is not much. Again, California is a prime example. It has spent over $4 billion on capital punishment in the modern death penalty era, with just thirteen executions to show for it.[107] On average, that is over $300 *million per execution* – take-your-breath-away expensive. That figure is lower in states with more executions and fewer inmates on death row. Florida, for example, spends an average of $24 million per execution.[108] But that is still outrageously high, especially for a state where more death row inmates die of natural causes and suicide than executions.[109] In practice, the death penalty today is mostly just an incredibly expensive form of life imprisonment.

That realization has broadened the base of those opposed to the death penalty. In the past, opposition to the death penalty rested primarily on humanitarian and due process–type grounds. Today, those opposed to the death penalty include fiscal conservatives and legislators in cash-strapped states.[110] Gone is the claim that opponents of the death penalty are "soft on crime."[111] The new narrative is that they are "smart on crime" – it makes no sense to have a death penalty that costs millions to maintain but almost never gets used.[112]

In sum, the finality of the death penalty led to a massive time lag between death sentences and executions, and that time lag, and the unprecedented scrutiny of capital convictions that it allowed, led to the discovery of innocents on death row – a good thing for the wrongfully convicted, but a bad thing for the death penalty's legitimacy. That time lag also led to a pile-up on death row, which in turn led to concerns about the inhumane conditions of long-term solitary confinement. Meanwhile, efforts to get the death penalty right led to skyrocketing costs at every turn, widening the ideological base of those willing to let the ultimate punishment go. As discussed next, these developments have led to yet more cascading effects, all with serious implications for the death penalty's long-term viability.

THINGS GOING WRONG LEAD TO STATES LETTING GO

The most recent developments of the modern death penalty era start with a massive drop in executions and death sentences, each a product of the accumulated developments discussed thus far. Those declines, along with the developments that caused them, have in turn undermined every penological justification for capital

---

[107] Corinna Barrett Lain, "The Virtues of Thinking Small," *University of Miami Law Review* 67 (2013): 397, 409.

[108] Mears, "Study: States Can't Afford Death Penalty"; Glossip v. Gross, 2776; David Von Drehle, "The Last Execution: Why the Era of Capital Punishment Is Ending," *Time*, April 2015, 29.

[109] Corinna Barrett Lain, "Passive-Aggressive Executive Power," *University of Maryland Law Review* 73 (2013): 229; Steiker and Steiker, "Cost and Capital Punishment," 120.

[110] Steiker and Steiker, "Cost and Capital Punishment," 120; Steiker and Steiker, "No More Tinkering," 419–20; Steiker and Steiker, "Capital Punishment: A Century," 662–68, 674.

[111] Lain, "The Virtues," 410.

[112] Ibid.; Steiker and Steiker, "Cost and Capital Punishment," 119.

punishment – incapacitation, deterrence, and retribution – while exacerbating some
of the death penalty's old problems and creating at least one new one. The result has
been calls to abandon the death penalty, which have prevailed in a number of state
legislatures across the country. *Things going wrong lead to states letting go.* And states
letting go, along with the reasons that take them there, are raising constitutional
concerns of their own.

Turning first to executions, 2016 saw just 20 of them.[113] That is less than half of the
53 executions that the nation saw ten years earlier in 2006, and a 70 percent decline
from the 66 executions the nation saw fifteen years earlier in 2001.[114] It is also a
39 percent decline from the 28 executions of 2015.[115]

Granted, part of the decline in executions over the last several years reflects the
difficulty states have had in procuring lethal injection drugs.[116] But the strong
downward trend in executions predates that development and is in large part a
reflection of decades of constitutional regulation of the death penalty. Today, the
single most likely outcome of a death sentence is reversal.[117] The next most likely
outcome varies state-to-state; nationally, death by execution and death by other
causes (natural and suicide) run neck and neck for second place.[118] Executions
require a strong institutional commitment, and pervasive doubts about the accuracy
of capital convictions have left few states with the will necessary nowadays to carry
them out.[119] The year 2016's executions illustrate the point. Eighty percent of those
executions – 16 of 20 – were conducted in just two states: Texas and Georgia.[120]

Even greater than the decline in executions has been the decline in death
sentencing. The year 2016 brought just 30 new death sentences – a record low for
the modern death penalty era.[121] That's a 76 percent decline from the 125 death
sentences we saw ten years ago in 2006, and an 81 percent decline from the 155 death
sentences we saw fifteen years ago in 2001.[122] It is also a 39 percent decline from the
49 death sentences issued in 2015, which was itself a record low at the time.[123] The
fact that death sentencing has fallen just over 80 percent over the past fifteen years

[113] Death Penalty Information Center, "Executions by Year," Death Penalty Information Center,
www.deathpenaltyinfo.org/executions-year.
[114] Ibid.
[115] Ibid.
[116] James Gibson and Corinna Barrett Lain, "Death Penalty Drugs and the International Moral
Marketplace," *Georgetown Law Journal* 103 (2015): 1217, 1251.
[117] Glossip v. Gross, 2768–69.
[118] Ibid.; Lain, "The Virtues," 410.
[119] Lain, "Passive-Aggressive," 229–30; Steiker, "The American Death Penalty from a Consequentialist Perspective," 216 n. 37.
[120] Death Penalty Information Center, "Executions by Year."
[121] Death Penalty Information Center, "Death Sentences in 2016," Death Penalty Information
Center, www.deathpenaltyinfo.org/2016-sentencing.
[122] Death Penalty Information Center, "Death Sentences in the United States from 1977 by State
and by Year," Death Penalty Information Center, http://www.deathpenaltyinfo.org/death-sen
tences-year-1977-present.
[123] Ibid.

speaks volumes about the state of the death penalty today, and the long-term viability of executions going forward.

Even more telling are the negligible death sentences coming out of states traditionally known as death penalty strongholds. Virginia is the third most executing state in the country, but has had no new death sentences in the last five years.[124] Oklahoma is the second most executing state in the country, but has had just eight new death sentences in the last five years.[125] Texas is by far the most executing state in the country, and had eleven new death sentences in 2014 alone. But in 2015 it generated only two, and in 2016 it generated only four.[126] And even 2014's 11 death sentences were less than half of the 23 death sentences the state produced ten years earlier in 2004, and 77 percent lower than the 48 death sentences it produced fifteen years earlier in 1999.[127]

Driving the extraordinary decline in death sentencing is a host of factors that make juries less likely to choose death, and prosecutors less likely to ask for it in the first place.[128] At the top of the list are reduced public confidence in the death penalty,[129] exorbitant costs,[130] reliably strong mitigating evidence in most every case,[131] the availability of LWOP as a sentencing option,[132] and the likelihood that hard-won death sentences will never be carried out.[133] All but one of these – the availability of LWOP[134] – are cascading effects set in motion by the Supreme Court's attempt to regulate the death penalty to get it right, which was itself driven by the Court's recognition of the uniquely consequential finality of death.

This precipitous decline in death sentences and executions has, in turn, undermined every penological justification of capital punishment. Incapacitation is no longer considered to be a primary purpose of capital punishment. The death penalty once assured that murderers would never have the opportunity to terrorize society again, but today we have LWOP for that – and it costs millions less to maintain.[135] Moreover, both public opinion polls and the sentences that juries choose in capital

---

[124] Ibid.

[125] Ibid.

[126] Ibid.

[127] Ibid.

[128] Steiker and Steiker, "Entrenchment and/or Destabilization," 240; Steiker and Steiker, "Capital Punishment: A Century," 671–72; Steiker and Steiker, "Cost and Capital Punishment," 142.

[129] Steiker, "The American Death Penalty from a Consequentialist Perspective" 216–18, 216 n. 37; Steiker and Steiker, "Entrenchment and/or Destabilization," 240; Steiker and Steiker, "No More Tinkering," 374–75.

[130] Steiker and Steiker, "Cost and Capital Punishment."

[131] Steiker and Steiker, "Entrenchment and/or Destabilization," 232.

[132] Ibid. 234.

[133] See discussion at supra note 117.

[134] Steiker and Steiker, "Entrenchment and/or Destabilization," 234.

[135] *Glossip v. Gross*, 2767 (Breyer, J., dissenting).

cases both suggest that when given the choice, between LWOP and the unposition of death, the public prefers LWOP.[136]

The deterrence rationale for the death penalty has also largely faded away. The death penalty's deterrent value has always been a point of sharp contention,[137] but never has it been more attenuated than today, when death sentences are disappearing and executions take decades to carry out, if carried out at all.[138] What Judge Kozinski said in 1995 is even more true now: "To get executed in America these days you have to be not only a truly nasty person but also very, very unlucky."[139] Only 1 percent of murderers end up on death row, and among those who do, the chance of being executed any given year is around 2 percent.[140] Nowadays, the death penalty's cost is also part of the mix; the question is not just whether the death penalty deters, but whether it deters more than the myriad of other crime control measures that those millions might buy instead.[141]

That leaves retribution, the chief justification for the death penalty today.[142] The idea that those who take a life should forfeit theirs, if only because they deserve it, has a certain intuitive appeal; but here again, the prolonged wait between death sentence and execution (if it ever comes) undermines the moral force of that claim.[143] Killing a killer might satisfy the retributive impulse, but killing a "poster child for redemption,"[144] a killer whose life decades later is marked by deep remorse, service to others, and religious devotion,[145] often lacks the same sense of satisfaction. Those executed are rarely the same people they were when they committed the crime, draining the retributive value of the execution while depriving victims' families of the cold-hearted killer whose execution they could feel good about (although some feel good about it anyway).[146] Moreover, to the extent "closure"

---

[136] Baze v. Rees, 78 (Stevens, J., concurring).

[137] John Donohue, "Does the Death Penalty Deter Killers?," *Newsweek*, August 19, 2015, www .newsweek.com/does-death-penalty-deter-killers-364164. For a recent report by the National Research Council of the National Academy of Sciences, Engineering, and Medicine concluding that research to date has not shown a deterrent effect and therefore should not be used to inform judgments about the death penalty, see National Research Council, "Deterrence and the Death Penalty," April 18, 2012, www.deathpenaltyinfo.org/documents/NatResCouncil-Deterr.pdf.

[138] Glossip v. Gross, 2768–69, 2770.

[139] Kozinski and Gallagher, "Death: The Ultimate Run-On Sentence," 25.

[140] "Capital Punishment in America," *The Economist*.

[141] Steiker and Steiker, "Capital Punishment: A Century," 676–77.

[142] Ibid. 676; Baze v. Rees, 79 (Stevens, J., concurring).

[143] Glossip v. Gross, 2769; Kozinski and Gallagher, "Death: The Ultimate Run-On Sentence," 4.

[144] "Former Inmates Plead for Clemency for Kelly Gissendaner, Who Gave Them Hope in Prison," Death Penalty Information Center, http://deathpenaltyinfo.org/node/6254; Jane Lampman, "A Saint on Death Row," *Christian Science Monitor*, April 7, 2009, www.csmonitor.com/Books/Book-Reviews/2009/0407/a-saint-on-death-row.

[145] Carol S. Steiker and Jordan M. Steiker, "Let God Sort Them Out? Refining the Individualization Requirement in Capital Sentencing," *Yale Law Journal* 102 (1992): 836–37.

[146] Steiker and Steiker, "Entrenchment and/or Destabilization," 230; Frank Green, "Powell Executed for 1999 Murder," *Richmond Times-Dispatch*, March 19, 2010.

for victims' families figures into the retributive calculus, today's death penalty falters for another reason as well: it revictimizes victims, prolonging their suffering and tormenting them with the ups and downs of multiple execution dates and last-minute stays.[147]

If the only consequence of the current administration of capital punishment was to cast its penological justifications into doubt that would be problematic enough. But as the death penalty has become more rare, it has also become more capricious, exacerbating old problems and creating at least one new one. The old problems include arbitrariness in death sentencing and executions,[148] racial disparities in the imposition of death,[149] and death sentences that say more about the lawyering than the crime.[150] The new problem is the influence of location. Today, the single biggest predictor of a death sentence is where the defendant is tried, a reflection of the death-seeking propensities of the local prosecutor.[151] In 2015, 21 counties – less than 1 percent of the nation's total – were responsible for all of the nation's executions; indeed, five were responsible for 40 percent of those executions alone.[152] Like race, the influence of location in death sentencing feeds into a larger problem with the death penalty's application: the factors that should explain the imposition of death don't, and the factors that shouldn't, do.[153]

In short, today's death penalty is marked by high costs and low returns – and that has led to calls to let it go. In 2009, the prestigious American Law Institute rescinded its model penal code on the death penalty, an important development in part because the provision served as the model for every death penalty statute in the modern era, and in part because of the ALI's reason for doing so: "the intractable and structural obstacles to ensuring a minimally adequate system of capital punishment."[154] Conservative opposition to the death penalty has also grown over time. Indeed, it has now given rise to Conservatives Concerned About the Death Penalty, a national organization whose rationale for repeal is perhaps best captured by the words of conservative commentator George Will: "There is no bigger government

---

[147] *Glossip v. Gross*, 2769; Kozinski and Gallagher, "Death: The Ultimate Run-On Sentence" 4; Ronald J. Trabak and J. Mark Lane, "The Execution of Injustice: A Cost and Lack-of-Benefit Analysis of the Death Penalty," *Loyola Louisiana Law Review* 23 (1989): 129–32.

[148] See the discussion at infra notes 167–69.

[149] *Glossip v. Gross*, 2761; Ian Millhiser, "Killing a White Person Is Almost the Only Reason Murderers Ever Receive the Death Penalty," *Think Progress*, September 23, 2015, http://thinkprogress.org/justice/2015/09/23/3704672/murderers-are-almost-never-executed-unless-they-kill-a-white-person/.

[150] *Glossip v. Gross*, 2761.

[151] Ibid. For an excellent report on the issue, see Fair Punishment Project, "America's Top Five Deadliest Prosecutors: How Overzealous Personalities Drive the Death Penalty," June 2016, http://fairpunishment.org/wp-content/uploads/2016/06/FPP-Top5Report_FINAL.pdf.

[152] Ibid.; Nina Totenberg, "Why Has the Death Penalty Grown Increasingly Rare?," NPR, December 7, 2015, www.npr.org/2015/12/07/457403638/why-has-the-death-penalty-grown-increasingly-rare.

[153] *Glossip v. Gross*, 2759–62.

[154] Steiker and Steiker, "No More Tinkering," 354.

program than the one that can kill you.["155] The media has chimed in as well, although in the last several years, its focus has shifted from reporting on the death penalty's problems to predicting its impending demise.[156]

But talk is cheap. The strongest indication of the death penalty's end is the number of states that have ended it. In the last decade, seven states have abandoned the death penalty as the ultimate sanction: New York, New Jersey, Illinois, New Mexico, Connecticut, Maryland, and Delaware.[157] Others have come close. Attempts to repeal the death penalty in Montana and New Hampshire failed by a single vote, and Nebraska's Republican-controlled legislature actually passed a repeal measure, only to have the governor lead a charge to bring it back.[158]

In all but one of the states that abolished the death penalty (Delaware), the cost of capital punishment – and what the state was getting for it – played a substantial part in the decision to let it go. Illinois reported that it had spent some $100 million on the death penalty in the ten years prior to abolition, but had no executions during that time.[159] New York had spent $170 million, and New Jersey $253 million, in the modern death penalty era, and like Illinois, neither had a single execution to show for it.[160] Connecticut and New Mexico had each executed one person in the modern era, but were paying $3–5 million a year to maintain their capital punishment systems.[161] And Maryland had executed five people during that time, but had

---

[155] Davis,"Faith and Fiscal Responsibility"; Clarence Page, "The Most Unlikely Death-Penalty Critics," *Chicago Tribune*, April 12, 2000, http://articles.chicagotribune.com/2000-04-12/news/0004120027_1_death-penalty-critics-executions-death-penalty-information-center.

[156] Von Drehle, "The Last Execution,"; Wolf and Johnson, "Courts, States Put Death Penalty on Life Support"; Lincoln Caplan, "Richard Glossip and the End of the Death Penalty," *New Yorker*, September 30, 2015, www.newyorker.com/news/news-desk/richard-glossip-and-the-end-of-the-death-penalty.

[157] Wolf and Johnson, "Courts, States Put Death Penalty on Life Support"; Steiker and Steiker, "No More Tinkering," 362–64. Delaware is the most recent state to make the move. In August 2016, the Delaware Supreme Court ruled that the state's death penalty statute was unconstitutional, and the state attorney general chose not to appeal the ruling. Randall Chase, "Delaware AG Won't Appeal Court Rejection of Death Penalty," *AP The Big Story*, August 15, 2016, http://bigstory.ap.org/article/8afa1b6bebbb447f92a8e3cdb7c9ac28/delaware-ag-wont-appeal-court-rejection-death-penalty.

[158] Katharine Q. Seelye, "Measure to Repeal the Death Penalty Fails by a Single Vote in the New Hampshire Senate," *New York Times*, April 17, 2014, www.nytimes.com/2014/04/18/us/in-new-hampshire-measure-to-repeal-death-penalty-fails-by-a-single-vote.html?_r=1; Amanda Terkel, "Bill to Abolish the Death Penalty Fails by Just One Vote in Montana House," *Huffington Post*, February 24, 2015, www.huffingtonpost.com/2015/02/24/montana-death-penalty_n_6744316.html. Nebraska reinstated its death penalty by referendum, with the governor contributing $300,000 from his own funds to help. Paul Hammel, "Nebraskans Vote Overwhelmingly to Restore Death Penalty, Nullify Historic 2015 Vote by State Legislature," *Omaha World-Herald*, November 9, 2016, www.omaha.com/news/politics/nebraskans-vote-overwhelmingly-to-restore-death-penalty-nullify-historic-vote/article_38823d54-a5df-11e6-9a5e-d7a71d75611a.html.

[159] Lain, "The Virtues," 408.

[160] Ibid.; Steiker and Steiker, "Cost and Capital Punishment," 121–23.

[161] Laura Bassett, "Connecticut Repeals Death Penalty," *Huffington Post*, April 25, 2012, www.huffingtonpost.com/2012/04/25/connecticut-repeals-death-penalty_n_1453331.html; the New

estimated its cost of doing so at just over \$32 million per execution.[162] Other considerations factored into the decision-making calculus as well – concerns about wrongful convictions, racial bias, and the intolerable conditions of death row among them.[163] But the fact that states were getting little bang for the buck appears to have been a tipping-point for repeal – an ominous sign for the death penalty's future, particularly in low-executing states.[164]

In addition, the cascading effects of decades of constitutional regulation of the death penalty have led to another development portending its demise: the prospect of judicial abolition. In 1972, the Supreme Court invalidated the death penalty because it was arbitrary and capricious as then administered.[165] A sentence of death was like being struck by lightning, Justice Stewart famously lamented[166] – and today that is literally true. In 2016, 20 people were executed; 36 were struck by lightning.[167]

But the problem then, as now, was not just arbitrariness; it was also the mere fact of the death penalty's infrequent use. As Justice White explained in 1972, it was a "near truism" that a punishment "could so seldom be imposed that it would cease to be a credible deterrent or measurably to contribute to any other end of punishment in the criminal justice system."[168] He went on to say that "[a] penalty with such negligible returns to the State would be patently excessive and cruel and unusual punishment violative of the Eighth Amendment."[169] In Justice White's mind, this was exactly what had become of the death penalty by the early 1970s; it had come to be "so infrequently imposed that the threat of execution [was] too attenuated to be of substantial service to criminal justice."[170] And that was 1972.

Fast-forward to 2016. The dramatic decline in death sentences and executions has made the death penalty even more arbitrary than it was 40 years ago, plus it has substantially negated the penological justifications that supported the death penalty in the first place. Over the years, various Supreme Court justices have bemoaned the death penalty's arbitrariness, as well as its failure to produce executions in a manner that would serve its deterrent and retributive purposes (the former complaint coming

---

Mexico Coalition to Repeal the Death Penalty, "Cost," www.nmrepeal.org/issues/cost; Steiker and Steiker, "Cost and Capital Punishment," 121–22.

[162] Ian Simpson, "Maryland Becomes Latest U.S. State to Abolish Death Penalty," *Reuters*, May 2, 2013, www.reuters.com/article/us-usa-maryland-deathpenalty-idUSBRE9410TQ20130502; Steiker and Steiker, "Cost and Capital Punishment," 120;

[163] Simpson, "Maryland Becomes Latest U.S. State"; Deborah Baker, "New Mexico Bans Death Penalty," *Huffington Post*, April 18, 2009, www.huffingtonpost.com/2009/03/18/new-mexico-bans-death-pen_n_176666.html.

[164] Steiker and Steiker, "Cost and Capital Punishment," 162.

[165] Furman v. Georgia, 408 U.S. 238 (1972).

[166] Ibid. 309–10.

[167] Death Penalty Information Center, "Executions by Year;" National Weather Service, "U.S. Lightning Deaths in 2016: 38," www.lightningsafety.noaa.gov/fatalities.shtml.

[168] Furman v. Georgia, 311.

[169] Ibid., 312.

[170] Ibid., 313.

from the left, the latter from the right).[171] But most recently, those complaints have converged into a constitutional catch-22. As Justice Breyer put the point:

> A death penalty system that seeks procedural fairness and reliability brings with it delays that severely aggravate the cruelty of capital punishment and significantly undermine the rationale for imposing a sentence of death in the first place.... In this world, or at least in this Nation, we can have a death penalty that at least arguably serves legitimate penological purposes or we can have a procedural system that at least arguably seeks reliability and fairness in the death penalty's application. We cannot have both.[172]

Fold in the fact that the Justices now consider societal trends – "evolving standards of decency" – in determining whether a punishment violates the "cruel and unusual punishments" clause and one can begin to see the constitutional case for abolition.[173]

Indeed, lower courts have already started making it. In 2015, the Connecticut Supreme Court struck down what was left of the state's death penalty after its legislative repeal.[174] And in 2014, a federal district court in California ruled that the state's death penalty was unconstitutional, in part because "the execution of a death sentence is so infrequent, and the delays proceeding it so extraordinary, that the death penalty is deprived of any deterrent or retributive effect it might once have had," and in part because in California, a sentence of death amounted to one "no rational jury or legislature could ever impose: life in prison, with the remote possibility of death."[175] Ironically, the Ninth Circuit Court of Appeals reversed the decision on procedural grounds.[176] The case had come to the district court on habeas, and procedural hurdles should have prevented it from ruling on the merits of the claim.[177]

So there we stand. The finality of the death penalty makes the stakes too high to impose the punishment without substantial protections, but those protections come with burdens and those burdens come with costs. Those costs have led to problems (or at least revealed them), and those problems have beget problems of their own. Put it all together and you get plummeting death sentences and executions, along with more costs, more burdens, and more dissatisfaction with the death penalty's negligible returns. States walk away, courts start taking notice, and even politicians are not campaigning on support for the death penalty like they once were.

---

[171] Steiker and Steiker, "Capital Punishment: A Century," 683; John Paul Stevens, "On the Death Sentence," *New York Review of Books*, December 23, 2010, www.nybooks.com/articles/2010/12/23/death-sentence/ (last accessed January 10, 2016); Glossip v. Gross, 2760, 2762, 2770; Callins v. Collins, 1130; Steiker and Steiker, "No More Tinkering," 388–89.

[172] Glossip v. Gross, 2772.

[173] Glossip v. Gross, 2773, 2749.

[174] State v. Santiago, 318 Conn. 1, 55–73 (2015).

[175] Jones v. Chappell, 1053, 1063.

[176] Jones v. Davis, 806 F.3d 538 (2015).

[177] Ibid., 538–53.

The train, it would seem, has left the station – but one can still imagine it getting derailed. A domestic terrorism attack (or other mass murder) might do it; retribution is a value one can tout at any cost. A Supreme Court ruling that invalidates the death penalty before the country is ready might also be a way to kick-start renewed enthusiasm for capital punishment. After all, the death penalty was dying once before; it was backlash in the wake of the Court's 1972 decision abolishing the death penalty that led to its revival in 1976.[178]

Only this much is clear – the trajectory we are on now. If we continue on this trajectory, the American institution of capital punishment will, over time, collapse under its own weight. It may take years, it may take decades, and it may be cut short by court intervention. But if current trends continue, it is only a matter of time – and time is so much of what today's death penalty is all about. Upon reflection, there is something strangely karmic in the way the death penalty is winding down, an irony in the fact that capital punishment itself is dying a painstakingly slow death on pragmatic grounds.

[178] Corinna Barrett Lain, "Furman Fundamentals," *Washington Law Review* 82 (2007): 46–55.

3

The Time It Takes to Die and the Death of the Death Penalty

Untimely Meditations on the End of Capital Punishment in the United States

Jennifer L. Culbert

A necessary assumption of modern death penalty jurisprudence in the United States is that "death is different."[1] The uniqueness of the penalty of death – what distinguishes it from any other penalty – is generally ascribed to two characteristics of death: its finality and its severity.[2] However, as many scholars of the death penalty have observed, the time it takes to die obscures and undermines the uniqueness of death as a punishment. Since people condemned to death are guaranteed certain procedural rights that people condemned to life in prison are not, when a person is condemned to death they are not condemned to die at the hands of the state as much as they are condemned to the *possibility* of being executed rather than dying in prison as others do.[3] In this essay, I echo the remarks of legal scholars who discuss the way in which "delayed" and "slow" death contribute to the demise of the difference of death. However, these remarks address only part of what the time it takes to die does to the modern system of capital punishment. The time it takes to die does not simply render a death sentence a sentence to die in confinement – perhaps by lethal injection or some other method of execution, or perhaps not. Nor does the time it takes to die simply remind us that death is a more or less painful process – one that can be exacerbated by procedures put in place ostensibly to reduce the dying person's suffering. The time it takes to die also reminds us that the image of death that guides the modern capital punishment system – an image of

---

[1] *Gregg v. Georgia*, 428 U.S. 153 (1976) at 188.

[2] *Garner v. Florida*, 430 U.S. 349 (1977) at 357. Jeffrey Abramson argues there is a third characteristic of death: the decision to impose death as a penalty is based on an "ethical" rather than a "legal" judgment. This is due to the fact that the penalty addresses matters of "moral guilt" as much if not more than legal culpability. See Jeffrey Abramson, "Death-Is-Different Jurisprudence and the Role of the Capital Jury," *Ohio State Journal of Criminal Law* 2:117 (2004): 119.

[3] *Jones v. Chappell*, Case CV 09-02158-CJC, July 2014. See also Angela April Sun, "'Killing Time' in the Valley of the Shadow of Death: Why Systematic Pre-execution Delays on Death Row Are Cruel and Unusual," *Columbia Law Review* 113 (2013): 1585, 1604.

death as immediate and total annihilation – is profoundly uncertain. As the history of the death penalty itself teaches, death has been and can be always imagined otherwise. In brief, I argue in this essay that the time it takes to die reminds us that death is related to time – not simply because death takes time, but because the way we imagine what it is to die and to be dead is not a matter of fact as much as it is a matter of speculation about a paradoxically unforeseeable future that, in itself, reflects the prejudices of our moment. While individuals sentenced to death often experience religious conversions that provide them with images of death other than the image assumed by modern death penalty jurisprudence – specifically ones where death is not, in some metaphysical way, really the complete end of life – the modern criminal justice system does not impose death as a penalty in order to hasten the moment when criminals will be brought before the judges of the next world where "real" justice can be done.[4] Death is imposed as the most absolute penalty that can be imposed in a secular society.[5] By calling attention to the relationship between time and death, the time it takes to die leads us to consider not simply or only the value of imposing death as a penalty but also the cogency of the figure of death that is assumed *and* required by the modern capital punishment system. Consequently, the time it takes to die unsettles not only the capital punishment system (as conventional critics would have it) and the criminal justice system (as criminal law professionals recognize), but also the understanding of "life" that is the alternative to "death," for when we imagine death differently, alternative possibilities for the way we imagine life may become more evident too.

"DEATH IS DIFFERENT"

How?

The Supreme Court has long recognized that "death is a different kind of punishment from any other which may be imposed in this country."[6] As noted above, the two aspects of death that are most often identified as distinguishing it from all other penalties are its severity and its finality. When the severity of the death penalty is at

---

4   Albert Camus, "Reflections on the Guillotine," in *Resistance, Rebellion, and Death*, trans. Justin O'Brien (New York: Vintage Books, 1988), 173–234. See also Daniel Lachance, "Some Find Redemption on Death Row, but Few Find Mercy," *The Conversation*, November 3, 2015, https://theconversation.com/some-find-redemption-on-death-row-but-few-find-mercy-49791, accessed May 31, 2016.

5   See *Gardner* v. *Florida*, 430 U.S. 349 (1977) at 357–58. "From the point of view of society, the action of the sovereign in taking the life of one of its citizens also differs dramatically from any other legitimate state action." What is more, in a self-governing community that understands that it gives law to itself rather than receiving it from a higher authority, death is imposed by the sovereign state as a manifestation of its monopoly of lethal violence and its "awe-inspiring" power. Walter Berns, *For Capital Punishment: Crime and the Morality of the Death Penalty* (Lanham, MD: University Press of America, 1991), 169.

6   *Gardner* v. *Florida*, 430 U.S. 349 (1977) at 357.

issue, it is the enormity of the penalty that is being emphasized. Death is the "ultimate sanction."[7] It is the most terrible punishment the state can impose. Death is unique in its gravity and harshness because of "its absolute renunciation of all that is embodied in our concept of humanity."[8] In brief, it is a "truly awesome punishment,"[9] inspiring a mixture of wonder and dread with the magnitude of the state's repudiation of the person being punished. Due to its severity, the Supreme Court is alert to the potential excessiveness of death as a punishment in relation to a particular crime. For this reason, the Court has insisted that the penalty be reserved for the most heinous crimes and justified in its application in terms of a valid penological purpose.[10]

The finality of the death penalty is difficult to distinguish from its severity. Still, the irreversibility of death is treated as a separate aspect of the death penalty that also sets it apart from all other punishments.[11] For once the penalty has been carried out, unlike other penalties, it cannot be annulled or voided; it is irrevocable.[12] When a person is executed, they can never be resuscitated and brought back to life. Death precludes the possibility of changing course, turning around and returning to an earlier moment. Should a mistake be made – regarding the facts of the case or the law that applies, regarding the way in which the trial is carried out or the way in which the sentence is determined – redress is impossible. The mistake cannot be rectified; there is no relief.[13] The finality of the death penalty calls then for accuracy (or at least a heightened need for "reliability"[14]) in the determination of legal responsibility and moral guilt.

Why the state should ever impose such a final and severe penalty is a question that is answered by the Supreme Court in *Gregg* v. *Georgia* (1976).[15] The Court states, "In part, capital punishment is an expression of society's moral outrage at particularly offensive conduct. This function may be unappealing to many, but it is essential in an ordered society that asks its citizens to rely on legal processes rather than self-help to vindicate their wrongs."[16] This statement betrays a number of assumptions about crime, anger, revenge, and law that reinforce and strengthen the idea that "death is different" from all other punishments imposed by the state. For example, the death penalty is explicitly recognized to be "expressive."[17] When

---

[7] *Furman* v. *Georgia*, 408 U.S. 238 (1972) at 286.
[8] *Furman*, 408 U.S. at 306.
[9] *Furman*, 408 U.S. at 290.
[10] *Gregg* v. *Georgia*, 428 U.S. 153 (1976) at 183.
[11] *Ring* v. *Arizona*, 536 U.S. 584 (2002) at 616.
[12] See *Furman*, 408 U.S. at 306; *Gregg*, 428 U.S. at 187; *Spaziano* v. *Florida*, 468 U.S. 447 (1984) at 468.
[13] *Furman*, 408 U.S. at 290.
[14] *Woodson* v. *North Carolina*, 428 U.S. 280 (1976) at 305.
[15] *Gregg*, 428 U.S.
[16] *Gregg*, 428 U.S. at 183.
[17] Joel Feinberg, "The Expressive Function of Punishment," *The Monist* 49:3 (July 1965): 397–423.

the Court says that capital punishment is an expression of society's moral outrage, the Court recognizes the death penalty to consist of more than "hard treatment"; in addition it has a "condemnatory aspect."[18] This means the death penalty is, adapting Joel Feinberg's description of punishment, "a conventional device for the expression of attitudes of resentment and indignation, and of judgments of disapproval and reprobation, either on the part of the punishing authority himself or of those 'in whose name' the punishment is inflicted."[19] In *Gregg*, the Court recognizes the death penalty as such a device. The Court also recognizes that what the death penalty expresses is not simply personal resentment or fury toward a person who commits some heinous act. According to the Court's statement in *Gregg*, the death penalty communicates a feeling of "moral outrage" or righteous anger, a feeling that is shared by the members of a community on the occasion when "someone has acted in a manner that is thought to be unjust."[20] Walter Berns argues that such a response is based on the opinion that "men are responsible, and should be held responsible, for what they do."[21] Indeed, according to Berns, "Anger recognizes that only men have the capacity to be moral beings and, in so doing, acknowledges the dignity of human beings."[22] In addition, and just as importantly, anger demonstrates that the members of a society are not just self-interested, calculating individuals who have consented to abide by a set of rules only because (and only to the extent that) they personally benefit from these rules. Feelings of anger that arise and are shared when others are betrayed or harmed demonstrate that people actually care about what happens to the other members of their society.[23] Berns helps us see that, to the extent a feeling of moral outrage is expressed by capital punishment, the "ordered society" to which the Court refers in *Gregg* is assumed to be a "moral community."

Of course, the Court admits that the expression of righteous anger articulated by capital punishment is not necessarily pleasing to everyone. Nevertheless, the Court insists that capital punishment is vital in a society that "asks" its citizens to defer to a central authority to get revenge rather than take justice in their own hands. Thus, the Court seems to assume the validity of an argument made by René Girard, that "vengeance is a vicious circle that is broken only when the power to seek reprisal is consolidated in a sovereign authority," specifically a judicial system in conjunction with a firmly established political power,[24] which is ultimately a power that can sacrifice lives.[25] The Court implies the promise to express outrage in the genre of lethal violence – specifically the threat to impose capital punishment – must be kept

---

[18] Feinberg, "The Expressive Function of Punishment," 397–423, 423.
[19] Feinberg, "The Expressive Function of Punishment," 397–423, 400.
[20] Berns, *For Capital Punishment: Crime and the Morality of the Death Penalty*, 153.
[21] Berns, *For Capital Punishment: Crime and the Morality of the Death Penalty*, 153.
[22] Berns, *For Capital Punishment: Crime and the Morality of the Death Penalty*, 154.
[23] Berns, *For Capital Punishment: Crime and the Morality of the Death Penalty*, 155.
[24] René Girard, *Violence and the Sacred*, trans. Patrick Gregory (Baltimore: Johns Hopkins University Press, 1972), 23.
[25] Girard, *Violence and the Sacred*, 17.

if "ordered society" is to continue foregoing the satisfactions of "self-help." The threat provides not only a substitute pleasure for those who might otherwise seek to "vindicate their wrongs," but also a warning to those who might otherwise engage in "offensive conduct" themselves in the pursuit of vindication.

Following Michel Foucault's account of the disappearance of torture as a public spectacle in *Discipline and Punish*, Austin Sarat explains in *Gruesome Spectacles* that the act of putting someone to death once contained a dramatic, awe-inspiring pedagogy of power.[26] In *Discipline and Punish*, Foucault points out that "Besides its immediate victim, the crime attacks the sovereign: it attacks him personally, since the law represents the will of the sovereign."[27] In other words, by engaging in conduct offensive to an "ordered society," the criminal harms not only the direct victim of their crime but also challenges the authority of the sovereign political power that guarantees the order of society. According to this understanding of the crime, execution has a "juridico-political function": "It is a ceremonial by which a momentarily injured sovereignty is reconstituted. It restores that sovereignty by manifesting it at its most spectacular."[28] In particular, the public execution "deploys before all eyes an invincible force. Its aim is not so much to re-establish as to bring into play, as its extreme point, the dissymmetry between the subject who has dared to violate the law and the all-powerful sovereign who displays his strength."[29]

Today, however, the execution not only takes place behind high walls and locked doors. It is also a "cool, bureaucratic operation,"[30] or at least it is supposed to be. According to Foucault, over time instead of demonstrating the superiority of the sovereign, excessive punishment "was thought to equal, if not exceed, in savagery the crime itself" so that instead of setting the sovereign apart and above the condemned criminal, torture and public executions came to make "the executioner resemble a criminal, judges murderers," and "the tortured criminal an object of pity or admiration."[31] Punishment then becomes the most hidden part of the penal process, and "justice no longer takes public responsibility for the violence that is bound up with its practice."[32]

While it may no longer take public responsibility for the violence the practice of justice requires,[33] Sarat argues that the state continues to work primarily to differentiate state killing from murder. What this means today is that "we seek a technology

---

[26] Austin Sarat, *Gruesome Spectacles: Botched Executions and America's Death Penalty* (Stanford, CA: Stanford University Press, 2014), 28.

[27] Michel Foucault, *Discipline and Punish: The Birth of the Prison*, trans. Alan Sheridan (New York: Vintage Books, 1995), 47.

[28] Foucault, *Discipline and Punish*, 48.

[29] Ibid., 48–49; cited in Sarat, *Gruesome Spectacles*, 8.

[30] Sarat, *Gruesome Spectacles*, 9.

[31] Foucault, *Discipline and Punish*, 9.

[32] Ibid.

[33] See Robert Cover, "Violence and the Word," *Yale Law Journal* 95 (1986): 1601.

that leaves no trace." We do so, Sarat claims, because the methods used to take life help us distinguish the death we call capital punishment from the death we call murder.

The Difference the Difference Makes

Because death is different in its severity and its finality, the procedures used in capital cases are held to a heightened standard of substantive and procedural fairness. After the Supreme Court ruled in *Furman* v. *Georgia* (1972) that capital punishment was unconstitutional because it was imposed arbitrarily, it was not certain the death penalty could ever be imposed in the United States again. However, in 1976, the Court determined the death penalty could be imposed without violating the Constitution when states sufficiently rationalized their sentencing processes. The sentencing schemes that passed muster at that time, shared two features. First, trials in capital cases were divided in two phases: the guilt phase and the sentencing phase. Second, during the sentencing phase, the sentencing authority was required to "weigh" aggravating and mitigating circumstances and base its sentencing decision on the outcome of the process. Law professor Margaret Jane Radin famously refers to this development in the jurisprudence of capital punishment as "a kind of super due process."[34] In capital cases, Radin argues, the Supreme Court has determined the process by which a death penalty is imposed, and not just the death penalty itself, may violate the Eighth Amendment's prohibition against cruel and unusual punishment. In brief, while death may be imposed as long as it is not "inhuman and barbarous" and does not "involve torture or a lingering death,"[35] the process by which death is determined to be the appropriate penalty in a particular case may itself be found to deny human dignity, thereby rendering the death penalty unconstitutional. While the Court has often admitted that it has not clearly identified what constitutes "cruel and unusual punishment," in *Trop* v. *Dulles* (1958) it claims, "The basic concept underlying the Eighth Amendment is nothing less than the dignity of man."[36] At the same time, the Court acknowledges that the words of the Amendment are not "precise" and their "scope is not static." Hence, "The Amendment must draw its meaning from the evolving standards of decency that mark the progress of a maturing society."[37] Consequently, a death sentence imposed under a sentencing scheme that was once accepted may now be challenged on the grounds that the procedure fails to treat persons with the degree of respect society has come to expect. This is what happened in *Woodson* v. *North Carolina* (1976).[38] In *Woodson*, the Supreme Court states, "North Carolina's

[34] Margaret Jane Radin, "Cruel Punishment and Respect for Persons: Super Due Process for Death," 53 *Southern California Law Review* 1143 (1980): 1148.

[35] *In re. Kemmler*, 136 U.S. 436 (1890) at 447.

[36] *Trop* v. *Dulles*, 356 U.S. 86 (1958) at 100.

[37] *Trop*, 356 U.S. at 101.

[38] *Woodson*, 428 U.S.

mandatory death penalty statute for first-degree murder departs markedly from contemporary standards respecting the imposition of the punishment of death and thus cannot be applied consistently with the Eighth and Fourteenth Amendments' requirement that the State's power to punish 'be exercised within the limits of civilized standards.'"[39] While the Court in a companion case allows that the death penalty may be imposed in the United States, in *Woodson* the Court finds North Carolina's death penalty statute deficient for the purpose. Indeed, not only does the statute depart from contemporary standards respecting the imposition of the punishment of death by making the punishment mandatory for persons found guilty of a capital crime[40] but it also fails to guide the discretion of the jury sentencing the defendant to death (as required by *Furman* to check the "arbitrary and capricious" exercise of "the power to determine which first-degree murderers shall live and which shall die.")[41] In addition, the statute fails to provide for "particularized consideration" of the character and record of the person found guilty of murder before the imposition of the death sentence (also required by *Furman* to insure that "death is the appropriate punishment in a specific case.")[42]

Over time the Supreme Court has insisted that death penalty sentencing schemes include some additional features. Recently, in *Hurst v. Florida* (2016), the Court declared that the jury in a death penalty case rather than the judge must find each fact necessary to impose a sentence of death.[43] In brief, judges are no longer to make independent decisions about what the defendant deserves, taking juries' recommendations into consideration only. Now, juries must find the facts necessary to sentence defendants to the ultimate punishment.

Another common feature of state death penalty statutes is the automatic appeal of any death sentence imposed to the state's supreme court. Not every state makes the appeal mandatory but no state precludes it. In *Gregg* v. *Georgia* (1976), the U.S. Supreme Court describes the automatic appeal provided for by Georgia's new statutory scheme as "an important additional safeguard against arbitrariness and caprice."[44] The statute charges the State Supreme Court "to review each sentence of death and determine whether it was imposed under the influence of passion or prejudice, whether the evidence supports the jury's finding of a statutory aggravating circumstance, and whether the sentence is disproportionate compared to those sentences imposed in similar cases."[45] The appeals process that has developed since 1976 is the focus of much attention in our present discussions of the time it takes to die.

---

[39] *Woodson,* 428 U.S. at 301.
[40] *Woodson,* 428 U.S. at 288–302.
[41] *Woodson,* 428 U.S. at 302–03.
[42] *Woodson,* 428 U.S. at 303–05.
[43] *Hurst v. Florida,* 136 S.Ct. 616 (2016).
[44] *Gregg,* 428 U.S. at 198.
[45] *Gregg,* 428 U.S. at 198.

THE TIME IT TAKES TO DIE

It is evident now that it takes a long time to die on death row. What is not evident are the reasons for the time it takes, responsibility for the delay, and the legal consequences of dying so slowly in the hands of the state.

"Delayed Death"

In 2009, the Supreme Court of the United States denied the petition for writ of certiorari in the case of *Thompson* v. *Florida*.[46] William Thompson had been on death row for thirty-two years. He petitioned the Court to determine whether the Eighth Amendment's prohibition of cruel and unusual punishments precludes the execution of a prisoner who has been on death row for such an extraordinary amount of time. Indeed, according to the Bureau of Justice Statistics, in 2013, the most recent year for which data have been published, the average elapsed time from sentence to execution of all inmates executed in the United States was 186 months or 15.5 years.[47] (In 2011, it was 198 months or 16.5 years.)

The statements made by Justices John Paul Stevens, Clarence Thomas, and Stephen Breyer in *Thompson* v. *Florida* discuss many of the reasons for the length of confinement under sentence of death. The first and most obvious reason has to do with the appeals process. While there are slight variations across states, the process is similar everywhere. After a death sentence is imposed there is a direct appeal to the state's highest court. If the court reverses or throws out the defendant's conviction or sentence, the case goes back to the trial court, and the whole process may start again. If the court allows the conviction and sentence to stand, the defendant may appeal to the U.S. Supreme Court. The Supreme Court is not obliged to take the case, but until it decides not to do so, the defendant's direct appeals process remains in effect.

More often than not, the Court decides not to take the defendant's case. The defendant may then return to the state to make one final appeal for a habeas corpus review of their case. Such a review is to examine the lawfulness of the defendant's detention or imprisonment. The defendant will argue that they should be released on the grounds of either a factual or a legal error. The error usually identified is the denial of a state constitutional right, such as the right to effective assistance of counsel. The defendant may also allege prosecutorial misconduct, or that any plea they made before trial was involuntary. If the state's highest court decides that such an error occurred, the case may go back to the trial court. If the court decides that no error occurred, the state's appeal process is over.

The defendant may then try to take their case to federal court. To do so, the defendant requests another habeas corpus review but this time in a district court that

---

[46] *Thompson* v. *McNeil*, 129 S.Ct. 1299 (2009).

[47] Tracy L. Snell, "Capital Punishment, 2013 – Statistical Tables," December 2014, NCJ 248448, U.S. Department of Justice, Office of Justice Programs, Bureau of Justice Statistics.

can consider a claim regarding the denial of a federal constitutional right. Again, the defendant is likely to make the claim that they were denied effective assistance of counsel. If the district court finds that the defendant has been denied a federal constitutional right or has been otherwise unlawfully detained, the case goes back to the state trial court. However, if the district court disagrees with the defendant's argument about the lawfulness of their detention, the appeals process is still not quite over. The defendant may challenge the district court's decision by filing an appeal with a federal court of appeals. If the appeals court agrees with the defendant, the case may be sent back to the state court. If the appeals court disagrees with the defendant, the defendant has still one last appeal to make. This appeal is made to the U.S. Supreme Court. Again, the Supreme Court is not obliged to take the case. But if the Court refuses to take the case this time, the defendant has exhausted the appeals process. With no other option, the defendant may then choose to seek clemency from the governor of the state in which they were originally tried.

The time it takes just to describe the appeals process gives some indication of how long the process takes to play out in the actual life of a person found guilty and sentenced to death for a capital crime. But while many people, and in particular supporters of the death penalty such as Justice Thomas,[48] blame the appeals process for the time it takes to see someone executed after they have been sentenced to death, other factors contribute as well. As law professor Dwight Aarons observes, a defendant is more likely to be on death row for an inordinate amount of time when their case is on the margins of death eligibility.[49] What is more, the dysfunctional administration of the criminal justice system is responsible for many delays. As Justice Stevens notes in *Thompson* v. *McNeil*, citing Justice Breyer in *Knight* v. *Florida*, "delays have multiple causes, including 'the States' failure to apply constitutionally sufficient procedures at the time of initial [conviction or] sentencing.'"[50] An ineffective and inefficient capital case processing system leads to delays in finding and appointing eligible counsel, for example. Fighting off execution warrants that are prematurely issued, ironically in an effort to facilitate faster executions, may also delay matters as attorneys are loathe to take cases under such pressure and inmates must then fight for stays of execution before they have even completed their state habeas proceedings. Delays may also be caused by incompetent counsel, or by uncertainty concerning the substantive criminal law and Eighth Amendment jurisprudence. Limits on the reimbursement of fees and expenses for appellate attorneys can slow things down as well.

---

[48] In *Thompson* v. *McNeil*, Justice Thomas reiterates, "I remain 'unaware of any support in the American constitutional tradition or in this Court's precedent for the proposition that a defendant can avail himself of the panoply of appellate and collateral procedures and then complain when his execution is delayed.'" *Thompson*, 129 S.Ct. at 1301, citing *Knight* v. *Florida*, 528 U.S. 990 (1999) at 990.

[49] Dwight Aarons, "Getting Out of This Mess: Steps toward Addressing and Avoiding Inordinate Delay in Capital Cases," *Journal of Criminal Law and Criminology* 89:1 (1998): 1.

[50] *Thompson*, 129 S.Ct. at 1300, citing *Knight*, 528 U.S. at 998.

In addition to the delays related to counsel, prosecutors may be responsible for some delays in the appellate review. For example, prosecutors may force courts to consider matters that are tangential to the question of the defendant's guilt or the appellate process. This may occur when prosecutors resist requests to release public records and documents, or when they seek to disqualify defense attorneys from representing inmates. As the attorneys responsible for a trial may not be the same attorneys responsible for the appeal and post-conviction work, the state can lose track of cases for a while. Actually, even when cases are carefully monitored, court records and other documents can get lost so that time must be spent searching for them or reconstructing testimony. Indeed, years may pass before the court reporter, court clerk, trial attorneys, and trial judge review a transcript of the original trial and certify it for appellate review.

Burdened by large caseloads both prosecutors and defense attorneys may ask for extensions. Additional delays may be due to the discovery of new facts and developments in the law. The good behavior of the inmate on death row may also provide additional arguments for appeal. Of course, the longer an inmate waits to be executed, the more time there is for these kinds of arguments to become salient. Finally, despite the aggressiveness with which defendants may be charged with and prosecuted for capital crimes, the state is not always ready or willing to execute those it convicts. In addition to having to marshal the resources necessary to get an inmate to the execution chamber, there are political reasons to limit the number of people executed in a state every year.

"Slow Death"

In addition to the appeals process that contributes to the delay between sentence and execution, there is another process identified with the modern system of capital punishment in the United States that is criticized for taking too much time: lethal injection. Lethal injection is the most common method of execution now used in the United States. In 1982, Texas was the first state to use it. At the time, lethal injection was lauded as a painless and quick method of execution. In addition, it had the advantage of giving an execution the appearance of a peaceful, medical procedure. Indeed, as retired warden Donald A. Cabana notes, lethal injection was often condemned by death penalty supporters as killing convicted criminals in a manner that was "better than they deserve."[51] At the same time, opponents of capital punishment objected to lethal injection on the grounds that lethal injection "sanitizes the whole execution process – makes it far too easy, too clean."[52] Death penalty opponent Robert Johnson observes that a "supine inmate, seemingly at rest, appears

[51] Donald A. Cabana, "The History of Capital Punishment in Mississippi: An Overview," http:// mshistorynow.mdah.state.ms.us/articles/84/history-of-capital-punishment-in-mississippi-an-over view#topofpage, accessed 6 March 2016.
[52] Cabana, "The History of Capital Punishment in Mississippi: An Overview."

to drift off into a sleep that merges imperceptibly with death."[53] This is, he claims, the ideal modern death, "a death that occurs in one's sleep, painlessly."[54]

Experience with lethal injection has shown that we have yet to be able to command such a death. Instead, lethal injection has proven to be one of the most complicated, least understood, and poorly administered criminal penalties used. It also takes a lot of time. Recent examples of what I am calling "slow death" abound. To take but one example, and not the most protracted, there is the death of Clayton Lockett. On April 29, 2014, Lockett was executed by the state of Oklahoma as punishment for the 1999 murder of nineteen-year-old Stephanie Neiman and the rape of her friend. Neiman was shot and buried alive. Lockett was executed by lethal injection. The first drug, midazolam, which acts as a sedative, was given at 6:23 pm and a doctor declared Lockett unconscious at 6:33 pm. However, when the next drugs were introduced, vercuronium bromide and potassium chloride, Lockett "raised his head up" and started "kind of jerking it," according to the court filing. Witnesses also claim he started moaning and trying to talk. The corrections director, Robert Patton, called off the execution at about 6:56 pm. As no life-saving measures were given to Lockett, he soon died. His time of death was recorded as 43 minutes after the execution started.

This neat number, horrifying as it is, obscures the fact that we don't know when the execution actually started and so cannot really say how long Lockett's execution took. According to the court filing, Lockett was pricked at least 16 times in an attempt to get the IV inserted for the lethal injection. The correct needle was unavailable, and the doctor used a 1.25 inch needle instead of a 2 to 2.25 inch needle to put an IV in Lockett's femoral vein. The doctor declined to set a second line because, the doctor said later, "We had stuck this individual so many times, I didn't want to try and do another line." It was acknowledged that Lockett was "in some pain" from all of the sticks. Later, when it became apparent that there was a problem with the IV, a doctor tried to set a new intravenous line in Lockett's groin area but hit an artery so blood squirted on his clothing. According to court documents filed by lawyers, the prison warden described the scene as "a bloody mess."

The question of when an execution actually starts is a serious one. In 2009, Romell Broom was put to death by lethal injection as punishment for the rape and murder of a fourteen-year-old girl, crimes for which he was convicted in 1985. Unfortunately, officials failed to get a needle into his veins. In a period of two hours, Broom was pricked 18 times to no avail. The governor finally called off the execution. In 2013, the Ohio Supreme Court agreed to consider whether a second attempt at executing Broom would be cruel and unusual punishment and violate double-jeopardy rules. In 2016, the Court ruled 4–3 that a second attempt to execute Broom

[53] Robert Johnson, *Death Work: A Study of the Modern Execution Process* (Belmont, CA: Wadsworth Publishing Co., 1998), 46.

[54] Johnson, *Death Work*, 46.

by lethal injection would not violate the double jeopardy clauses of the federal and state constitutions. According to the Court, the law makes clear that "the execution commences when the lethal drug enters the IV line."[55] As the procedure in Broom's case was never able to proceed to this point, there is "no violation of the Fifth Amendment protection against double jeopardy, [and] the state is not barred from a second attempt to execute."[56] With regard to the argument that a second attempt at executing Broom would be cruel and unusual punishment, the Ohio Supreme Court argued, "The state's intention in carrying out the execution is not to cause unnecessary physical pain or psychological harm."[57] Although the Court recognized that the state had failed to follow its execution protocol in 2009, it noted that since then the state had revised the protocol and successfully executed 21 death-row inmates.[58] On these grounds, the Court concluded that Broom had not convincingly established that "the state in carrying out a second attempt is likely to violate its protocol and cause severe pain."[59] In addition, the Court claimed, "the pain and emotional trauma Broom already experienced do not equate with the type of torture prohibited by the Eighth Amendment."[60] Consequently, the state is not barred from seeking to execute Broom a second time.

Again, while it is difficult to remember now, lethal injection was originally greeted with ambivalence by Americans *not* because it was understood to be such a difficult procedure but, on the contrary, as Cabana notes, because it was considered "too easy."[61] However, the "tidy appearance" of lethal injection is a distinct part of its appeal, according to law professor Deborah Denno. While it is true that the condemned person may not appear to suffer when they are executed by lethal injection and, consequently, their death may not satisfy the desire for revenge expressed by their victim's loved ones, the appearance of controlled, painless death is important for the state, particularly when there is increasing pressure from the public to televise executions.[62]

In the context of such a possibility, communications scholar Catherine Langford's argument about the use of the body-as-gauge metaphor is particularly relevant.[63] Langford argues that capital punishment discourse is guided by a metaphor – "the body-as-gauge."[64] In brief, the body is figured as a measuring device that can be read

[55] *State* v. *Broom*, 146 Ohio St.3d 60, 2016-Ohio-1028 at 26.
[56] *State*, 146 Ohio St.3d at 26.
[57] *State*, 146 Ohio St.3d at 46.
[58] *State*, 146 Ohio St.3d at 52.
[59] *State*, 146 Ohio St.3d at 53.
[60] *State*, 146 Ohio St.3d at 46.
[61] Cabana, "The History of Capital Punishment in Mississippi: An Overview."
[62] Deborah Denno, "When Legislatures Delegate Death: The Troubling Paradox behind State Uses of Electrocution and Lethal Injection and What It Says about Us," *Ohio State Law Journal* 63 (2002): 92 note 181.
[63] Catherine L. Langford, "Tinkering with the Machinery of Death: The Body-as-Gauge in Discourses about Capital Punishment," *Argumentation and Advocacy* 51 (Winter 2015): 153–170.
[64] Langford, "Tinkering with the Machinery of Death," 154.

for signs of pain or suffering. This figure, she says, appears in the discourse of all parties concerned with capital punishment; abolitionists, prosecutors, defense attorneys, judges deciding cases, the people in charge of administering the death penalty, and policymakers all use the body-as-gauge metaphor to evaluate the different methods the state uses to kill. A body that writhes, sits up, or bleeds sets off alarms, and the courts are obliged to consider the Eighth Amendment.[65]

Arguing that problems with electrocution and asphyxiation (the gas chamber) led the states broadly to adopt lethal injection as the preferred method of execution, she shows how the body-as-gauge metaphor culminates in the three-drug protocol. Although the first execution by lethal injection took place in 1982 in Texas, Oklahoma was the first state to adopt lethal injection as a means of execution in 1977.[66] The protocol developed then in Oklahoma called for the use of three drugs: sodium thiopental, an anesthetic which renders the inmate unconscious; pavulon or pancuronium bromide, which paralyzes the inmate and stops them from breathing; and potassium chloride, which finally stops the inmate's heart. Langford argues that these drugs work to disengage and then disconnect the body-as-gauge. According to Langford, the first step, the anesthetic, "*disassociates* the mind from the body. . . . [I]f the mind is not conscious of pain, the body-as-gauge will not register suffering." The second step, the pancuronium bromide, "*masks* pain if the first step is not successful. By paralyzing the muscular system, the body will not respond to the pain experienced if the brain is cognizant of it." The third and final step stops the inmate's heart terminates life, obviously, "ending the ability of the body-as-gauge to function."[67]

While methods of execution are often critically evaluated in terms of the suffering they (appear to) cause, it is also the case that they may be constitutionally challenged if they simply take too long. In *In re Kemmler* (1890), the Court holds that "Punishments are cruel when they involve torture or a lingering death."[68] In other words, it is understood that death takes time but it is also constitutionally required that death come quickly. The question then is how quickly. Is there a tipping point in time where the courts must step in and say "enough is enough"?[69]

According to Langford, and despite the Ohio Supreme Court's finding in 2016, we are "confident" that "executions extending one to two hours should be considered torture." But when, on the basis of the body-as-gauge metaphor, Langford claims, "18 minutes is acceptable; 25 minutes is too long," as Langford

---

[65] Langford, "Tinkering with the Machinery of Death," 154.

[66] "So Long as They Die: Lethal Injections in the United States," www.hrw.org/reports/2006/us0406/3.htm, accessed March 14, 2016.

[67] Langford, "Tinkering with the Machinery of Death," 163.

[68] *In re. Kemmler*, 136 U.S. at 447. "Cruel" may also be defined in terms of proportionality so that a punishment may be rendered unconstitutional if it is found excessive with regard not only to the crime for which it is being imposed but also with regard to the pain involved.

[69] Erin Simmons, "Challenging an Execution after Prolonged Confinement on Death Row [Lackey Revisited]," *Case Western Reserve Law Review* 59, no. 4 (2009): 1249, 1250.

acknowledges, "Where the constitutional line of protection is drawn within the seven minutes that exists in-between is uncertain."[70]

The problem seems to have become more pressing now that some of the drugs used for the three-drug protocol are no longer available.[71] At the end of 2010, manufacturers of sodium thiopental in Europe refused to allow it to be used in capital punishment, and in 2011, the European Commission imposed new restrictions on the export of anesthetics used to execute people.[72] Most recently, the pharmaceutical company Pfizer imposed controls on the distribution of its drugs to ensure that none are used in lethal injections.[73] One response to the difficulties states have had getting the drugs they need to conduct executions has been to move to a one-drug protocol. In 2012, Yokamon Hearn in Texas was the first person in the United States to be executed using such a protocol. However, compared with the three-drug method, "executing with the one-drug method takes longer."[74]

Another response has been to use replacements for the drugs that can no longer be legally supplied for executions. In *Glossip* v. *Gross* (2015), the Supreme Court ruled that death row inmates in Oklahoma may be executed using midazolam instead of sodium thiopental as a sedative in combination with other lethal injection drugs.[75] After Pfizer's decision in 2016, this course of action may become even more difficult.

As an alternative to experimenting with new drugs and protocols, states have begun reinstating methods of execution as back-ups that were once rendered obsolete by lethal injection. States acknowledge they are moved to do so to reduce the physical pain and suffering of the people executed. But they are also troubled by

[70] Langford, "Tinkering with the Machinery of Death," 157. In this regard, it would seem that "cruel and unusual" punishment is like hard-core pornography; we know it when we see it. See Justice Potter Stewart's concurring opinion in *Jacobellis* v. *Ohio*, 378 U.S. 184 (1964).

[71] However, it was already apparent then that there were problems occurring with the three-drug protocol. In a Memorandum of Intended Decision in the case of *Morales* v. *Tilton* (2006), Judge Jeremy Fogel noted concerns that inmates may have been conscious when they were injected with pancuronium bromide and potassium chloride, and indicated that if an inmate was conscious when these drugs were injected, it was agreed that the inmate would suffer an unconstitutional level of pain. The cause of the concerns he noted was not a lack of sodium thiopental but was rather "a number of critical deficiencies" in the protocol and its implementation in California. See *Morales* v. *Tilton*, No. C 06 219 & 926 JF RS, U.S. Dist. Ct. for N. Dist. of Calif., Dec. 15, 2006 (Memorandum).

[72] Ed Pilkington, "Europe Moves to Block Trade in Medical Drugs Used in US Executions," *The Guardian*, December 20, 2011, www.theguardian.com/world/2011/dec/20/death-penalty-drugs-european-commission, accessed March 14, 2016.

[73] Erik Eckholm, "Pfizer Blocks the Use of Its Drugs in Executions," *New York Times*, May 13, 2016, www.nytimes.com/2016/05/14/us/pfizer-execution-drugs-lethal-injection.html?_r=0, accessed June 5, 2016.

[74] Nick Welsh, "The Death Penalty Is Experiencing Technical Difficulties. Your Execution May Not Resume Shortly. How Legal Wrangling over the Chemicals Used in Lethal Injection Could Shut Down Capital Punishment," *Pacific Standard*, November/December (2012): 48–53, 53.

[75] *Glossip* v. *Gross*, 576 U. S. __ (2015).

the time it takes for the people executed to die. This focus of concern is made explicit in an article published on the NBC News website entitled "Firing Squad to Gas Chamber: How Long Do Executions Take?"[76] The occasion of the article was Utah's decision to bring back the firing squad as an execution method. The decision was made in the wake of yet another "botched" execution, this time in Arizona. At 1:52 pm on July 23, 2014, Joseph Wood was put to death by lethal injection. However, instead of appearing to quietly go to sleep, for 25 minutes Wood seemed to gasp, snort, and convulse. An hour into the procedure, his lawyers filed an emergency appeal with the Supreme Court requesting that the execution be stopped. The appeal was denied, but by that time Wood had been pronounced dead. A process that was supposed to take ten minutes took one hour and 57 minutes.

In this context, it is not surprising that the NBC News article discusses different methods of execution that have been used in the United States and highlights how long each method takes. According to the article, guillotine and firing squad kill most quickly; they are tied at less than a minute. The electric chair can take two to 15 minutes or more. Hanging and the gas chamber are similarly unpredictable; hanging takes four to 11 minutes, and the gas chamber takes ten to 18 minutes. By far the most unpredictable, however, is lethal injection. Depending on the chemicals used, the physiology of the inmate and other factors, the article reports that lethal injection can take anywhere from five minutes to two hours.

LEGAL CHALLENGES

Both "delayed death" and "slow death" have provided grounds for challenging the constitutionality of capital punishment in the United States. However, as of yet, the Supreme Court has not been persuaded that the time it takes to die renders capital punishment unconstitutional.

What "cruel and unusual" means has been and continues to be difficult to decide, as the Supreme Court itself remarks in *Wilkerson v. Utah* (1879).[77] In *In re Kemmler* (1890), the Court nevertheless attempts to clarify the Eighth Amendment.[78] Holding that "Punishments are cruel when they involve torture or a lingering death," the Court explains that "cruel" implies "something more than the mere extinguishment of life," something "inhuman and barbarous."[79] In other

---

[76] Tracy Connor, "Firing Squad to Gas Chamber: How Long Do Executions Take?," nbcnews .com, March 25, 2015, www.nbcnews.com/news/us-news/firing-squad-gas-chamber-how-long-executions-take-n329371, accessed February 28, 2016.

[77] See *Wilkerson v. Utah*, 99 U.S. 130 (1879), 135–36. "Difficulty would attend the effort to define with exactness the extent of the constitutional provision which provides that cruel and unusual punishments shall not be inflicted."

[78] *In re. Kemmler*, 136 U.S. at 447.

[79] *In re. Kemmler*, 136 U.S. at 447. "Cruel" may also be defined in terms of proportionality so that a punishment may be rendered unconstitutional if it is found excessive with regard not only to the crime for which it is being imposed but also with regard to the pain involved.

words, death is not itself cruel, although what exactly renders a punishment "inhumane and barbarous" is still unclear. Indeed, over half of a century later, in *Trop* v. *Dulles* (1958) the Court admits that it has not yet detailed "the exact scope of the constitutional phrase 'cruel and unusual.'"[80] This time, however, in addition to acknowledging that "the words of the Amendment are not precise," the Court claims the scope of these words "is not static." In effect, the Supreme Court says the meaning of the words of the Eighth Amendment may change over time. In fact, it suggests that such change is to be expected when it determines, "The Amendment must draw its meaning from the evolving standards of decency that mark the progress of a maturing society."[81]

Delayed Death

In 1995, the Supreme Court denied the petition for writ of certiorari in the case of Clarence Lackey.[82] This was the first of many petitions to be denied that raise the question "whether executing a prisoner who has already spent some 17 [or more] years on death row violates the Eighth Amendment's prohibition against cruel and unusual punishment."[83] In 1995, Lackey's petition was "novel" but "not without foundation."[84] According to Justice Stevens, that foundation was laid in *Gregg* v. *Georgia* (1976). In *Gregg* v. *Georgia*, Justice Stevens says, the Supreme Court found that the Constitution does not prohibit the death penalty on the grounds that "(1) the death penalty was considered permissible by the Framers," and "(2) the death penalty might serve 'two principal social purposes: retribution and deterrence.'"[85] Both grounds are challenged by a delay of 17 years or more, Justice Stevens claims. First, such a delay would be unthinkable to the Framers, therefore "the practice of the Framers would not justify a denial of petitioner's claim."[86] Second, it is arguable whether any social purpose is served by executing someone after they have been on death row for 17 years or more. With regard to retribution, Justice Stevens suggests, "after such an extended time, the acceptable state interest in retribution has arguably been satisfied by the severe punishment already inflicted."[87] As for deterrence, "the additional deterrent effect from an actual execution now, on the one hand, as compared to

---

[80] *Trop*, 356 U.S. at 100.
[81] *Trop*, 356 U.S. at 100.
[82] *Lackey* v. *Texas*, 514 U.S. 1045 (1995).
[83] Following *Lackey*, 514 U.S., the Court denied the petition for writ of certiorari in *Elledge* v. *Florida*, 525 U.S. 944 (1998) (23 years); *Knight* v. *Florida*; *Moore* v. *Nebraska* 528 U.S. 990 (1999) (25 and 19 years, respectively); *Foster* v. *Florida*, 537 U.S. 990 (2002) (more than 27 years), *Smith* v. *Arizona*, 552 U.S. 297 (2007) (30 years), and *Thompson*, 129 S.Ct. (32 years).
[84] *Lackey*, 514 U.S. at 1045.
[85] *Lackey*, 514 U.S. at 1045.
[86] *Lackey*, 514 U.S. at 1045.
[87] *Lackey*, 514 U.S. at 1045.

17 years on death row followed by the prisoner's continued incarceration for life, on the other, seems minimal."[88]

In addition to the claims suggested by the Court's decision in *Gregg*, Justice Stevens offers two more reasons to take up the question posed by the petitioner in Texas. First, it is clear that an execution after prolonged confinement is inconsistent with international norms, as "the highest courts in other countries have found arguments such as petitioner's to be persuasive."[89] Second, it is possible that execution after "inordinate delay" would be found to infringe the prohibition against cruel and unusual punishment included in the Eighth Amendment.[90]

Fourteen years later in *Thompson* v. *McNeil* Justice Stevens observes, "While the length of petitioner's confinement under sentence of death is extraordinary, the concerns his case raises are not unique."[91] In brief, in the fourteen years since *Lackey* an argument that once seemed novel has become familiar. Indeed, the grounds for arguing that substantially delayed executions violate the Eighth Amendment's prohibition against cruel and unusual punishment have not changed. Despite the persistence of the issue (and the probability that the average time between sentencing and execution will only increase[92]), the Supreme Court has yet to grant writ of certiorari in a case of delayed death.

While procedural and substantive barriers may prevent federal courts from hearing a *Lackey* claim,[93] in "'Killing Time' in the Valley of the Shadow of Death: Why Systematic Pre-execution Delays on Death Row Are Cruel and Unusual," Angela April Sun argues that all efforts so far to argue before the Supreme Court that prolonged pre-execution stays on death row are unconstitutional under the Eighth Amendment's cruel and unusual clause have failed because the Court claims that insofar as the state is responsible for these prolonged stays there is no evidence of *deliberate* delay.[94] In so far as the defendant is responsible – that is to say, insofar as the defendant makes use of the appellate and collateral procedures available to him to scrutinize the legality of the penalty imposed – the Court sees no reason to encourage people on death row to use these procedures to delay executions further, which it would do if it recognized the legitimacy of a *Lackey* claim.

As an alternative line of attack on the constitutionality of keeping people on death row for long periods of time, Sun considers briefly a case-by-case approach

[88] *Lackey*, 514 U.S. at 1046.

[89] *Lackey*, 514 U.S. at 1047.

[90] *Lackey*, 514 U.S. at 1046–47.

[91] *Thompson*, 129 S. Ct. at 1299.

[92] Simmons, "Challenging an Execution after Prolonged Confinement on Death Row [Lackey Revisited]," 1249, 1268.

[93] Erin Simmons explains there are both procedural and substantive barriers that prevent federal courts from hearing the *Lackey* claim. Nevertheless, she argues, these barriers can be overcome. See Simmons, "Challenging an Execution after Prolonged Confinement on Death Row [Lackey Revisited]," 1249.

[94] Sun, "'Killing Time' in the Valley of the Shadow of Death: Why Systematic Pre-execution Delays on Death Row Are Cruel and Unusual," 1585, 1604.

concerned with the deliberate, discrete actions of officials in particular cases. However, this approach fails to focus on the systematic reasons for the delay, and consequently she dismisses it pretty much out of hand. Instead, Sun argues for a completely different strategy. She argues that the Court must be confronted with the fact that given the delays, the death penalty is not the sentence at issue. What is at issue is an unconstitutional punishment, the punishment that is *actually* being imposed in all of the ostensibly "capital" cases: the sentence of "life in the 'shadow of death.'"

Such a sentence is unconstitutional not because the death penalty is unconstitutional but because the sentence imposed is cruel and unusual on its own terms. For instance, "life in the 'shadow of death'" violates the Eighth Amendment in several ways. It is cruel in so far as there is a substantial period of time before death to anticipate and reflect on it. It is unusual by comparison to punishment in other states. It is disproportionate as it inflicts gratuitous mental suffering, and it is inherently arbitrary and capricious. What is more, it is unlegislated. Therefore it is not sanctioned by any common law or statute.

Sun is not cited, but for all intents and purposes her argument is adopted by United States District Judge Cormac Carney in his opinion in *Jones* v. *Chappell* (2014).[95] In his opinion, Judge Carney argues that the death penalty in California today violates the Eighth Amendment's prohibition against cruel and unusual punishment. It does so because "systemic delay has made...execution so unlikely that the death sentence...has been quietly transformed into one no rational jury or legislature could ever impose: *life in prison, with the remote possibility of death.*" While a random few may be executed, Judge Carney claims, "they will have languished for so long on Death Row that their execution will serve no retributive or deterrent purpose and will be arbitrary." In brief, while the judge does not go as far as Sun to describe executions as delayed systematically, which implies that executions are delayed methodically or in keeping with a system, he does observe that the delay is systemic and concludes from this observation that any penalty that is actually carried out under these circumstances will serve no penological purpose. Noting that the Eighth Amendment proscribes a state from randomly selecting which members of the criminal population it will sentence to death, Judge Carney argues that the Eighth Amendment cannot then allow a state to randomly select from among the few sentenced to death someone to actually execute. "Arbitrariness in execution is still arbitrary, regardless of when in the process the arbitrariness arises."

In November 2015, in a unanimous decision, a three-judge panel of the U.S. 9th Circuit Court of Appeals rejected Carney's ruling on the grounds that federal judges may not consider new constitutional theories in cases of habeas corpus. In the panel's decision, Judge Susan B. Graber validates speculation that Carney adopted

---

[95] *Jones v. Chappell*, Case CV 09-02158-CJC, July 2014.

Sun's argument in his holding when she reminds the lower court that the purpose of habeas corpus is to ensure that the conviction complied with federal law that existed at the time, "not to provide a mechanism for the continuing reexamination of final judgments based upon later emerging legal doctrine." However, as the *Los Angeles Times* reports, all the issues raised in Carney's holding in *Jones v. Chappell* are far from settled.

In the future, legal challenges to delayed death may well address issues before the California Supreme Court on which it has not yet ruled, including one of the issues in *Jones v. Chappell* – whether arbitrary delay deprives the death penalty of any deterrent value. Should another panel in California in another case at another time choose to take up such issues, the case could go to the California Supreme Court and the constitutionality of delayed death could finally be decided, at least at the state level. In brief, the constitutional question of delayed death remains open, and life on death row goes on.

Slow Death

In cases of slow death, legal challenges concern lethal injection and focus on two areas of concern. The first is the pain and suffering caused by the drugs used in a lethal injection. The second is the pain and suffering attributable to the way in which a lethal injection is carried out.

As noted above, most states employ lethal injection as their primary method of execution, and most of them use a three-drug protocol. The first drug renders the prisoner unconscious and insensate; the second paralyzes the muscles and prevents the prisoner from breathing; the third stops the heart. In *Baze v. Rees* (2008), the petitioners argued that this protocol was unconstitutional because it creates an intolerable risk that the condemned prisoner will suffer unnecessary pain.[96] The pain would occur as a result of the first drug, sodium pentothal, being administered incorrectly with the consequence that the prisoner would not be completely unconscious and so would be able to feel the effects of the drugs that follow. Due to the fact that the second drug is a paralytic agent, there would be no way for the condemned prisoner to communicate their suffering, but should the first drug be incorrectly administered or fail, the second drug would cause the prisoner excruciating pain. All agree that the experience of this pain would violate the Eighth Amendment's prohibition of cruel and unusual punishment. Indeed, for this reason, vets are prohibited from using a paralytic agent when they euthanize animals.

The seven-member majority decision against the petitioners was supported by six separate opinions. Chief Justice John Roberts, joined by Justices Anthony Kennedy and Samuel Alito, writes first, noting that to prevail on such a claim "there must be a 'substantial risk of serious harm,' an 'objectively intolerable risk of harm' that

[96] *Baze v. Rees*, 553 U.S. 35 (2008).

prevents prison officials from pleading that they were 'subjectively blameless for purposes of the Eighth Amendment.'"[97] The Chief Justice states that the petitioners fail to show the existence of such a risk, and with this point most of the concurring opinions agree. In his opinion, Chief Justice Roberts dismisses all of the reasons the petitioners offer in support of the claim that the risk exists. For example, they state that doses are difficult to mix into solution form and are hard to load into syringes. Chief Justice Roberts answers by pointing out that the instructions for reconstituting the drug are on the package insert. The petitioners also claim there are no clear instructions about the administration of the drug such as the rate at which it should be injected to prevent the failure of the IV. In addition, the petitioners worry, without proper training and supervision, the IV could be set so as to infiltrate into surrounding tissues and an inadequate amount of the drug would be delivered to the vein. Chief Justice Roberts replies that Kentucky has put in safeguards such as requiring that the members of the IV team have at least one year of experience in the medical field (as EMTs, paramedics, military corpsmen, etc.) and that the members of the team must participate in at least 10 practice sessions per year. To assuage concerns about the training of the members of the IV team, Chief Justice Roberts notes that during these sessions, team members practice setting up primary and backup lines. They also prepare two sets of the lethal injection drugs before the execution starts. Finally, the petitioners claim there are no reliable means available or prescribed for monitoring the "anesthetic depth of the prisoner after the sodium thiopental has been administered." To this claim Chief Justice Roberts responds that the warden and the deputy warden are present in the execution chamber and are supposed to be looking out for what they have been told will be the "very obvious" signs of IV problems, including infiltration. In any case, if the inmate doesn't lose consciousness within a minute, the Kentucky protocol requires the warden to redirect the flow of the drug to the back-up IV site.

A second set of legal challenges to lethal injection has been more successful, at least at the federal district court level. This set of challenges does not focus on the administration of a single drug but rather casts doubt on the reliability of the entire lethal injection process. Most famously, in the case of *Morales* v. *Tilton* (2006), Judge Jeremy Fogel undertakes a thorough review of California's lethal injection protocol as it is actually administered and concludes that lethal injection in California is "broken."[98] More precisely, he concludes that "absent effective remedial action by the Defendants," the lethal injection protocol in California creates an undue and unnecessary risk that an inmate will suffer pain so extreme that it offends the Eighth Amendment. While Judge Fogel does not go so far as to suggest lethal injection is fatally flawed as a method of execution, he does determine that

97 Citing *Farmer* v. *Brennan*, 511 U. S. 825 (1994) at 842, 846, and n. 9.
98 See *Morales* v. *Tilton*, No. C 06 219 & 926 JF RS, U.S. Dist. Ct. for N. Dist. of Calif., Dec. 15, 2006 (Memorandum).

no executions can take place in California until the lethal injection protocol is revised and problems that have been identified are addressed. In the particular case of Michael Morales, he said in an earlier ruling that if California wanted to go ahead with the execution it would have to reduce the risk that the inmate would be conscious when he was injected with pancuronium bromide and potassium chloride. To this end, the judge suggested the state develop a protocol that uses only sedatives. As an alternative, he suggested the state designate a person or persons with training to monitor the inmate's level of consciousness during the execution and to insure that all the proper steps were taken if Morales was not unconscious when the second and third drugs were injected. When two anesthesiologists who had been recruited by the state to participate in the execution refused to do so at the last minute, Morales's execution was postponed. When Human Rights Watch asked the California Attorney General's public spokesperson why the corrections department had not chosen a single massive dose of sodium thiopental, the sedatives option, he responded, "[The execution] would take too long."[99]

In the earlier ruling the judge had ordered a review of California's lethal injection protocol to take place whether Morales was executed or not in order to look into the issues raised by Morales's appeal. In an essay on his experience in lethal injection litigation, Judge Fogel discusses what the review discovered.[100] One thing the review brought to light in particular is the fact that execution team members receive minimal and inconsistent training. In addition, and particularly troubling given Chief Justice Roberts's argument in *Baze* v. *Rees* published two years later, execution team members "apparently made no effort to comply with the manufacturer's directions for mixing the sodium thiopental used in executions."[101] Actually, team members are directed by the protocol to proceed in a manner contrary to those directions, according to Judge Fogel.[102] In addition, execution team members keep irregular and at times illegible records of condemned inmates' vital signs. Many problems are exacerbated by the conditions in which the members of the execution team work, the judge says. For example, San Quentin's gas chamber has been modified so that lethal injections can take place there, and the awkward physical space as well as the dim lighting make it difficult for team members to verify if equipment is working properly and for anyone to observe how the condemned inmate is responding to the drugs as they are applied. The presence of prison officials and dignitaries at an execution makes

---

[99] Cited in Human Rights Watch, "So Long as They Die: Lethal Injections in the United States," *Human Rights Watch Report* 18, no. 1 (April 2006), www.hrw.org/report/2006/04/23/so-long-they-die/lethal-injections-united-states, accessed 10 June 2016, part V.

[100] Jeremy Fogel, "In the Eye of the Storm: A Judge's Experience in Lethal-Injection Litigation," *Fordham Urban Law Journal* 35 (2008): 735.

[101] Fogel, "In the Eye of the Storm: A Judge's Experience in Lethal-Injection Litigation," 735, 746.

[102] Ibid.

matters only worse, as there is little room for team members to work then and it is not easy to see what is going on.

Perhaps in response to the issues raised by the *Morales* case, and the failure of the state to be able to find any medical professionals to assist in carrying out the existing lethal injection protocol, in November 2015 California proposed a new one-drug lethal injection protocol. The approval process will take at least a year, and legal challenges are expected after that.[103] In the meantime, California will not execute anyone.

California is not alone in temporarily suspending executions. A number of states have put executions on hold, either by court or executive order, while legal challenges to the execution process are being heard or addressed.[104] Some observers suggest this may be a sign of the end of capital punishment in the United States. Others are more skeptical. One of the more skeptical observers, law professor Deborah Denno, notes that those who wish to save the death penalty may criticize a particular method of execution as vociferously as those who wish to the see the death penalty abolished. She calls this phenomenon the "execution methods paradox" and describes it as the result of the fact that "friends and foes of the death penalty align both sides of the execution methods debate, despite their different goals."[105] According to Denno, historically, legislatures do not change from one method to another out of concern for the suffering of the inmate to be executed. Legislatures propose these changes because the acceptability of the death penalty process itself becomes jeopardized.[106] In other words, "legislatures typically change an execution method to stay one step ahead of a looming constitutional challenge to that method."[107] In the case of California's proposed lethal injection protocol, the new one-drug protocol is being described as "humane and dignified" as well as a way to reduce the risk of the person being executed experiencing "inhumane suffering."[108] Of course, according to Denno, "legislatures and courts have consistently claimed that the change from one method of execution to another provides the condemned the most humane and decent means of death possible given our knowledge of human science."[109]

[103] Maura Dolan and Paige St. John, "California Proposes New Single-Drug Method for Executions," *LA Times*, November 6, 2015; www.latimes.com/politics/la-me-pol-ca-execution-protocol-20151105-story.html, accessed 11 June 2016.
[104] www.deathpenaltyinfo.org/death-penalty-flux, accessed 10 June 2016.
[105] Denno, "When Legislatures Delegate Death: The Troubling Paradox behind State Uses of Electrocution and Lethal Injection and What It Says about Us," 65.
[106] Ibid.
[107] Ibid.
[108] Maura Dolan and Paige St. John, "California Proposes New Single-Drug Method for Executions," *LA Times*, November 6, 2015; www.latimes.com/politics/la-me-pol-ca-execution-protocol-20151105-story.html, accessed 11 June 2016.
[109] Denno, "When Legislatures Delegate Death: The Troubling Paradox behind State Uses of Electrocution and Lethal Injection and What It Says about Us," 65.

IS DEATH SO DIFFERENT?

Given the legal system's lack of willingness to address how long is too long to die at the hands of the state – indeed, allowing the time between sentence and execution to go on indefinitely by refusing to consider one way or another the constitutionality of delayed death, or by embracing alternative protocols of lethal injection, in principle at least, that may actually extend the time between execution and death – is death really so different from life in prison? What difference does death actually make?

In 2015, journalists Frank R. Baumgartner and Anna W. Dietrich conducted a study based on a review of every death sentence since 1973, the beginning of the modern era of the death penalty.[110] According to their study, "Execution is in fact the third most likely outcome following a death sentence. Much more likely is the inmate to have their sentence reversed, or to remain for decades on death row."[111] Reiterating the numbers from the review, Baumgartner and Dietrich note that 8,466 death sentences were imposed across the United States from 1973 to 2013; during this time, 3,194 sentences were overturned on appeal when the underlying statute was declared unconstitutional, the conviction was overturned, or the death penalty was overturned but guilt was sustained. In addition, 392 had their sentences commuted by the governor to life in prison, and 33 were removed from death row for some other reason. Between 1973 and 2013, 1,359 people were executed; during the same period, 509 died of natural causes or suicide. In 2013, 2,979 people remained on death row.

Among other things, what these numbers say is that if a person was sentenced to death between 1973 and 2013, they were more likely not to be executed than they were to be executed. What is more, if they died in prison, there was a significant chance that they did not suffer the punishment the state imposed on them. In the period of the review, 16 percent of people sentenced to be executed died at the hands of the state and 6 percent died of natural causes or by their own hand. These numbers may not be accurate, however, as it is unclear if inmates who "volunteered" to be executed should be counted as suicides or as competent individuals who accepted the justness of their punishment and chose to waive their appeals.[112] If, as law professor John Blume suggests, at least some volunteers may be motivated by suicidal desires (rather than acceptance of the justness of their punishment), the number of people executed would go down and the number of people who die of

---

[110] Frank R. Baumgartner and Anna W. Dietrich, "Most Death Penalty Sentences Are Overturned. Here's Why That Matters," *Washington Post*, March 17, 2015; www.washingtonpost.com/blogs/monkey-cage/wp/2015/03/17/most-death-penalty-sentences-are-overturned-heres-why-that-matters/, accessed 11 June 2016.

[111] Baumgartner and Dietrich, "Most Death Penalty Sentences Are Overturned. Here's Why That Matters."

[112] John H. Blume, "Killing the Willing: 'Volunteers,' Suicide and Competency," www.deathpenaltyinfo.org/documents/BlumeVolunteerArticle.pdf, accessed 11 June 2016, 28.

other causes while on death row would go up. As it is, more than a third as many people died in prison under sentence of death as died by execution. Of course, over 42 percent of people originally sentenced to death suffered another punishment or were exonerated and released.

With these statistics in mind, it is worth considering how the unique appeals process that contributes to the reversal of sentences in death penalty cases distinguishes death from other penalties. Certainly, this appeals process is costly. As a result death is much more expensive than other penalties. In California, for example, it has cost $4 billion to execute 13 people.[113] And, of course, the longer it takes to put someone to death, the more it costs.[114] Criminal lawyers, law professionals, and law professors agonize about the resources that are absorbed by the death penalty, for it is not simply a matter of money that is involved but the time and energy of people and institutions. One such institution is the Supreme Court itself, which has been described by Douglas Berman as having a "troublesome affinity for obsessing over capital cases."[115] What he means by this is that the Supreme Court has not only invested considerable energy and effort in capital punishment but that the Court may also be "caught up in a 'culture of death,' which leads the Justices to 'waste' an extraordinary amount of its scarce time and energy to reviewing capital cases and adjudicating the claims of death row inmates."[116]

As a consequence, the Supreme Court may not give "sufficient attention to noncapital criminal justice issues."[117] Indeed, as Berman points out, Eva Nilsen argues that the "death is different" doctrine has gutted the Eighth Amendment as far as other sentences go.[118] Berman cites Nilsen at length, when she explains "minimum security is far different from segregation in a supermax facility, and imprisonment for a term of years is not the same as imprisonment for life without possibility of parole. Each sentence contains particular hardships, pain, and loss, thus each should be subject to meaningful Eighth Amendment scrutiny considering both circumstances

---

[113] Arthur L. Alarcón and Paula M. Mitchell, "Executing the Will of the Voters? A Roadmap to Mend or End the California Legislature's Multi-Billion-Dollar Death Penalty Debacle," *Loyola of Los Angeles Law Review* 44, no. S41 (2011): S212.

[114] According to Alarcón and Mitchell, several states have conducted cost-benefit analyses of their death penalty statutes and as a result have either abolished or severely limited capital punishment. Those states are New Jersey, New Mexico, Maryland, and Illinois. In 2011, they note that twelve more states were undergoing cost studies. Those states are Colorado, Connecticut, Indiana, Kansas, Missouri, Montana, Nebraska, Nevada, New Hampshire, North Carolina, Oregon, and Tennessee. Alarcón and Mitchell, "Executing the Will of the Voters?," S207.

[115] Douglas A. Berman, "A Capital Waste of Time? Examining the Supreme Court's 'Culture of Death,'" *Ohio Northern University Law Review* 34 (2008): 861, 861.

[116] Ibid., 861, 869.

[117] Ibid., 861, 879.

[118] Eva S. Nilsen, "Decency, Dignity, and Desert: Restoring Ideals of Humane Punishment to Constitutional Discourse," *U.C. Davis Law Review* 41 (2007): 111.

of the offender and the crime."[119] According to Nilsen, "Sentences for terms of years do not get adequate scrutiny under current Eighth Amendment law; and the Court's excessive deference to legislatures leaves no room for conscience or moral compunction in its decisions."[120]

According to a report by Richard Dieter, the Executive Director of the Death Penalty Information Center, the "culture of death" affects more of the criminal justice system than just the Supreme Court.[121] The report notes that states are spending millions of dollars on the death penalty while at the same time, courts are less open, trials are delayed, and police are being furloughed.[122] With regard to the police, Dieter says, "Where studies have been done, the excess expenditures per year for the death penalty typically are close to $10 million per state. If a new police office (or teacher, or ambulance driver) is paid $40,000 per year, this death penalty money could be used to fund 250 additional workers in each state to secure a better community."[123] An alternative formulation of the opportunity costs of the death penalty and the culture of death to which it has given rise concerns prosecutors, public defenders, and judges. According to Dieter, "If it takes 1,000 hours of state-salaried work to arrive at a death sentence and only 100 hours to have the same person sentenced to life without parole, the 900 hours difference is a state asset. If the death penalty is eliminated, the county or the state can decide whether to direct those employee-hours to other work that has been left undone, or choose to keep fewer employees."[124]

What this discussion of cost suggests is that death is different not because people die at the hands of the state and therefore suffer a uniquely final and severe punishment. Instead, it indicates how the phenomenon Berman calls the "culture of death" sucks up all the financial, intellectual, and temporal resources of the jurisdictions that impose the death penalty. Insofar as death is different, then, it is so because a "culture" or perhaps a "cult" has taken hold of the criminal justice system and attributed to death unique qualities that the cult or culture then itself makes true. For example, Berman argues that death as a penalty is assumed to make a "unique impression on the imagination."[125] Indeed, this assumption justifies the use

---

[119] Berman, "A Capital Waste of Time? Examining the Supreme Court's 'Culture of Death,'" 861, 880. Nilsen, "Decency, Dignity, and Desert: Restoring Ideals of Humane Punishment to Constitutional Discourse," 111.

[120] Berman, "A Capital Waste of Time? Examining the Supreme Court's 'Culture of Death,'" 861, 880.

[121] Richard C. Dieter, "Smart on Crime: Reconsidering the Death Penalty in a Time of Economic Crisis," Death Penalty Information Center, Washington, DC (October 2009); www .deathpenaltyinfo.org/documents/CostsRptFinal.pdf, accessed 11 June 2016.

[122] Ibid.

[123] Ibid.

[124] Ibid.

[125] See Berman, "A Capital Waste of Time? Examining the Supreme Court's 'Culture of Death,'" 861, 870.

of the death penalty as a deterrent. Of course, there is no evidence that the death penalty actually works as a deterrent.[126] Instead, as Berman shows, there is clear evidence, as shown above, that the impression death makes "uniquely impacts the behavior and attitudes of all persons who operate or assess criminal justice institutions."[127] Similarly, Berman says death as a penalty is assumed to be of unique "societal interest."[128] As such, Berman claims, it elicits a disproportionate amount of media and political attention.[129] This interest makes it unsurprising then that "Supreme Court Justices and their clerks, prodded by lawyers, public policy groups and the media, will always be inclined to give particularly careful, cautious and conscientious attention to any and every death penalty case brought their way."[130] However, it isn't clear in Berman's account of society's unique interest in the death penalty whether media and political attention reflect or create this interest. Once again, the *assumption* that death is different explains the difference that makes death different.

Yet, from another vantage point, specifically from the perspective of prisoners sentenced to death, death is not all that different and, as time passes, seems to be becoming even less so. For death sentences are lived in prison and, in most places, the conditions in which these lives are lived are not different from lives lived in maximum security or solitary confinement. Indeed, the ACLU entitles a report on solitary confinement on death row, "A Death before Dying." In this title, the ACLU describes the profound loss experienced by prisoners who are held in isolation, in small cells for 22–24 hours a day, with reduced or no natural light, and little human interaction, let alone human contact, in terms of the end of being alive, a ceasing to exist, or a passing away. This passing away occurs before death, or what is sometimes referred to as "physical death," is formally pronounced. Summarizing research on the effects of solitary confinement on prisoners, the ACLU reports lists a horrifying array of negative physiological and psychological conditions, among them hyper-sensitivity to external stimuli, perceptual distortions and hallucinations, increased anxiety and nervousness, fears of persecution, lack of impulse control, severe and

---

[126] In 2012, the National Research Council published a report on deterrence and the death penalty. A Committee on Law and Justice concluded, "research to date is not informative about whether capital punishment decreases, increases, or has no effect on homicide rates. Therefore, these studies should not be used to inform deliberations requiring judgments about the effect of the death penalty on homicide. Claims that research demonstrates that capital punishment decreases or increases the homicide rate or has no effect on it should not influence policy judgments about capital punishment." See Daniel S. Nagin and John V. Pepper, "Deterrence and the Death Penalty," Committee on Law and Justice at the National Research Council, April 2012.

[127] Berman, "A Capital Waste of Time? Examining the Supreme Court's 'Culture of Death,'" 861, 870.

[128] Ibid., 861, 871.

[129] Ibid., 861, 871.

[130] Ibid., 861, 871.

chronic depression, heart palpitations, withdrawal, blunting of affect and apathy, talking to oneself, headaches, problems sleeping, confused thought processes, night-mares, dizziness, self-mutilation, and lower levels of brain function. "Most people in isolation will fall apart," a prison psychiatrist cited by the report notes.

The philosopher Lisa Guenther observes the same phenomenon but puts it differently. Starting with the insight that "there is no individual without relations, no subject without complications, and no life without resistance,"[131] Guenther concludes from her study of solitary confinement, "Persons who are structured as intentional consciousness but are deprived of a diverse open-ended perceptual experience of the world, or who are structured as transcendental intersubjectivity but are deprived of concrete relations to others, have the very structure of their Being-in-the-world turned against them and used to exploit their fundamental relationality."[132] Guenther argues that solitary confinement does not just effect prisoners' "mental health" but their whole capacity to relate to objects within the world, to coconstitute with others a sense of shared reality, and to participate in a common situation.[133] In brief, solitary confinement renders people "socially dead."[134]

Recently, however, prisoners sentenced to death are claimed to experience solitary confinement differently than those who have been sentenced to some other severe penalty. What death row prisoners are said to experience is called "death row phenomenon," which is defined as "the harmful effects of the conditions experi-enced on death row, including solitary confinement and the mental anxiety prison-ers experience whilst waiting for their death sentence to be imposed."[135] The concept of this phenomenon has been used internationally to prevent extradition of individuals who are facing the possibility of being sentenced to death in the United States.[136] Death row phenomenon is distinguished from the harmful effects

---

[131] Lisa Guenther, *Solitary Confinement: Social Death and Its Afterlives* (Minneapolis: University of Minnesota Press, 2013), xv.

[132] Ibid., xv.

[133] Ibid., 156.

[134] "Social death" is a term that has been used by a variety of scholars in different fields to refer to an experience of extreme or profound loss. To retain its theoretical integrity, Jana Králová argues that the term is best understood to refer to a set of particular losses – a loss of social identity, a loss of social connectedness, and losses associated with the disintegration of the body – and its use should be limited only to the most extreme circumstances, in which the majority or all of its facets are severely compromised and/or lost. See Jana Králová, "What Is Social Death?," *Contemporary Social Science* 10, no. 3 (2015): 235–48, 246; http://dx.doi.org/10.1080/21582041.2015.1114407, accessed June 11, 2016.

[135] "Death row phenomenon" and "death row syndrome" are often used interchangeably, but "death row syndrome" properly refers to "the consequential psychological illness that can occur as a result of death row phenomenon." See Karen Harrison and Anouska Tamony, "Death Row Phenom-enon, Death Row Syndrome, and Their Affect on Capital Cases in the U.S.," *Internet Journal of Criminology* (2010); www.internetjournalofcriminology.com, accessed 12 June 2016, 2.

[136] Patrick Hudson, "Does the Death Row Phenomenon Violate a Prisoner's Rights under International Law?," *EIJL* 11 (2000): 833–56.

of the conditions experienced in solitary confinement by "the ever present and mounting anguish of awaiting execution and the death penalty," which is to say, "the unique stresses of living under sentence of death."[137] Curiously, however, "the anguish and mounting tension of living in the ever-present shadow of death" has not been empirically established.[138] Nor has "death row syndrome," the drastic psychological and psychiatric reactions that inmates have experienced to life on death row.[139] Perhaps for this reason, it is unclear what, if any, implications death row phenomenon has for capital punishment in the United States.

However, the point here is not that we should undertake empirical studies of death row inmates' experiences on the grounds that "it seems likely that individuals awaiting execution experience some kind of powerful psychological reaction to knowing death is imminent."[140] The point is rather to acknowledge that experiences of "life" and "death" in prison are not so distinct. Indeed, the suggestion that empirical studies are necessary to establish a difference between them makes the point.

What may seem just as likely as one of the "unique stresses" of a death sentence to render the experience of living with a death sentence different than living with a sentence of life is the *hope* the appeals process may inspire in prisoners who appreciate how few people are ultimately put to death, and consequently, the *possibility* that their sentence will be modified or even set aside. To the extent that this is so, the appeals process and the ardour with which it is undertaken appears again to be what distinguishes death from other penalties. As Douglas Berman observes, even as the Supreme Court reduces the number of cases it considers every year, "Death penalty cases continue to assume a large part of the Supreme Court's docket because, in the capital context and only in the capital context, the Justices and their clerks seem eager to correct any and every error they perceive in each and every capital case."[141]

Of course, the eagerness of the Court and its affiliates to correct errors in capital cases does not mean that the errors made in capital cases are unique to that context. It is the eagerness to identify and fix these errors that makes death different, not the character of the mistakes made in the process of investigating a crime, charging someone with having committed it, trying the suspect, finding the prisoner guilty,

---

[137] Amy Smith, "Not Waiving but Drowning: The Anatomy of Death Row Syndrome and Volunteering for Execution," *Boston University Public Interest Law Journal* 17 (2008): 237–254, 242.

[138] Caycie D. Bradford, "Waiting to Die, Dying to Live: An Account of the Death Row Phenomenon from a Legal Viewpoint," *Interdisciplinary Journal of Human Rights Law* 5, no. 1 (2010–2011): 77–96, 80.

[139] Bradford, "Waiting to Die, Dying to Live: An Account of the Death Row Phenomenon from a Legal Viewpoint," 83.

[140] Smith, "Not Waiving but Drowning: The Anatomy of Death Row Syndrome and Volunteering for Execution," 237–254, 251.

[141] Berman, "A Capital Waste of Time? Examining the Supreme Court's 'Culture of Death,'" 861, 876.

and sentencing them for what they have done. Certainly, the scrutiny brought to bear on death penalty cases reveals miscarriages of justice that are familiar to anyone who studies criminal law.

To take but one example, evidence presented in *McCleskey* v. *Kemp* (1987) famously demonstrates that a disparity in the imposition of death sentences in Georgia based on the murder victim's race and, to a lesser extent, on the race of the offender.[142] Despite assuming the validity of this evidence, the majority of the Supreme Court finds the petitioner failed to show that racial considerations played any part in the sentencing process in his trial. Writing for the majority, Justice Lewis Powell argues that no evidence is presented of purposeful discrimination in McCleskey's case. While the statistics may be correct, they do not substantiate the claim that the outcome of McCleskey's case was influenced by racial bias. As Nilsen points out, the Supreme Court makes a similar argument in *United States* v. *Armstrong* (1996), when it denied discovery of disproportionate prosecutions of minorities for crack cocaine as opposed to powder cocaine because the petitioners could not show, in the absence of discovery, that there was discrimination against the particular defendant in the case.[143] As Nilsen again points out, "Death sentences may well demand 'super due process,' but other sentences surely demand much more than the virtual blank check issued by the Supreme Court to the legislatures."[144]

Nilsen argues explicitly that the Court's hands-off doctrines have ensured that the law presently provides no realistic remedy even when a sentence is based wholly or partly on the race of the defendant.[145] But her argument also implies that what is made evident in death penalty cases argued before the Supreme Court – whether or not the death row inmate prevails – is the injustice of the entire system rather than of the death penalty system per se. Super-due process may be accessible only to those sentenced to death but what is revealed by this process is not the uniqueness of death. Rather, what is revealed are the limits of the human criminal justice system. What is more, in his *McCleskey* opinion, Justice Powell admits as much. According to Justice Powell, if the Supreme Court accepted McCleskey's claim that racial bias has impermissibly tainted the capital sentencing decision, "we could soon be faced with similar claims as to other types of penalty. Moreover, the claim that his sentence rests on the irrelevant factor of race easily could be extended to apply to claims based on unexplained discrepancies that correlate to membership in other minority groups, and even to gender.... If arbitrary and

---

[142] *McCleskey* v. *Kemp*, 481 U.S. 279 (1987); see Samuel R. Gross, "David Baldus and the Legacy of *McCleskey* v. *Kemp*," *Iowa Law Review* 97 (2012): 1905.

[143] *United States* v. *Armstrong*, 517 U.S. 456 (1996); Nilsen, "Decency, Dignity, and Desert: Restoring Ideals of Humane Punishment to Constitutional Discourse," 111, 155.

[144] Nilsen, "Decency, Dignity, and Desert: Restoring Ideals of Humane Punishment to Constitutional Discourse," 152.

[145] Ibid., 155.

capricious punishment is the touchstone under the Eighth Amendment, such a claim could – at least in theory – be based upon any arbitrary variable, such as the defendant's facial characteristics, or the physical attractiveness of the defendant or the victim, that some statistical study indicates may be influential in jury decision-making. As these examples illustrate, there is no limiting principle to the type of challenge brought by McCleskey."[146] While Justice Powell may be trying to denigrate race by equating membership in a particular racial group with member-ship in a group distinguished by the mere appearance of its members, he is effectively admitting that all sentencing decisions are susceptible to the charge that they are irrational, given, as I have argued elsewhere, he provides no other reason to believe that the criminal justice system would be swamped with appeals should the Court find for McCleskey.[147]

Despite such examples, there are other kinds of appeals that will be pursued in death penalty cases that might not be pursued in other cases. Given the Supreme Court's concern to fix errors in death penalty cases, appeals on the grounds of actual innocence would presumably be one of these kinds. Indeed, according to the Death Penalty Information Center, since 1973, 156 people who were sentenced to death have been exonerated and released from prison. The average time between sentence and exoneration is a little over 11 years.[148] However, it turns out that in 2015 alone, according to the National Registry of Exonerations, 149 people who were convicted of a crime and later officially declared innocent were exonerated.[149] These 149 defendants served on average 14-and-a-half years in prison. As there are so many more people sentenced to severe penalties other than death, it is not easy to compare the absolute numbers of exonerations cited above. As of January 2106, the National Registry of Exonerations had recorded 1733 known exonerations since 1989; what is more, according to the National Registry of Exonerations, "By any reasonable accounting, there are tens of thousands of false convictions each year across the country, and many more that have accumulated over the decades." However, reiterating a view expressed by the critics of the judicial system's "culture of death," the report comments, "We average nearly three exonerations a week, and most get little attention." In brief, the work done to review and investigate post-conviction claims of innocence that do not involve the death penalty is pretty much overlooked. Nevertheless, "Conviction Integrity Units" or CIUs are being established around the United States in prosecutors' offices to do this work, and the National Registry of Exonerations takes this as a sign of recognition that convicting the innocent is a

---

[146] *McCleskey v. Kemp*, 481 U.S. 279 (1987) at 315–18.

[147] See Jennifer L. Culbert, *Dead Certainty: The Death Penalty and the Problem of Judgment* (Stanford: Stanford University Press, 2008), 65.

[148] Death Penalty Information Center, "The Innocence List," www.deathpenaltyinfo.org/innocence-list-those-freed-death-row; accessed 13 June 2016.

[149] "The National Registry of Exonerations: Exonerations in 2015," National Registry of Exonerations, February 3, 2016; www.law.umich.edu/special/exoneration/Documents/Exonerations_in_2015.pdf, accessed 11 June 2016.

serious public problem that requires proactive government attention.[150] Again, death gets a lot more attention, but the problems that are revealed in the criminal justice system by that attention do not distinguish death from other penalties.

Waiting for the criminal justice system to do its work also does not distinguish death. Consider the now infamous case of Kalief Browder. The Sixth Amendment (1791) states, "In all criminal prosecutions, the accused shall enjoy the right to a speedy and public trial...." In *Barker* v. *Wingo* (1972), the Supreme Court developed a four-part test by which to determine, on a case-by-case basis, if the right to a speedy trial has been violated.[151] In 1974, the Speedy Trial Act established time limits for completing various stages of a federal criminal prosecution. Many states also have constitutional provisions or statutes that guarantee a defendant the right to a speedy trial. Usually, the prosecution has 60 to 120 days to bring an imprisoned defendant to trial. Nevertheless, it was possible for sixteen-year-old Browder to spend three years in prison on Rikers Island before robbery charges against him were dropped.

As Jennifer Gonnerman explains in an article about Browder's experience, some states have a version of the "speedy-trial" law called the "ready rule."[152] In the state of New York this rule requires that "all felony cases (except homicides) must be ready for trial within six months of arraignment, or else the charges can be dismissed." However, the clock can stop for many reasons so that "the amount of time that is officially held to have elapsed can be wildly different from the amount of time that really has." As Gonnerman explains in a second article published after Browder's death, he had been arrested in the spring of 2010, at age sixteen, for a robbery he insisted he had not committed. Then he spent more than one thousand days on Rikers waiting for a trial that never happened. During that time, he endured about two years in solitary confinement, where he attempted to end his life several times.[153] After he left Rikers, he attempted suicide at least once more and then, two years later, he succeeded.

Required in light of the assumption that "death is different," the procedures put in place to respect this difference distinguish the death penalty from all other penalties. However, as time goes on, the effects of these procedures seem to render the experience of prisoners on death row less distinguishable from the experience of other prisoners. As the example of Kalief Browder suggests, not even the experience of suffering the delay of the penalty separates inmates accused of minor crimes from those found guilty of committing the most heinous. Death is different because it was *made* different, but time is eroding what was once thought done.

---

[150] "The National Registry of Exonerations: Exonerations in 2015," 2.
[151] *Barker* v. *Wingo* 407 U.S. 514 (1972).
[152] Jennifer Gonnerman, "Before the Law," *The New Yorker*, October 6, 2014.
[153] Jennifer Gonnerman, "Kalief Browder, 1993–2015," *The New Yorker* June 7, 2015; www.new yorker.com/news/news-desk/kalief-browder-1993–2015, accessed 13 June 2016.

IMPLICATIONS OF THE APPARENT DECLINE OF DEATH'S DIFFERENCE

I have just argued that the time it takes to die undermines the difference between the *experience* of the death penalty and other severe penalties imposed by the state. Now I want to suggest that the experience of the death penalty undermines the image of death on which the capital punishment system is predicated, the image on which the "culture of death" described by Berman is focused.

This image comes to us from the nineteenth century, when, as Jonathan Strauss argues, death became "a sheer and unredeemable absence, an unconsolable loss, and a confrontation with pure negativity."[154] In brief, prior to the Enlightenment, in the West death was not assumed to be an absolute. For a long time before then, death was, according to Philippe Ariès, "the awareness by each person of a *Destiny* in which his own personality was not annihilated but *put to sleep – requies, dormitio.*"[155] When death is conceived as repose in a realm of shadows, a vague fading away into a twilight in which distinctions are not easily drawn, the time before and the time after death is not obvious. Nor is it significant, for death "was both familiar and near, evoking no great fear or awe."[156] To understand this attitude, Ariès suggests it is important to appreciate that in death, "man encountered one of the great laws of the species, and he had no thought of escaping it or glorifying it."[157] Only in the Middle Ages did death become the occasion when man was most able to reach an awareness of himself, as an individual with his own story, his own attachments to the world, and his own reckoning for the conduct of his life.[158] Later the individual's death became a matter of social concern, giving rise to a "cult of the dead." While this cult was easily accommodated in Christian faith, its "exalted and emotive" nature actually had a "positivist origin," Ariès claims, as it emerged from a combination of concerns having to do with the dead body. These concerns included worries about public health – specifically, fear of the dead literally poisoning the living as the dead were haphazardly buried beneath the flooring of the churches in which the living worshipped[159] – as well as a desire to possess the remains of the beloved dead as survivors became unwilling "to accept the departure of their loved one."[160] According to Ariès, this powerful sentiment was ultimately transformed into a wish to spare the dying person knowledge of their imminent death, which became a kind of shame about death and dying.[161] This shame then contributed to the

---

[154] Jonathan Strauss, "Preface: The State of Death," *Diacritics* 30, no. 3 (Fall 2000): 3–11, 3.
[155] Philippe Ariès, *Western Attitudes toward Death: From the Middle Ages to the Present*, trans. Patricia M. Ranum (Baltimore: Johns Hopkins University Press, 1974), 104.
[156] Ibid., 13.
[157] Ibid., 28.
[158] Ibid., 46.
[159] Ibid., 70.
[160] Ibid.
[161] Ibid., 86.

notion that dying was a failure, from which it followed that death was forbidden, as was any acknowledgement of death. Grief or any other emotion related to death had to be hidden or was otherwise disparaged as "morbid."

Elements of all of these ideas of death are present in the image that guides contemporary capital punishment. However, the most influential idea is the one that death is not a state into or out of which a person can slip, but rather is a total negation of the possibility of being at all. Such an idea informs the view, expressed by Hegel, that "Death. . .is of all things the most dreadful,"[162] a view reiterated by Justices on the Supreme Court when they describe death as "the ultimate sanction"[163] and as "the absolute renunciation of all that is embodied in our concept of humanity."[164]

In *Being and Time*, Martin Heidegger provides a philosophical account of death that could underpin this view.[165] As summarized by Simon Critchley, Heidegger proposes, "being is time and time is finite. For human beings, time comes to an end with our death. . . .If our being is finite, then an authentic human life can only be found by confronting finitude and trying to make a meaning out of the fact of our death."[166] "Being-toward-death" in this way entails four principles. First, death is non-relational. This means not only that one dies alone but also that one cannot share or experience death through or with the death of another. Second, death is certain. There is no evading death. Life ends with death and this end cannot be avoided. Third, despite the fact that death is certain, death is indefinite. One knows it will happen but one does not know exactly when. Finally, fourth, death is a limit that cannot be overcome or overtaken. It is the end of possibility, the termination of what might be. At this limit, whatever one may become one has already become and may become no other and no more. Death cannot be surpassed.

The image of death provided by this account complements the tales commonly told of death row conversions, stories about condemned inmates who, when confronted with certain death, are "born again" and live the remainder of their lives as "authentic" human beings for the first time until the (indefinite) moments of their executions. Indeed, an important justification for the sentence of death in the seventeenth and eighteenth centuries in the United States was to facilitate the criminal's change of heart so that they might know remorse and ask for forgiveness.[167] Executions were even delayed to allow for sufficient time for the prisoner to repent and "prepare for death."[168] As the historian Daniel Lachance observes, as the time between sentence

---

[162] Cited in Strauss, "Preface: The State of Death," 3–11, 3.

[163] *Furman*, 408 U.S. at 286.

[164] Ibid. at 306.

[165] Martin Heidegger, *Being and Time*, trans. John Macquarrie and Edward Robinson (New York: Harper & Row, 1962).

[166] Simon Critchley, "Being and Time Part 6: Death," *The Guardian*, July 13, 2009; www.theguar dian.com/commentisfree/belief/2009/jul/13/heidegger-being-time, accessed June 13, 2016.

[167] Stuart Banner, *The Death Penalty: An American History* (Cambridge, MA: Harvard University Press, 2002), 16.

[168] Banner, *The Death Penalty: An American History*, 18.

and execution gets longer, the more time prisoners on death row have to change. They become religious and preach the Gospel, like Karla Faye Tucker, or devote themselves to the welfare of young people, like Stanley "Tookie" Williams.

Perhaps to avoid the implication that such conversions might be authentic, and that people might genuinely understand death in terms other than those used by the Supreme Court, the transformations that occur on death row are often greeted with cynicism.[169] True, even in the young United States, it was recognized that people on death row might try to manipulate appearances to escape death. Stuart Banner, a historian of capital punishment in the United States, comments, "There were few things as useful in obtaining executive clemency as a conspicuous repentance, especially one achieved in the company of ministers who had the ear of the government."[170] What is more, according to Banner, "This incentive casts some doubt on the sincerity of many of the execution-eve conversions so prized by the ministers."[171] In any case, concern about such doubt, if not the doubt itself, is evident in the public statements even of supporters of death row inmates who petition for clemency on the grounds that they are no longer the person who committed the crime for which they were sentenced to die. Take, for example, Karla Faye Tucker. In 1984, Tucker was sentenced to death in Texas for killing two people with a pickaxe. On death row she became a deeply religious born-again Christian. The televangelist Pat Robertson, a proponent of capital punishment in most cases, lead the charge to save Tucker's life, calling her an "extraordinary woman" whose "authentic spiritual conversion" cries out for mercy.[172] The description of her conversion as "authentic" betrays the fact that her transformation might be considered suspect, however. A Texas newspaper certainly seemed skeptical about her when it reported, "Karla Faye Tucker, the 38-year-old pickax murderer who charmed television audiences worldwide with her coquettish smile and talk of Jesus, was executed Tuesday despite an all-out legal blitz to spare her life."[173]

---

[169] In "Some Find Redemption on Death Row, but Few Find Mercy," Daniel Lachance makes a very different argument about the reception of death row transformations by the state, arguing instead that people in the United States may, perhaps without knowing it, feel that capital punishment "brings closure not only to the family members of victims, but also to the condemned themselves." Lachance proposes that such sentiments may explain why it is so difficult to abolish capital punishment in the United States. See Daniel Lachance, "Some Find Redemption on Death Row, but Few Find Mercy," *The Conversation*, November 3, 2015; https://theconversation.com/some-find-redemption-on-death-row-but-few-find-mercy-49791, accessed 10 June 2016.

[170] Banner, *The Death Penalty: An American History*, 19.

[171] Ibid., 19–20.

[172] Jesse Katz, "Should Karla Faye Tucker Be Executed?," *LA Times*, January 9, 1998; http://articles.latimes.com/1998/jan/09/news/mn-6616, accessed 14 June 2016.

[173] Kathy Walt, "Tucker Dies After Apologizing; Despite Legal Blitz, Woman Executed for Pickax Slayings," *Houston Chronicle*, February 3, 1998; www.clarkprosecutor.org/html/death/US/tucker437.htm, accessed 14 June 2016.

What if Tucker's and others' conversions were taken seriously, though? This question is posed not to suggest that we embrace the religious views death row inmates propound but rather to suggest that we consider the possibility that they are embracing valid alternative conceptions of death.[174] Death is, after all, impossible to speak about. As the philosopher Matteo Cestari observes, "From Heraclitus on, theoretical thinking has generally been conceived in terms of an activity deriving from the exercise of common *Lògos* and the philosopher has to 'follow the common' (*hèpesthai tò ksunò*) and not one's own personal wisdom (*phrònesis*). How could there be philosophy – which speaks the universal tongue of reason – about death, which allegedly is a matter of unique, unrepeatable singularity? . . . How can we find a general, impersonal truth about death (but which death?), if the question is not death in general or the category of death, but every single death?"[175]

In light of the difficulty of speaking about death, another way to present the suggestion that we consider more thoughtfully the experience of death on death row is to propose that we take *time* seriously. Drawing from the work of the philosopher Henri Bergson, we could attend to time as "duration," an experience of ongoing and immeasurable movement rather than of a succession of discrete units or moments that seem to follow one after the other in a line.[176] This movement does not traverse space but rather consists in a temporal heterogeneity, in which "several conscious states are organized into a whole, permeate one another, [and] gradually gain a richer content."[177] As Bergson himself notes, to describe these states as "several" is to speak of them as if they were separate from one another,[178] set side by side instead of simultaneously occurring as differences of a whole experience that unfolds in an indeterminate and always changing flow. It is not possible to isolate and capture or measure a moment of time; as soon as the attempt is made, it is gone.

In the context of a discussion to take time seriously as it is lived on death row, the proposal is that we attend to time as "duration," setting aside, for a moment at least, the idea that death is the end of time. Instead, we might imagine death in time, a transformation that unfolds in time, with time, through time. In brief, death is change rather than an end. This idea may sound familiar from arguments made that death row inmates should be entitled to a legal appeal – not just an appeal for clemency made to a political authority – to demonstrate how they have changed

---

[174] See Kristin Zeiler, "Deadly Pluralism? Why Death-Concept, Death-Definition, Death-Criterion and Death-Test Pluralism Should Be Allowed, Even Though It Creates Some Problems," *Bioethics* 23, no. 8 (2009): 450–459.

[175] Matteo Cestari, "'Each Death Is Unique'. Beyond Epistemic Transfiguration in Thanatology," Academia. www.academia.edu/1928487/_Each_Death_is_Unique_._Beyond_Epistemic_Transfiguration_in-Thanatology, accessed June 14, 2016.

[176] Henri Bergson, *Time and Free Will: An Essay on the Immediate Data of Consciousness*, trans. F. L. Pogson (Mineola, NY: Dover Publications, 2001).

[177] Ibid., 122.

[178] Ibid.

during their time on death row.[179] This legal argument does not question the principle that death is a defining limit, however. What is more, it reiterates the assumption that working with and against this limit is how people change and become more "authentic" human beings. A dialectic with absolute negativity is presumed as the prisoner is transformed for the better through an encounter with their finitude. By contrast, the idea proposed here tries to take seriously the experience of inmates on death row who know they are going to die – as we all do – and do not know when – again, like everyone else – but who also die *slowly*, thereby inviting us to question the presumption of a single final moment when the end takes place and time is up.

Certain familiar but perplexing aspects of death on death row may be illuminated when we attend more closely to time as duration rather than finite. For instance, in *Furman* v. *Georgia* (1972) the Supreme Court insisted that the penalty serve a legally recognized purpose, and identified deterrence and retribution as the purposes it might serve. While deterrence has always been controversial, retribution has not. As Claire Finkelstein observes, "public rhetoric in support of the death penalty, for example, is nearly always retributivist."[180] Retributivism is a theory of punishment that states punishment can never be inflicted on a person for any reason other than the fact that that particular person committed a crime. What is more, as Kant insists in his influential discussion of retribution, justice requires the criminal's punishment be determined by the principle of equality. The principle of equality states that "whatever undeserved evil you inflict on another within the people, that you inflict upon yourself."[181] This means not only that the criminal may not be made to suffer for something they have not done but also that they may not be made to suffer more pain than they inflicted through their criminal actions. This is the doctrine of *lex talionis*, often translated as "an eye for an eye." This doctrine lends itself to the idea of "closure," and the notion that a death sentence concludes the ordeal for the victim's family, allowing them to move on.[182] However, many people no longer expect the death penalty to provide closure. On the contrary, people like Bill and Denise Richard, whose eight-year-old son was killed in the 2013 Boston Marathon bombing, argue "the continued pursuit of that punishment could bring years of appeals and prolong reliving the most painful day of our lives."[183] The Richards experience the penalty of death as an extension rather than as a conclusion of the time of their son's death and their suffering. Death is not the end.

---

[179] See Meghan J. Ryan, "Death and Rehabilitation," *U.C. Davis Law Review* 46 (2013): 101.

[180] Claire Finkelstein, "Death and Retribution," *Criminal Justice Ethics* (Summer/Fall 2002): 12–21, 12.

[181] Immanuel Kant, *The Metaphysics of Morals* (1797), trans. Mary Gregor (Cambridge: Cambridge University Press, 1991), 141.

[182] See John Marsh, "Does Death Penalty Bring Closure?," *cnn.com*, May 201, 2015; www.cnn.com/2015/05/20/opinions/marsh-tsarnaev-forgiveness/, accessed 13 June 2016.

[183] See Marsh, "Does Death Penalty Bring Closure?."

Indeed, the "moment of death" actually eludes the understanding of physical time. As the philosopher D. F. M. Strauss observes, "Whatever criteria are used by the biologist, only once they have been applied and the living entity (plant, animal or human being) is declared 'dead' the physicist may look at a physical clock and not the (thus externally correlated) 'moment of death.'"[184] Medical personnel attending executions are well acquainted with the ambiguity of the so-called "moment of death," and for that reason, it is difficult to find trained people not only to assist with the actual execution but also to make the pronouncement of death. The Council on Ethical and Judicial Affairs of the American Medical Association makes a strong distinction between *determining* death and *certifying* death. According to a Council Report entitled "Physician Participation in Capital Punishment," determining death "includes monitoring the condition of the condemned during the execution and determining the point at which the individual has actually died. Certifying death includes confirming that the individual is dead after another person has pronounced or determined that the individual is dead."[185] The Council finds that determining death may "require physician involvement in the actual execution process" and therefore that determining death is "unethical" for a physician who has taken the Oath of Hippocrates. Among other scenarios the Council imagines is one in which an execution attempt fails and the physician charged with determining death would have to indicate that death has not been "achieved." In such a case, the physician would have to "indicate that the execution attempt must be repeated" and in so doing would participate in the execution.[186]

When we attend more closely to time as duration the most significant insight we gain is the fragility of the power of a state that is predicated on a particular image of death. As Sarat has argued, the time it takes for the death penalty to be carried out is necessary to distinguish the state from the murderer it is punishing. During this time, it is verified that the penalty is imposed by the rule of law, not men, and the penalty is deserved. But the time it takes to impose the penalty does not distinguish the state from the murderer as the prisoners who die under sentence of death die by chance, like everyone does, anticipating a possibly painful process with an uncertain outcome. In brief, the state fails to make death – or at least the death it promulgates – happen.

CONCLUSION

In this essay, I have suggested that the time it takes die leads us to consider the possibility that death isn't "death" as we often imagine it at law and as the modern capital punishment system assumes and requires it to be. Indeed, the time it takes to

[184] D. F. M. Strauss, "Do We Really Comprehend Time?" *South African Journal of Philosophy* 29:2 (2010): 167, 173.

[185] Council on Ethical and Judicial Affairs, American Medical Association, "Council Report: Physician Participation in Capital Punishment," *JAMA* 270, no. 3 (July 21, 1993): 365–368, 368.

[186] Council on Ethical and Judicial Affairs, American Medical Association, "Council Report: Physician Participation in Capital Punishment," 365–368, 367.

die undermines the difference between "life" and "death," letting us consider seriously not simply or only the value of imposing death as a penalty but also the validity of the image of death that informs the American criminal justice system. This means also that the time it takes to die challenges our understanding of "life" as an alternative to "death."

More specifically, death is not as definitive as the capital punishment system and the American system of jurisprudence takes for granted. Recognizing the non-definitiveness of death challenges the stranglehold this conception of death has on our thinking of being but also of law and sovereignty. Thus, the time it takes to die begins to unsettle us not only because it threatens capital punishment practice (i.e. makes it unconstitutional on the grounds of being cruel and unusual) but also because it threatens a view of death that profoundly shapes our understanding of the meaning of life.

4

Grand Finality

Post-Conviction Prosecutors and Capital Punishment

Daniel S. Medwed[1]

INTRODUCTION

In the years since the United States Supreme Court permitted reinstatement of the death penalty in 1976, scholars have paid close attention to the question of why prosecutors charge a crime as a capital offense. We now have a sense of the political variables that affect the decision; we have explored the racial characteristics of perpetrators and victims to divine trends; and we have analyzed geographic disparities to better understand when and where the ultimate penalty is sought. We have also examined the results of those charging decisions in depth. We know the number of plea bargains, the percentage of trials that yielded death sentences, and the reversal rate achieved through the appellate and post-conviction process.

But the scholarly community has largely ignored some related questions. Why do many prosecutors assigned to handle the appellate and post-conviction phases of a capital case – those entrusted with the task of defending death – fight tooth-and-nail to preserve the trial outcome? Even more, why might those prosecutors reject defense overtures to join in a request for an evidentiary hearing or new trial in situations where they had nothing to do with the original charging decision and have misgivings about the propriety of the trial proceedings?

These reactions clash with the gallant image of the American prosecutor so often portrayed in judicial opinions and the canons of legal ethics. For more than a century, observers have painted a picture of the American prosecutor as a "minister of justice," an attorney with duties separate and apart from other lawyers.[2] Unlike

[1] I am grateful to Austin Sarat for soliciting this paper as part of a symposium he organized at the University of Alabama School of Law as well as to my fellow presenters at that event. I would also like to thank the participants in law faculty workshops at the University of Utah and Northeastern University at which I presented earlier versions of this chapter.
[2] See, e.g., Bruce A. Green, "Why Should Prosecutors 'Seek Justice'?," *Fordham Urban Law Journal* 26 (1998): 607, 612–18.

defense counsel, whose sole responsibility is to champion their clients' interests, prosecutors are quasi-judicial officers who bear a dual obligation: to serve as zealous advocates for the government's position and neutral public servants concerned with justice for all, including criminal defendants.[3] Why, then, might appellate and post-conviction prosecutors turn a blind eye to trial-level injustices and fail to realize the minister-of-justice ideal in death penalty cases?

On the one hand, this failure makes sense – and may even come from honorable impulses. Although prosecutors do not formally represent victims' families in death penalty cases, they may serve as the *de facto* point of contact for supplying information to the victim community and fielding questions as the litigation marches into the appellate and post-conviction arena. Post-conviction prosecutors might develop an affinity for victims through these interactions and become loath to upset the apple cart by consenting to an evidentiary hearing or new trial.[4]

Post-conviction prosecutors might also perceive their primary role in the adversary system as that of zealous advocate for the trial result. This justification has populist overtones. The legislature has implemented the will of the people by giving prosecutors the option to pursue the death penalty in certain instances; the chief prosecutor has exercised this option by choosing to file capital charges in a case; and the jury has spoken by rendering a death sentence. In line with this vision, the post-conviction prosecutor becomes the defender of democracy, as embodied in the jury verdict, while the other side now bears the burden of overturning that outcome. Furthermore, capital cases involve the most heinous offenses in our society. Prosecutors drawn to the ranks of law enforcement through a wish to fight crime may view resistance to a convicted capital defendant's pleas as part of their public safety calling.[5]

On the other hand, the fact that many appellate and post-conviction prosecutors refuse to express openness to viable defense claims in the capital context may reflect less principled motivations. As I have discussed in depth elsewhere, these motivations are both institutional and individual. Professional and political incentives to preserve convictions, along with psychological pressures, influence how prosecutors approach their jobs after trial.[6] The research on cognitive biases in particular helps explain why post-conviction prosecutors defend death sentences with gusto. Relevant biases include the confirmation bias and the aversion to cognitive dissonance.[7]

This chapter asserts that another explanation should be added to the mix: how the value of "finality" plays a key role in prompting prosecutors to neglect to reexamine

---

[3] Daniel S. Medwed, *Prosecution Complex: America's Race to Convict and Its Impact on the Innocent* (New York: New York University Press, 2012): 2.

[4] See Daniel S. Medwed, "The Zeal Deal: Prosecutorial Resistance to Post-Conviction Claims of Innocence," *Boston University Law Review* 84 (2004): 125, 145–46.

[5] Ibid. at 139.

[6] See generally Medwed, *Prosecution Complex*.

[7] See infra notes 96–109 and accompanying text.

capital convictions. A prosecutor's customary belief in the need for finality in the litigation process is heightened in the capital punishment context, generating what I deem a search for "grand finality." The idea that disputes must at some point reach a final resolution in order to achieve peace for litigants, victims, and witnesses, and to make room in the system for new disputes, takes on added significance in a death penalty case because the prospect of true finality is attainable. As others have famously noted, there is no appeal from the grave.[8] A post-conviction prosecutor striving for finality may ignore a defendant's legitimate demand to re-open a capital case. This can prolong injustices – and help produce wrongful executions.

I am not suggesting that prosecutors should abandon their advocacy yearnings and acquiesce whenever the defense raises viable doubts about the propriety of a death penalty trial. That would be unrealistic. My more modest claim is that prosecutors who aspire to exemplify the minister-of-justice ethos should be amenable to evidentiary hearings or new trials in capital cases when warranted. The best way to ensure these events occur is for a prosecutor to join in the defense request for a full airing of its claims and thereby put pressure on judges to act.[9]

I begin this chapter with an evaluation of how and why prosecutors file capital charges at the outset, and then delve into the work of appellate and post-conviction prosecutors assigned to defend any ensuing death sentences. Next, I take a close look at the explanations for prosecutorial intransigence to appellate and post-conviction claims of error in death penalty cases. After that discussion, I tackle the topic of grand finality and prosecutors' reliance on that principle to justify efforts to maintain death sentences. Ultimately, I put forth potential remedies targeted at thwarting the dependence on grand finality by prosecutors.

CHARGING DEATH

Any discussion about how appellate and post-conviction capital prosecutors approach their work should begin with an overview of how death penalty cases arise. Thirty-one states and the Federal government allow for capital punishment in particular cases.[10] In order for a crime to be "death-eligible," it must contain one or more special circumstances as determined by the legislature that elevate a murder to a capital offense. Those circumstances vary depending on the jurisdiction and may encompass the killing of a police officer, a child, multiple victims, or other abhorrent crimes. At the state level, the decision to pursue capital charges in a death-eligible

---

8   See, e.g., James R. Acker et al., "No Appeal from the Grave: Innocence, Capital Punishment, and the Lessons of History," in *Wrongly Convicted: Perspectives on Failed Justice*, ed. Saundra D. Westervelt & John A. Humphrey (New Brunswick, NJ: Rutgers University Press, 2001), 154–73.

9   See generally Medwed, "Zeal Deal."

10 See Death Penalty Information Center, "States with and without the Death Penalty," available at www.deathpenaltyinfo.org/states-and-without-death-penalty (as of November 9, 2016).

matter generally falls within the discretion of the chief prosecutor in the county in which the crime occurred, and the prosecution must provide the defendant with notice of its intent to seek the death penalty in a timely fashion.[11]

In theory, prosecutorial discretion to charge a case as a capital crime is not unbound. Legislators outline the criteria on which prosecutors should base their choices; judges and ethics boards monitor those choices. But the legislative criteria are amorphous, which in practice leaves prosecutors with vast autonomy to weigh whether to file capital charges. What is more, the judiciary normally defers to prosecutors in all facets of their charging power, and disciplinary agencies seldom sanction prosecutors for ethical violations of any sort.[12] These external controls over capital charging (legislative guidance, judicial oversight, and disciplinary body supervision) are often supplemented by internal controls within prosecutors' offices. Some chief prosecutors have instituted committees or other formal processes for capital charging decisions.[13]

Despite the presence of external and internal controls, disparities about whether to seek the death penalty exist within jurisdictions because of the predilections of individual county prosecutors, the overwhelming majority of whom are elected, and the political tastes of the local electorate.[14] Take New York. The Empire State reinstated capital punishment in 1995, ushering in a brief experiment with the death penalty. Some prosecutors filed capital charges quite readily. Others – most notably, Robert Johnson, the District Attorney for Bronx County in New York City – rejected the option as a matter of principle.[15] This meant the odds of capital charges differed

[11] See, e.g., GrassRoots Investigation Project of Equal Justice USA & National Death Row Assistance Network, "Capital Defense Handbook," available at http://ndran.org/capital%20defense%20handbook.htm.

[12] Daniel S. Medwed, "Emotionally Charged: The Prosecutorial Charging Decision and the Innocence Revolution," *Cardozo Law Review* 31 (2010): 2187.

[13] Barbara LaWall, the chief prosecutor in Pima County, Arizona (Tucson), installed a panel of seven people to determine whether to file capital charges. After the creation of the panel system, the rate of capital filings declined in that jurisdiction. See Kim Smith, "For Pima County Attorneys, Panel, Death Penalty Never a 'Slam Dunk,'" *Arizona Daily Star*, May 20, 2007.

[14] Jonathan DeMay, "A District Attorney's Decision to Seek the Death Penalty: Toward an Improved Process," *Fordham Urban Law Journal* 26 (1999): 767. More than forty states elect their chief county prosecutors. David A. Graham, "Most States Elect No Black Prosecutors," *The Atlantic*, July 7, 2015. At the federal level, the Attorney General and U.S. Attorneys in each district are appointed. For a discussion of decision-making by federal prosecutors, see Bruce A. Green & Fred C. Zacharias, "The 'U.S. Attorneys Scandal' and the Allocation of Prosecutorial Power," *Ohio State Law Journal* 69 (2008): 187. Prosecutors' decisions about whether to seek the death penalty are inevitably affected by politics, including the proximity of the next election and the level of electoral competition. See Isaac Unah, "Electoral Incentives and Prosecutorial Decision to Seek the Death Penalty" (manuscript on file with author).

[15] In 1996, Robert Johnson refused to seek the death penalty against a defendant accused of killing a police officer, prompting Governor George Pataki of New York to remove Johnson from prosecuting the case, claiming this reflected a "blanket policy" that violated death penalty law. See Richard C. Dieter, "Killing for Votes," October 1996, available at www.deathpenaltyinfo.org/killing-for-votes. See also Christopher Dunn, "The Death Penalty Skips across County

based on where within the state, even within New York City, the crime occurred. The state's highest court found the death penalty law unconstitutional in 2004.[16]

Data reveal that other states experience large county-by-county disparities in the frequency with which death is pursued. More than half the death cases in Texas come from four large counties, and most of the state's counties have never produced a capital verdict.[17] This trend surfaces elsewhere too. A 2013 study by the Death Penalty Information Center posited that only 2 percent of the nation's counties account for most state death penalty cases.[18] A single county – Riverside County in California – generated 16 percent of the death sentences imposed nationwide in 2015, more than any *state* in the country except for Florida.[19]

Variations in funding levels exacerbate disparities in capital charging practices. Counties with ample funds can afford to litigate capital cases. That pursuit is self-reinforcing; those prosecutors are trained in death penalty matters, succeed in obtaining death sentences, perceive death as an appropriate punishment, and are inclined to seek death in subsequent cases. Other counties lack the resources and the experience to develop an appetite for the death penalty.[20] The federal government's capital punishment regime is designed to limit inconsistency. But, as at the state level, local idiosyncrasies produce discrepancies in federal death penalty charges.[21]

Lines," *New York Newsday*, February 25, 2003 (observing that Johnson had not yet pursued capital punishment in any death-eligible cases whereas District Attorney Richard Brown of Queens County had filed capital charges in four cases).

[16] Death row was empty three years later. See Death Penalty Information Center, "New York," available at www.deathpenaltyinfo.org/new-york-1.

[17] Elahe Izadi, "American Sniper Trial: Why Prosecutors Often Don't Seek the Death Penalty," *Washington Post*, March 6, 2015.

[18] Death Penalty Information Center, "The 2% Death Penalty: How a Minority of Counties Produce Most Death Cases at an Enormous Cost to Us All," October 2013, available at www.deathpenaltyinfo.org/documents/TwoPercentReport.pdf. See also Simone Seiver, "Why Three Counties That Loved the Death Penalty Have Almost Stopped Pursuing It: A Closer Look at Get-Tough DAs," *The Marshall Project*, August 11, 2015, available at www.themarshallproject.org/2015/08/11/why-three-counties-that-loved-the-death-penalty-have-almost-stopped-pursuing-it.

[19] Timothy Williams, "Executions by States Fell in 2015, Report Says," *New York Times*, December 16, 2015. See also Adam M. Gershowitz, "Statewide Capital Punishment: The Case for Eliminating Counties' Role in the Death Penalty," *Vanderbilt Law Review* 63 (2010): 307, 314–18.

[20] See Gershowitz, "Statewide Capital Punishment," 319–23.

[21] Authority over whether to file federal capital charges resides with "Main Justice," the headquarters of the Department of Justice in Washington, D.C., and eventually rests with the Attorney General. Yet the local United States Attorney in the district where the crime took place must make recommendations to Washington about whether a case warrants the death penalty. Those recommendations are influential. For a discussion of federal death penalty practices, see Robin Campbell, "Issues of Consistency in the Federal Death Penalty: A Roundtable Discussion on the Role of the U.S. Attorney," Vera Institute of Justice, 2002, available at www.vera.org/sites/default/files/resources/downloads/Issues_of_consistency.pdf.

Not only do decisions about whether to file death charges differ within particular jurisdictions, but those decisions are fraught with racial overtones. Concerns about racial discrimination in the administration of capital punishment provided crucial context to the Supreme Court's 1972 decision in *Furman* v. *Georgia* to abolish that penalty.[22] Numerous states reacted to *Furman* by modifying their systems to curb the jury's discretion in reaching a death penalty verdict.[23] These modifications proved vital to the Supreme Court's 1976 ruling in *Gregg* v. *Georgia* that resurrected the death penalty.[24] *Furman* did not directly target the issue of prosecutorial discretion in charging, but *Gregg* did. The Court in *Gregg* suggested, however, that states need not restrict the autonomy of prosecutors in choosing to file capital charges beyond classifying the types of crimes suitable for the death penalty.[25]

Evidence of racial discrimination persists today in the application of the death penalty.[26] Studies reveal that the race of the victim in a death-eligible crime is a potent variable in a prosecutor's decision to treat a case as a capital one. Although homicides with white victims and African-American perpetrators constitute a relatively small subset of crimes eligible for the death penalty, those cases are overrepresented in the percentage of cases in which prosecutors seek death.[27] Research indicates that racial gaps regarding the death penalty may even exist within a single county. A recent study of Alameda County in California, a large and diverse region that includes

[22] *Furman* v. *Georgia*, 408 U.S. 238 (1972); David C. Baldus & George Woodworth, "Race Discrimination in the Administration of the Death Penalty: An Overview of the Empirical Evidence with Special Emphasis on the Post-1990 Research," *Criminal Law Bulletin* 41 (Spring 2005): ART 11, n. 13.

[23] Many legislatures altered their sentencing regimes by listing statutory aggravating factors that juries must affirmatively find as a precondition to a death sentence or mandating that juries engage in a balancing of precise factors. David C. Baldus et al., "Racial Discrimination and the Death Penalty in the Post-*Furman* Era: An Empirical and Legal Overview, with Recent Findings from Philadelphia," *Cornell Law Review* 83 (1998): 1638.

[24] *Gregg* v. *Georgia*, 428 U.S. 153 (1976); Baldus & Woodworth, "Race Discrimination Post-1990 Research" 11 n.13.

[25] See Baldus et al, "Racial Discrimination Philadelphia" 1649–50.

[26] Implicit racial bias permeates the exercise of discretion by many prosecutors. See, e.g., Baldus & Woodworth, "Race Discrimination Post-1990 Research." Indeed, much of the racism in our criminal justice system is unconscious, and scholars have explored this conundrum for decades. See, e.g., Charles Lawrence, "The Id, the Ego, and Equal Protection. Reckoning with Unconscious Racism," *Stanford Law Review* 39 (1087): 317, 322. See also Darren Lenard Hutchinson, "'Continually Reminded of Their Inferior Position': Social Dominance, Implicit Bias, Criminality, and Race," *Journal of Law & Policy* 46 (2014): 23, 35–41; Jerry Kang et al., "Implicit Bias in the Courtroom," *UCLA Law Review* 59 (2012): 1124, 1141–1142; Sean D. O'Brien & Kathleen Wayland, "Implicit Bias and Capital Decision-Making: Using Narrative to Counter Prejudicial Psychiatric Labels," *Hofstra Law Review* 43 (2015): 751; Robert J. Smith & Justin D. Levinson, "The Impact of Implicit Racial Bias on the Exercise of Prosecutorial Discretion," *Seattle University Law Review* 35 (2012): 755; Robert J. Smith et al., "Implicit White Favoritism in the Criminal Justice System," *Alabama Law Review* 66 (2015): 871.

[27] See John H. Blume et al., "Explaining Death Row's Size and Racial Composition," *Journal of Empirical Legal Studies* 1 (2004): 165. The "race-of-the-victim" effect also surfaces in the statistics about which people are executed. Williams, "Executions by States Fell in 2015."

Oakland, detected immense "race of neighborhood" differences in death-charging. After analyzing 473 first-degree murder convictions spanning a 23-year period, Steven Shatz and Terry Dalton determined that prosecutors were far more inclined to pursue death for murders that took place in South County, a region where whites were three times more likely to be homicide victims than blacks, than in North County.[28]

Race is not the only improper element that affects the death penalty charging calculus. Socioeconomic class and gender have an impact, too, with poor men the most probable candidates to encounter the threat of execution.[29] Studies further demonstrate that many of those charged and convicted of capital offenses suffer from severe mental illnesses.[30]

This review of capital charging shows that prosecutors have massive discretion in selecting the ultimate penalty and that bias can creep into those decisions.[31] Prosecutors also wield discretion over the next key point in a capital case: whether to offer a plea bargain.[32] If the case is not resolved by a plea, it goes to trial where juries typically serve as fact-finders in the guilt and sentencing phases. After a jury returns a death sentence, the case moves into the appellate and post-conviction sphere in which prosecutors are put in the position of defending death. The rest of this chapter will focus on how prosecutors react to the scenario of defending death after trial and what prompts those reactions, especially when the verdict may have involved egregious procedural and constitutional errors or perhaps an innocent defendant.

PROSECUTORS DEFENDING DEATH

The ultimate penalty deserves the ultimate process. To that end, there are a series of appellate and post-conviction remedies available to those convicted of capital offenses. These procedures are not endless. And they do not always catch mistakes.

---

[28] Steven F. Shatz & Terry Dalton, "Challenging the Death Penalty with Statistics: *Furman, McCleskey*, and a Single County Case Study," *Cardozo Law Review* 34 (2013): 1227.

[29] See, e.g., DeMay, "A District Attorney's Decision," 782–83. A 2010 study of the federal death penalty concluded that capital defendants whose financial resources fall at the lower end of the scale are twice as likely to receive death sentences as their more affluent peers. See Jon B. Gould & Lisa Greenman, "Update on the Cost and Quality of Representation in Federal Death Penalty Cases," Report to the Committee on Defender Services, Judicial Conference of the United States, September 2010, available at www.uscourts,gov/file/2945/download.

[30] The nonprofit group Death Penalty Focus cites, as a conservative estimate, that 5–10 percent of those on death row have a serious mental illness. Death Penalty Focus, "Mental Illness on Death Row," available at https://death.rdsecure.org/article.php?id=53.

[31] Ninety-five percent of chief county prosecutors are white. What is more, 79 percent of them are white men; three in five states have no elected black prosecutors. Graham, "Most States."

[32] Kent S. Scheidegger, "The Death Penalty and Plea Bargaining to Life Sentences," Criminal Justice Legal Foundation Working Paper 09–01, February 2009, available at www.cjlf.org/publications/papers/wpaper09-01.pdf. A study of cases in Georgia from 1993–2000 found that the threat of capital punishment boosted the likelihood of a plea bargain by 20 to 25 percent across various models. Sherod Thaxton, "Leveraging Death," *Journal of Criminal Law & Criminology* 102 (2013): 475.

These procedures include the direct appeal;[33] post-conviction or "collateral" remedies,[34] which are often grounded in the ancient writs of habeas corpus[35] and coram nobis;[36] requests for executive clemency;[37] and the equitable remedy of a stay of execution.[38] Death row prisoners denied relief after exhausting their state

[33] After a defendant is sentenced to death and post-trial motion skirmishes occur, the case advances to the direct appeal. Even if a capital defendant persuades an appellate court that an error happened below, that does not always generate a reversal. A conviction will be overturned usually only where the appeals court concludes the mistake was not harmless. See Medwed, "Prosecution Complex" 110, 113–14, 125. In states with two layers of appellate courts, the appeal in a capital case often automatically ascends to the state's highest court. See, e.g., Utah Courts, "An Overview of the Utah Supreme Court," available at www.utcourts.gov/courts/sup/overview.htm. Sometimes the direct appeal is heard first in the intermediate appellate court. See Council of Chief Judges States Courts of Appeal, "The Role of State Intermediate Appellate Courts," 4 n. 6, November 2012, available at www.sji.gov/wp/wp-content/uploads/Report_5_CCJSCA_Report.pdf. In those situations, assuming the intermediate court upholds the conviction, the defendant generally may petition for further review in the state court of last resort. After a defendant exhausts the state appellate remedies, there is the option of asking the U.S. Supreme Court to consider the case.

[34] For the most part, states have codified versions of these writs in an effort to rationalize, clarify, and control the availability of post-conviction remedies. Some judges look beyond those statutes and draw upon these ancient writs as common law remedies where justice requires. See Daniel S. Medwed, "Up the River without a Procedure: Innocent Prisoners and Newly Discovered Non-DNA Evidence in State Courts," *Arizona Law Review* 47 (2005): 655, 681–86.

[35] The writ of habeas corpus emerged in medieval England as a mechanism for people jailed by the Crown to dispute the lawfulness of their confinement. The scope of habeas corpus was quite narrow when it crossed the pond to the United States. The "Great Writ" permitted challenges based on jurisdictional and, eventually, constitutional errors; claims of factual mistakes were usually beyond the pale of habeas review. Some American jurisdictions removed this barrier over time, acknowledging that courts may entertain newly discovered evidence claims via habeas corpus. Also, applicants for habeas relief historically were required to be in the custody of the state, with petitions filed in a court in the county where the defendant was confined. A grant of habeas corpus often produced absolute release from custody and banned any further proceedings against the petitioner. Ibid. at 674–75.

[36] The writ of error coram nobis arose in sixteenth-century England as a way for courts to rectify their own significant errors of fact. Available in the original trial court, defendants used coram nobis to assert facts unknown to the judge at the time of judgment that called the soundness of the conviction into doubt. This writ lacked a statute of limitations – though claimants needed to show they had proceeded with reasonable diligence – and a judge conferring relief under coram nobis typically vacated the conviction while giving the government permission to re-try the case. Ibid. at 669–70.

[37] Prisoners on the cusp of execution may try to invoke the executive clemency power to issue a pardon or sentence commutation. The Governor exerts this authority in most states, but it is normally channeled through an agency that evaluates applications. Studies indicate that clemency requests seldom succeed and that, when state executives do acquiesce, their motives are often questionable. See Michael Heise, "The Death of Death Row Clemency and the Evolving Politics of Unequal Grace," *Alabama Law Review* 66 (2015): 949; Michael Heise, "Mercy by the Numbers: An Empirical Analysis of Clemency and Its Structure," *Virginia Law Review* 89 (2003): 239. See also Jodi Wilgoren, "Citing Issue of Fairness, Governor Clears Out Death Row in Illinois," *New York Times*, January 12, 2003.

[38] Courts enjoy broad discretion in choosing whether to accommodate requests for a stay, and there are few bright-line rules. Some scholars have decried the stay process for its inconsistent results. See, e.g., Eric M. Freedman, "No Execution if Four Justices Object," *Hofstra Law*

remedies may seek further aid through the federal courts' habeas corpus
jurisdiction.[39]

These remedies are marked by a series of procedural and substantive barriers. In
general, the direct appeal is confined to issues presented to the trial court and
adequately "preserved" for review.[40] Unlike the direct appeal, in a post-conviction
petition a defendant may introduce issues never heard below.[41] Yet post-conviction
remedies are often subject to rigid statutes of limitations as well as obstacles to filing
successive petitions, appealing denials, and receiving evidentiary hearings. Defendants wishing to develop claims of innocence based on newly discovered evidence
bear heavy burdens in proving that, among other things, the information is truly
"new" and material to the case.[42] The nature of the prosecutorial response to defense
challenges on appeal and in post-conviction filings can dramatically affect the
outcome.[43] A prosecutor's willingness to join a request for an evidentiary hearing
or new trial makes it much harder for judges to hold firm – and much easier to
reverse a conviction in an atrocious, high-profile case.[44]

There is little research regarding how capital appeals and post-conviction motions
are handled administratively by prosecutors. What is clear is that the prosecution
team at each stage of a capital case usually consists of multiple attorneys, often at
great expense to taxpayers.[45] In most states, the district attorney's office in the county
in which the crime occurred will prosecute the trial while a different agency
(typically the state attorney general's office) will carry the laboring oar for the

---

Review 43 (2015): 639; Rebecca R. Sklar, "Executing Equity: The Broad Judicial Discretion to
Stay the Execution of Death Sentences," *Hofstra Law Review* 40 (2012): 771.

[39] State inmates may allege factual innocence based on new evidence, but that claim alone is
generally insufficient to support relief in a federal habeas action. Medwed, "Prosecution
Complex," 126. The passage of the Antiterrorism and Effective Death Penalty Act (AEDPA)
of 1996 has produced ample scholarly commentary, much of it critical. See, e.g., Lee Kovarsky,
"AEDPA's Wrecks: Comity, Finality, and Federalism," *Tulane Law Review* 82 (2007): 443.

[40] Legal issues usually must be initiated at the trial level – offers of proof made, objections
registered, arguments leveled – to preserve them for appeal. See, e.g., Larry Cunningham,
"Appellate Review of Unpreserved Questions in Criminal Cases: An Attempt to Define the
'Interests of Justice,'" *Journal of Appellate Practice & Process* 11 (2010): 285.

[41] Medwed, "Prosecution Complex," 125.

[42] See generally Medwed, "Up the River."

[43] I have studied this issue extensively in the context of post-conviction claims of innocence. See
Daniel S. Medwed, "The Prosecutor as Minister of Justice: Preaching from the Post-
Conviction Pulpit," *Washington Law Review* 84 (2009): 35; Medwed, "Zeal Deal."

[44] The prosecutorial response not only provides a public benefit to judges – cover, if you will – but
judges and prosecutors often have a cozy professional relationship. As Ion Meyn has put it,
"[i]nstitutional biases at play also favor the prosecutor. Judges and prosecutors share workplace
history. Prosecutorial offices tend to be embedded in the courthouse and judicial staff work
hard to coordinate prosecutorial scheduling." Ion Meyn, "The Lightness of the Prosecutor's
Burden," University of Wisconsin Law School Legal Studies Research Paper Series Paper
No. 1360, 40 (manuscript on file with author).

[45] See, e.g., Death Penalty Information Center, "Costs: $978,000 and Eight Prosecutors Allocated
for New Hampshire Death Penalty Trial," available at www.deathpenaltyinfo.org/node/2296.

appellate and post-conviction phases. Alabama employs this model with the Capital Litigation Division of the Attorney General's Office bearing responsibility for all proceedings after the trial.[46] In a handful of jurisdictions, one office – e.g., a special unit within the attorney general's office – will shepherd the case through the trial, appellate, and post-conviction process.[47] The county prosecutor occasionally handles all stages of capital litigation in state court.[48]

Sometimes the division of labor is not so clearly delineated. Many states establish a formal separation of duties between the county trial team and the state-level appellate and post-conviction unit, but make this line permeable by allowing the attorney general's office to intervene at trial either on its own volition or by invitation from the county.[49] Conversely, states may permit county prosecutors to assist in post-conviction proceedings by serving as specially designated attorneys general.[50] Responsibilities may even shift between the direct appeal and the post-conviction process, with the state controlling the former and the

---

[46] Office of the Attorney General of Alabama, "Alabama's Death Penalty Appeals Process," available at www.ago.state.al.us/File-Death-Penalty-Appeals-Process. Oregon takes this approach as well. E-mail from Jeffrey Ellis, Attorney, Oregon Capital Resource Counsel, February 13, 2016 (on file with author).

[47] Some smaller jurisdictions gravitate to this model, likely out of necessity. Consider New Hampshire, where lawyers from the Homicide Prosecution Unit of the state Attorney General's Office "are involved in murder cases from the first call of a suspicious death, through the trial of the case in the superior court, and the appeal of the conviction in the supreme court. The attorneys work closely with state and local police and oversee all investigations in cases of murder." See New Hampshire Department of Justice, Office of the Attorney General, "Criminal Justice," available at http://doj.nh.gov/criminal/index.htm. See also State of Delaware, Attorney General Matt Denn, "Criminal Division," available at http://attorneygeneral.dela ware.gov/criminal/index.shtml ("The Criminal Division of the Department of Justice is responsible for the prosecution of criminal cases throughout the State from misdemeanors to murders.").

[48] In Ohio, the county assumes responsibility for all state-level phases of a capital case. According to veteran defense attorney Jeff Gamso: "In the ordinary course of things, all state level process - trial, direct appeal, & post conviction - at all levels (through cert to SCOTUS) is handled by the elected county prosecutor's office. The AG will often assist, provide, amicus help, and likely try to take over any case that would actually get into the Supreme Court. But the county prosecutor can refuse the takeover." E-mail from Jeff Gamso, February 13, 2016 (on file with author); Ohio Rev. Code § 309.08(A). The Capital Crimes Unit of the state Attorney General's Office in Ohio customarily represents the warden in federal habeas actions. E-mail from David Stebbins, Federal Defenders, February 16, 2016 (on file with author).

[49] In California, the state constitution provides that "[W]hen required by the public interest or directed by the Governor, the Attorney General shall assist any district attorney in the discharge of the duties of that office." Cal. Const. Art. V, §13. In Kentucky, local prosecutors may, at any time, request help from the Attorney General, or in the absence of such a request the Attorney General can "intervene or direct [a] criminal proceeding. . .[Or] whenever requested in writing by the Governor, or by any of the courts or grand juries of the Commonwealth, or upon receiving a communication from a sheriff, mayor, or majority of a city legislative body stating that his participation in a given case is desirable to effect the administration of justice and the proper enforcement of the laws." Ky. Rev. Stat. Ann. 15.200.

[50] E-mail from Eric M. Freedman, Professor, Hofstra University-Maurice A. Deane School of Law, February 11, 2016 (on file with author).

county the latter.[51] North Carolina takes this a step further: counties defend state post-conviction filings while the task of handling federal habeas claims falls on the attorney general's office.[52]

Regardless of the allocation of responsibility in each death penalty jurisdiction, a different set of lawyers normally represents the government on appellate and post-conviction matters than the squad deployed for trial. For one thing, appellate and post-conviction chores require different skill sets from those utilized in trying a case. For another, ethical issues may come into play if a lawyer involved in the trial were asked to contest charges of prosecutorial misconduct in subsequent proceedings in that case.

Although capital cases are overturned by courts at a high rate, prosecutorial opposition at the appellate and post-conviction stages can lengthen the process and prevent the correction of certain injustices. One study of state death penalty cases from 1973–1995 revealed serious errors in more than 60 percent of capital cases; state courts reversed 47 percent of death sentences in that sample, and federal courts tossed out 40 percent of the remaining ones during habeas review. A consequence of the error and reversal rates, not to mention the protracted review process itself, was that less than 5 percent of capital defendants sentenced to death during this period were actually executed.[53] Another study analyzed nearly 7,500 defendants sentenced to death from 1973–2004 and determined that 37.4 percent of those defendants were removed from death row. The authors of that study estimated that 4.1 percent of those defendants were innocent, an appraisal they deemed "conservative."[54] State-specific studies buttress these find-ings. Capital sentences in Kentucky from 1976–2012 had a reversal rate of

---

[51] In North Carolina, the county prosecutor litigates the trial, the attorney general's office handles the direct appeal, and then control over state post-conviction proceedings technically reverts back to the county. County prosecutors, in turn, might seek assistance from the attorney general's office with the state post-conviction process. Apparently, any federal habeas actions are then fielded by the attorney general's office. E-mail from Elizabeth Hambourger, Staff Attorney, Center for Death Penalty Litigation, February 13, 2016 (on file with author). Missouri has a similar system. Experienced Kansas City defense lawyer Elizabeth Unger Carlyle explains that: "The appeal is handled by the attorney general, as are all felony appeals in Missouri. The first level post-conviction hearing (not called habeas in Missouri) goes back to the trial court. Again, either the local prosecutor or an assistant AG handles that." E-mail from Elizabeth Unger Carlyle, February 13, 2016 (on file with author).

[52] See supra note 51 and accompanying text.

[53] See James S. Liebman et al., "A Broken System: Error Rates in Capital Cases, 1973–1995," June 12, 2000, available at www2.law.columbia.edu/instructionalservices/liebman/liebman_final.pdf; James S. Liebman et al., "Capital Attrition: Error Rates in Capital Cases, 1973–1995," *Texas Law Review* 78 (2000): 1839. See also Michael O. Finkelstein et al., "A Note on the Censoring Problem in Empirical Case-Outcome Studies," *Journal of Empirical Legal Studies* 3 (2006): 375.

[54] See Samuel R. Gross et al., "Rate of False Conviction of Defendants Who Are Sentenced to Death," 111 *Proceedings of the National Academy of Sciences U. S. A.* 111, no. 20 (2014): 7230–35, available at www.pnas.org/content/111/20/7230.full.

64 percent,[55] and defendants sentenced to death in North Carolina from 1977–2009 had their cases overturned nearly 70 percent of the time.[56]

These statistics signal that courts tend to look more closely at capital cases than others, and are more willing to brand a mistake as reversible error. But that does not excuse the behavior of prosecutors who fight extended, likely losing battles in defending shaky death sentences. Time and time again, capital prosecutors after trial continue to wage war when they could have acquiesced to a claim for a new trial early on.

The saga of Kennedy Brewer is a glaring example of intransigence by appellate and post-conviction capital prosecutors. In May 1992, a three-year-old girl was abducted from her home in rural Noxubee County, Mississippi. Two days later she was discovered dead in a creek near her home with signs she had been raped. Kennedy Brewer, the African American boyfriend of the girl's mother, immediately surfaced as the main suspect. He had been babysitting the girl at the time of her disappearance. While there was no sign of forced entry, a broken window could have offered access to an assailant. A semen sample retrieved from the girl's body failed to yield a DNA profile. The police nevertheless arrested Brewer, and the longtime chief prosecutor in Noxubee, a white man, announced he would seek the death penalty. Brewer remained in jail until the case went to trial three years later in neighboring Lowndes County, where it was transferred ostensibly due to excessive pretrial publicity in Noxubee.[57]

The prosecution's case at trial was circumstantial except for some dubious forensic evidence. The medical examiner who conducted the autopsy of the girl's body found blemishes that he thought were "bite marks" from the perpetrator. Noxubee County prosecutors put Dr. Michael West on the stand, a bite mark analyst who had been suspended by the field's trade group, the American Board of Forensic Odontology. West testified that nineteen marks on the girl's body "indeed and without a doubt" came from Brewer's teeth. Notably, he asserted that Brewer's top two front teeth alone had inflicted this damage. The defense disagreed with this account and presented its own expert who concluded that (1) the marks stemmed from insect bites that had accumulated as the body wallowed in a Mississippi creek and (2) that producing these injuries without the assistance of bottom teeth was

---

[55] Opinion, "Ky. Prosecutors: Capital Punishment Unfair," *Lexington Herald-Leader*, March 7, 2012.

[56] Frank R. Baumgartner, "In N.C., only 20 percent of condemned are executed," *Charlotte Observer*, March 5, 2010.

[57] For a compelling and thorough evaluation of the Brewer case, see Tucker Carrington, "Mississippi Innocence: The Convictions and Exonerations of Levon Brooks and Kennedy Brewer and the Failure of the American Promise," *Georgetown Journal of Legal Ethics* 28 (2015): 123. See also Valena Elizabeth Beety, "The Death Penalty: Ethics and Economics in Mississippi," *Mississippi Law Journal* 81 (2012): 1437, 1465–70; E-mail from Tucker Carrington, July 23, 2015 (on file with author); Medwed, "Prosecution Complex," 161–62.

farfetched.[58] The jury sided with the prosecution, convicting Brewer of murder and sexual battery, and sentenced him to death.[59]

The Mississippi Attorney General's Office defended this outcome on appeal in spite of the weakness of the prosecution case. Two assistant attorneys general argued that the evidence supported the conviction and disputed a range of errors alleged by the defense, including those related to the admissibility of the bite mark evidence, the use of peremptory challenges to strike six black jurors during voir dire, and improper comments by the trial prosecutor. The Supreme Court of Mississippi unanimously affirmed the conviction in 1998,[60] and the U.S. Supreme Court declined to hear Brewer's case the following year.[61] The State requested an execution date.[62]

This represented the end of the direct appeal, thrusting the case into the post-conviction process. Brewer sought the appointment of a post-conviction attorney. In response, the Mississippi Supreme Court denied the state's motion for an execution date and sent the case to the trial court for assignment of counsel.[63] As his first post-conviction salvo, with newly appointed counsel on hand, Brewer claimed the state had failed to thoroughly test the available biological evidence in order to obtain an exculpatory DNA profile. The Attorney General's Office balked, insisting the government had no obligation to search for and unearth all potentially exculpatory evidence. In March 2000, the Supreme Court of Mississippi denied relief to Brewer once again, yet hinted in a footnote that the defendant should return to the trial court and ask to retest the evidence.[64]

Shortly after the 2000 decision, Brewer petitioned for a rehearing in the state Supreme Court on the grounds that, absent a remand and direction to the trial court, he lacked a procedural vehicle for acquiring funds to have the DNA material tested. The state's highest court agreed. It stayed the proceedings in December 2000, dispatching the matter to the trial court "for such proceedings as necessary to allow Brewer access to the DNA evidence in this case and funds for the testing of same."[65] Brewer subsequently filed a motion with the trial court to test the DNA evidence at the expense of the state, which was granted in 2001.[66] Those DNA tests *excluded* Brewer as the source of the material and revealed a genetic profile of an unknown man. The state compared the results of those tests to those performed on several of

[58] Medwed, "Prosecution Complex," 161–62. See also Radley Balko, "'Indeed, and without a Doubt,'" *Reason*, available at http://reason.com/archives/2007/08/02/indeed-and-without-a-doubt.

[59] For a dramatic description of the scene in the courthouse when Brewer was informed of his death sentence, see Carrington, "Mississippi Innocence," 125–26.

[60] *State v. Brewer*, 725 So. 2d. 106 (Miss. 1998).

[61] *Brewer v. Mississippi*, 526 U.S. 1027 (1999).

[62] Beety, "Ethics and Economics in Mississippi" 1467.

[63] Ibid.

[64] *Brewer v. State*, 819 So. 2d 1165 (Miss. 2000).

[65] *Brewer v. State*, 819 So. 2d 1169, 1171–72 (Miss. 2002).

[66] Ibid. at 1172.

Brewer's friends and relatives, but no match emerged. Other than that, it seems as if law enforcement did nothing to reinvestigate the crime.[67]

State prosecutors instead clung to the belief in Brewer's involvement. They even contested the jurisdiction of the Mississippi Supreme Court to order a new trial based on the DNA discovery, arguing that the trial court should have fielded this request.[68] In 2002, the state Supreme Court remanded the matter to the trial court to hold an evidentiary hearing on the issue of whether the DNA test results warranted a new trial.[69] A Lowndes County judge vacated Brewer's conviction, removed him from death row, and gave the prosecution permission to re-try him back in Noxubee.[70]

For five long years, Noxubee County prosecutors mused about whether to pursue a new trial – while Brewer awaited the decision behind bars in county lockup. Citing conflicts of interest, the state assigned a different county's chief prosecutor to the case in 2007. The substitute announced he would neither seek the death penalty in a new trial nor oppose an application for bail. In August 2007, a judge granted Brewer bail. Yet the prospect of a new murder trial still loomed.[71]

At the request of the Innocence Project in New York City, the authorities allowed the physical evidence from the rape kit to undergo additional DNA tests by a lab in California. The lab compared the DNA profile obtained from the previous round of testing with genetic material gleaned from cheek swabs taken from other suspects in the case. This process verified that the profile from the girl's rape kit matched that of Justin Albert Johnson, who was one of the original suspects in the case before Brewer became the focus.[72]

Lacking confidence that Noxubee prosecutors would provide assistance, the defense team disclosed these results to the Mississippi Attorney General's Office, which launched a reinvestigation. In a dramatic moment, investigators converged on Johnson at his cottage near the crime scene. Johnson admitted guilt and acknowledged he had acted alone. He proceeded to the victim's house where he showed law enforcement how he had approached the girl's bedroom window, abducted her and then, after sexually assaulting and strangling her, discarded her in the creek while she was still alive. Johnson also confessed to the rape of another three-year-old girl, a crime for which a man named Levon Brooks had been convicted and sentenced to death. In 2008, prosecutors dropped the case against Brewer and a lower court judge formally dismissed the charges – almost sixteen years after the rape-murder took place, thirteen years after the trial, and seven years after

---

[67] Medwed, "Prosecution Complex" 161–62.

[68] Brewer, 819 So. 2d at 1173.

[69] Ibid.

[70] Medwed, "Prosecution Complex," 161–62. See also Jimmie E. Gates, "Suspect's 4th Murder Trial Set for November 26; Court Has Thrown Out Three Prior Convictions on Appeal," *Clarion Ledger* (Jackson, MS), August 20, 2007.

[71] Medwed, "Prosecution Complex," 161–62.

[72] Ibid. Carrington, "Mississippi Innocence," 166–68.

DNA testing excluded him as the source of the genetic material from the crime scene.[73]

The Mississippi Attorney General's Office eventually did the right thing by confronting Johnson with the newfound evidence and agreeing with the decision to drop the charges. Its performance also stands in contrast to that of county prosecutors who not only took a weak, circumstantial capital murder case to trial, but antagonized Brewer's representatives to the point where they felt uncomfortable revealing the DNA evidence against Johnson to anyone in a position of power in Noxubee. Still, that begs the question of why it took appellate and post-conviction prosecutors from the most formidable law enforcement agency in the state *so long* – essentially a decade – to come to grips with the flaws in Brewer's case.

I admit that it is easy now, with the benefit of hindsight, to chastise state prosecutors for failing to acknowledge Brewer's innocence. But the case contained blatant warning signs from the start: a prosecution grounded on circumstantial evidence buttressed only by a discredited bite mark specialist with an odd theory. That's not much to go on in any case, let alone a capital one. And keep in mind that the Attorney General's Office opposed Brewer's direct appeal and contested at least two post-conviction motions, the second of which occurred after DNA tests initially demonstrated that someone other than the defendant had supplied the semen in the victim's rape. There is also no indication the Attorney General's Office intervened to convince county prosecutors to abandon a possible retrial while Brewer endured the indignities of continued detention from 2002 until his 2007 release on bail. Only after the Innocence Project delivered the name of the true perpetrator on a silver platter did the prosecution take any initiative to correct a palpable injustice.

As noted at the outset of this chapter, the canons of legal ethics hold that prosecutors should serve as "ministers of justice" committed to enforcing the law and safeguarding the rights of the accused.[74] Prosecutors in the Brewer case failed on both fronts. By neglecting to enforce the law, prosecutors allowed Justin Albert Johnson to remain at large; by failing to safeguard the rights of Kennedy Brewer, an innocent man lost years of freedom. Although Noxubee County prosecutors bear a large part of the blame, the state prosecutors who handled the appeal and post-conviction proceedings deserve their fair share too. Removed from the political and social dynamics of Noxubee, lawyers from the state Attorney General's Office in theory were supposed to view the case with clear eyes. In practice, however, their vision seemed clouded by a presumption of Brewer's guilt and a fundamental inability to look at the case objectively.

The story of Kennedy Brewer is not unique. After trial, newly assigned prosecutors across the nation far too frequently defend a conviction with vigor when the facts

---

[73] Carrington, "Mississippi Innocence," 166–68; Medwed, "Prosecution Complex," 161–62. See also Jerry Mitchell, "'Without DNA, He'd Be Dead' Conviction in Similar Case May Also Be Tossed," *Clarion Ledger* (Jackson, MS), February 16, 2008.

[74] See generally Medwed, "Prosecution Complex."

point to major errors in the case, even evidence of innocence.[75] This is worrisome any time it occurs, and tragic in cases where the ultimate penalty is at stake. Kennedy Brewer was lucky in the end; he lived. How many innocent or otherwise unjustly convicted prisoners have died in the execution chamber due in part to obstinacy by appellate and post-conviction prosecutors?

PROSECUTORS AND THE CONTINUED PURSUIT OF THE DEATH
PENALTY: PRACTICALITIES, POLITICS, AND COGNITIVE BIASES

A range of factors explain why appellate and post-conviction prosecutors might ignore possible miscarriages of justice and persevere in defending death sentences. These include the explanations I identified at the beginning of this chapter: (1) a fondness for victims, (2) a perception of the role of the prosecutor in the adversary system as predominantly that of advocate, and (3) a belief in the democratic process in general and the jury system in particular. Consider the basic issue of job security as well, both institutional and individual. An office delegated with the responsibility to handle appeals and post-conviction matters usually derives its funding from the legislative body that made this assignment. A failure to fulfill this obligation could hurt an agency where it hurts most: its budget.

So, for both practical and principled reasons, the official default position in prosecutors' offices is to defend any resulting conviction.[76] Even if some prosecutors in an office express misgivings about defending a capital conviction, there are likely others willing to proceed.[77] And a skeptical prosecutor may feel compelled to follow the boss's marching orders because rejecting a command from the top brass could doom a person's career. In the 1990s, supervisors in the Illinois Attorney General's Office asked an assistant state prosecutor, Mary Kenney, to challenge the appeals of Rolando Cruz, a man convicted of murder and sentenced to death for a crime to which another man had confessed. Kenney resigned in 1992 because of qualms about defending a death sentence imposed on someone she believed to be innocent.

[75] Although prosecutors sometimes cooperate with post-conviction DNA testing requests, they often do so only when confronted with the specter of litigation. One study of defendants exonerated by post-conviction DNA testing revealed that 49 percent of them received access to biological evidence for testing only after a court order by a judge. Brandon L. Garrett, *Convicting the Innocent: Where Criminal Prosecutions Go Wrong* (Cambridge, MA: Harvard University Press, 2011): 11–13.

[76] According to the Department of Justice, it is government policy to defend all cases on appeal and in post-conviction proceedings: "[i]f a defendant is convicted, the United States Attorney must prepare and present evidence at the defendant's sentencing hearing and defend the conviction at post-trial hearings and on appeal." United States Attorney, Department of Justice, "FY 2014 Performance Budget, Congressional Submission," available at www.justice.gov/sites/default/files/jmd/legacy/2014/08/22/usa-justification.pdf.

[77] See Patricia Wen, "Some Federal Prosecutors Reluctant to Bring Capital Punishment Cases," *Boston Globe*, March 15, 2015.

The Illinois Supreme Court later overturned Cruz's conviction, and he was acquitted at retrial.[78]

Appellate and post-conviction prosecutors might not only be concerned about the negative professional consequences of refusing to defend a conviction, but also motivated by the upside of succeeding in that defense. In a profession where job performance is difficult to gauge, a prosecutor's conviction rate – or, in the post-trial sphere, affirmance rate – can serve as a quantifiable proxy for success. Doing justice does not lend itself to metrics; measuring outcomes that advance the government's advocacy position does. The problem with focusing on outcomes is that it incentivizes prosecutors to strive for a result that disfavors the defendant regardless of whether that result is justified on the merits. Worse yet, it perpetuates a false and simplistic duality: that obtaining or preserving a conviction is a "win" and anything else a "loss."[79]

It almost goes without saying that litigators are renowned for their competitive personality traits. As one scholar put it more than a half century ago:

> Litigation is a process that thrives upon a competitive spirit ... There is a close congeniality between the psychological qualities of litigation and the attorney whose personality is marked by zealousness and aggressiveness. The attorney who takes a friendly and conciliatory attitude, assuming this to be a fixed need and propensity rather than a tactic, is most likely to find that his personality is a liability in litigation.[80]

That "competitive spirit" is fostered by an adversary system predicated on the theory that aggressive, zealous advocacy produces the most accurate outcomes.[81] The prospect of preserving a conviction, then, might satisfy an appellate or post-conviction prosecutor's hunger for a "win" and also advance the values of the adversary system.

The annals of criminal law are rife with anecdotes of offices rewarding trial prosecutors for obtaining convictions, and appellate and post-conviction prosecutors for defending them. In one notorious example, a district attorney in Colorado essentially instituted a "cash for convictions" program, doling out financial bonuses to prosecutors who secured guilty verdicts in 70 percent of their criminal trials.[82] Similar efforts are typically more nuanced.[83] It is small wonder that appellate and

---

[78] See Dieter, "Killing for Votes"; Ben Protess, "In 90s, Burris Sought Death Penalty for Innocent Man," *ProPublica*, December 31, 2008, available at www.propublica.org/article/in-90s-burris-sought-death-penalty-for-innocent-man-1231.

[79] See generally Medwed, "Zeal Deal."

[80] Robert S. Redmount, "Attorney Personalities and Some Psychological Aspects of Legal Consultation," *University of Pennsylvania Law Review* 109 (1961): 972, 979.

[81] Fred C. Zacharias, "Structuring the Ethics of Prosecutorial Trial Practice: Can Prosecutors Do Justice?," *Vanderbilt Law Review* 44 (1991): 45, 53–54.

[82] Medwed, "Prosecution Complex," 77.

[83] Ibid. ("Examples include publicizing individual conviction rates in the form of batting averages or listing attorneys on a bulletin board with stickers next to each name, green for wins and red for losses.").

post-conviction prosecutors see a professional advantage in toeing the party line and fighting to maintain a death sentence. Anything less could be seen as "soft" on crime, a mark of incompetence, or even treason against the chief prosecutor.[84]

Political variables enter the calculus as well. Shifting public opinion propels much of the debate in states on the verge of dismantling the death penalty. For instance, Pennsylvania Governor Tom Wolf announced a moratorium on executions in 2015. Most Pennsylvanians appeared to back this bold decision based on a poll indicating that a slim majority of the state's voters preferred a sentence of life to one of death for convicted murderers.[85] In right-leaning Nebraska, the legislature's choice to abolish the death penalty in May 2015 was preceded by a poll finding that 58.5 percent of state voters favored alternatives to capital punishment.[86] Nationwide, the percentage of Americans backing the death penalty dwindled from 76 percent in 1996 to 56 percent in 2015.[87] But in jurisdictions committed to the death penalty, capital punishment remains popular. A 2012 poll in Texas determined that only 21 percent of the electorate opposed the death penalty, while a resounding 73 percent either strongly or somewhat supported its availability as a punitive measure.[88]

Governors and state legislators are not the only politicians who care about public opinion when it comes to the death penalty. It matters for prosecutors too. Voters in 43 states elect their state Attorney General, who is the top law enforcement officer in the jurisdiction.[89] Chief county prosecutors are elected in 45 states, with Alaska, Connecticut, Delaware, New Jersey, and Rhode Island the only outliers that embrace an appointment model.[90] State and county prosecutors often have political ambitions that extend beyond their current posts – ambitions that might shape their views on the death penalty. Serving as an elected prosecutor is a time-tested path to higher office, as reflected by the old adage that "AG" stands for "Almost Governor."[91]

[84] Ibid. at 130.
[85] Jan Murphy, "Death penalty losing public support in Pa., poll shows," *PennLive.com*, March 25, 2015, available at www.pennlive.com/politics/index.ssf/2015/03/life_in_prison_preferred_over.html.
[86] The American Civil Liberties Union conducted this poll. Editorial Board, "The Death Penalty Ends in Nebraska," *New York Times*, May 28, 2015.
[87] Seiver, "Why Three Counties." The 49 death sentences rendered across the country in 2015 constituted a 33 percent decrease from the previous year, the lowest total since 1973. Williams, "Executions by States Fell in 2015." What is more, the number of executions in 2015 (28) fell from that of the previous year (35). Ibid.
[88] Ross Ramsey, "UT/TT Poll: Texans Stand behind the Death Penalty," *Texas Tribune*, May 24, 2012.
[89] Ben Wieder, "Big Money Comes to State Attorney-General Races," *The Atlantic*, May 8, 2014.
[90] These five states have slightly different models. See Ronald F. Wright, "Beyond Prosecutor Elections," *SMU Law Review* 67 (2014): 593, 598–99. Sometimes Delaware and Rhode Island are not included in the list of states that appoint county prosecutors. See Graham, "Most States"; Medwed, "Prosecution Complex," 130 n. 36.
[91] See Wieder, "Big Money."

Some assistant prosecutors share the political drive of their employers, hoping to ride the coattails of a well-liked chief prosecutor to an elected spot for themselves.

As a matter of political survival, then, savvy prosecutors often cultivate a persona that resonates with the local electorate. Prosecutors understandably gravitate toward "tough-on-crime" rhetoric. First, most potential voters identify more with being potential crime victims than criminal defendants. Second, prosecutorial elections are often overshadowed by higher-profile races, which forces candidates to adopt pithy themes that are accessible to the average person. The minister-of-justice principle is not easily reduced to a sound bite.[92]

In communities where capital punishment remains in vogue, prosecutors can sharpen their tough-on-crime political message by charging gruesome cases as capital offenses and defending any ensuing death sentence with vigor.[93] In fact, the political ideologies of self-professed law-and-order district attorneys seem to dictate approaches to capital cases almost as much as the wishes of the public in counties that rely heavily on capital punishment. As of 2015, Duval County, Florida, contained about 5 percent of the state's population, yet had generated roughly a quarter of the state's death sentences in recent years. Observers attribute Duval's outsized role in the production of capital cases to the ideology of its chief prosecutor at the time, Angela Corey, and the aggressiveness of her staff.[94] Consider three other counties that have accounted for an enormous number of death sentences since 1976: those encompassing Houston, Oklahoma City, and Philadelphia. In those jurisdictions the rate of capital sentences declined precipitously after chief prosecutors who were fierce proponents of the death penalty left office.[95] Appellate and post-conviction prosecutors presumably know the ideology of the chief prosecutor in the county that yielded a death sentence and may take that perspective into account in defending death.

[92] Medwed, "Prosecution Complex," 78, 142; David Alan Sklansky, "The Nature and Function of Prosecutorial Power," *Journal of Criminal Law & Criminology* 117 (forthcoming): 40, available at http://papers.ssrn.com/sol3/papers.cfm?abstract_id=2770815 (noting that "much of what we want from prosecutors is fairness, and that is [a] hard issue to debate in a political campaign"); Juleyka Lantigua-Williams, "Are Prosecutors the Key to Justice Reform?," *The Atlantic*, May 18, 2016.

[93] See generally Kenneth Bresler, "Seeking Justice, Seeking Election, and Seeking the Death Penalty: The Ethics of Prosecutorial Candidates' Campaigning on Capital Convictions," *Georgetown Journal of Legal Ethics* 7 (1994): 941.

[94] One of Corey's lieutenants, Bernie de la Rionda, led the push to obtain ten death sentences between 2008 and 2015. The Florida Supreme Court reversed three of those sentences, and overturned a previous capital conviction on the basis that de la Rionda commented on the defendant's sexual preferences despite warnings from the trial court to stop. See Robert J. Smith, "America's Deadliest Prosecutors," *Slate*, May 14, 2015, available at www.slate.com/articles/news_and_politics/jurisprudence/2015/05/america_s_deadliest_prosecutors_death_pen alty_sentences_in_louisiana_florida.html. In 2016, Corey lost her bid for reelection, falling to a challenger in the Republican primary. See Steph Solis, "Angela Corey Lost Her Primary, and the Internet Is Celebrating," *USA Today*, September 2, 2016.

[95] See Seiver, "Why Three Counties."

Psychological principles reinforce the institutional factors noted above – the practicalities of office funding, professional goals, and politics – to spur prosecutors to defend death sentences after trial regardless of concerns about capital punishment in general or its application in a particular case. The literature on cognitive bias is especially instructive. The term "confirmation bias" describes the human tendency to seek out and treasure information that confirms a person's initial hypothesis. Trial prosecutors who file capital charges might succumb to this bias after making that decision, overvaluing evidence of guilt and discounting any facts to the contrary.[96] Studies show that the formation of a strong initial theory of a case can have a lasting effect. This phenomenon is known as "belief perseverance." In short, people are reluctant to jettison their beliefs, even when confronted with legitimate reasons for doing so, and may embrace them despite mounting contrary evidence.[97]

Once a jury later decides to convict a defendant and impose a death sentence, a phenomenon known as the "status quo bias" may take shape. The jury has now validated the prosecutor's decision, a potent form of corroboration. It may take even more countervailing evidence than before to shift a person's viewpoint away from its original position.[98] Research also demonstrates that confidence in the truth of an assertion rises as that claim is repeated. Each time a jury, judge, or appellate tribunal affirms the defendant's guilt it produces a "reiteration effect" that can enhance a prosecutor's faith in that outcome.[99]

The status quo bias is most pronounced for prosecutors involved from the start of a case, but it has traction with lawyers who come on board later too. A prosecutor assigned to post-trial matters inherits a result sanctioned by the lawyers who charged and tried the case, the judge who let it proceed to a final outcome, and the jury that rendered a death verdict. It is natural for the incoming prosecutor to begin with the presumption that the decision at trial was correct and balk at any signs to the contrary.[100] In the words of Alafair Burke, the presumption of guilt becomes "stickier" after a conviction at trial.[101]

As the presumption of guilt becomes stickier over time, post-conviction and appellate prosecutors might engage in what psychologists call "top-down processing." Prosecutors inclined toward this mode of evaluating information after trial perceive the evidence mainly through the lens of the defendant-guilty theory and neglect or discount new evidence presented by the defendant. This contrasts with

---

[96] Medwed, "Prosecution Complex," 127.

[97] See, e.g., Keith A. Findley, "Tunnel Vision," in *Conviction of the Innocent: Lessons from Psychological Research*, ed. Brian L. Cutler (Washington, DC: American Psychological Association, 2012): 309–10.

[98] Medwed, "Prosecution Complex," 127.

[99] See Findley, "Tunnel Vision," 312.

[100] Medwed, "Prosecution Complex," 127.

[101] Alafair S. Burke, "Improving Prosecutorial Decision Making: Some Lessons of Cognitive Science," *William & Mary Law Review* 47 (2006): 1587, 1612.

"bottom-up processing," a more rigorous form of assessing information that is driven by the raw data and facts as opposed to overreliance on a preexisting theory.[102]

Even if capital trial prosecutors and those handling appellate and post-conviction litigation belong to different agencies, there might be an affinity among them based on their shared experience. Scholars talk about this in terms of "conformity effects." People within the same profession, not just the same office, have psychological incentives to act in line with peers based on overlapping roles and self-identity. Conformity effects might be heightened within prosecutors' ranks given that the nature of the work – "crime-fighting" – lends itself to self-righteousness.[103]

The pressure to conform to a peer's decision is likely enhanced when that peer had access to more information, as when a post-conviction prosecutor in a capital case reviews the conduct of her trial predecessor who interacted with witnesses and the police closer in time to the crime itself. The trial lawyer's link to the case was far stronger than that of an appellate or post-conviction attorney whose job is to offer a more clinical look at the case years down the road. This may prompt the newly assigned prosecutor to defer to the trial team's strategic choices and tactics or merely look askance at any defense claims.[104] The involvement of multiple lawyers might also lead to a diffusion of responsibility in which post-conviction prosecutors refuse to take ownership of the outcome of the case.[105]

On a more fundamental level, capital prosecutors may engage in what psychologists call "groupthink." Prosecutors in all phases of a death penalty case share an overarching objective: to represent the government in the enforcement of the law against violators in the most heinous matters. This mentality breeds cohesion within the group writ large (trial, appellate, and post-conviction branches). And this cohesion could generate efforts to minimize conflict and promote consensus, even across offices.[106] My colleague Deborah Ramirez uses the phrase "Team Prosecution" to explain why prosecutors from different offices and jurisdictions tend to embrace the party line and neglect to criticize each other's actions. This phrase is apt. Trial, appellate, and post-conviction prosecutors play various positions on the field, but they wear the same uniform with "law enforcement" splashed across their chests.

One's innate aversion to cognitive dissonance also helps shape prosecutorial responses in defending capital sentences. Cognitive dissonance surfaces when there is a conflict between one's self-image and the reality of one's actions. People often develop a healthy self-regard as a survival mechanism and interpret information in a

---

[102] See Andrew M. Smith et al., "An Investigation of Top-Down vs. Bottom-Up Processing in Post-Appellate Review of a Criminal Case," *Albany Law Review* 74 (2010–11): 1365.

[103] Medwed, "Zeal Deal," 139.

[104] Medwed, "Prosecution Complex," 128.

[105] See Barbara O'Brien & Keith Findley, "Psychological Perspectives: Cognition and Decision Making," in *Examining Wrongful Convictions: Stepping Back, Moving Forward*, ed. Allison D. Redlich et al. (Durham, NC: Carolina Academic Press, 2014): 35, 43–44.

[106] See Aviva Orenstein, "Facing the Unfaceable: Dealing with Prosecutorial Denial in Postconviction Cases of Actual Innocence," *San Diego Law Review* 48 (2011): 401, 427.

way that enhances an internal view of themselves as good, ethical actors. Defending an unjust conviction secured by fellow prosecutors clashes with that positive self-image. As a consequence, appellate and post-conviction prosecutors may hold fast to the original theory of guilt to harmonize their beliefs with their behavior. Acknowledging that Team Prosecution led an ignoble charge toward executing a person without sufficient justification may prove psychologically taxing. The weight of the cognitive stress could be too heavy to carry.[107]

In addition, prosecutors might experience an escalation of commitment to a death sentence as a case wends its way through the appellate and post-conviction process and marches toward completion. As the execution date nears, the internal pressure to preserve the outcome intensifies. Rather than viewing their previous work and that of their colleagues as sunk costs, prosecutors in the latter stages of a capital case may feel a rising attachment to the prospect of execution as a means of validating years of hard work.[108] Finally, implicit racial bias may affect the behavior of appellate and post-conviction prosecutors, as it does with respect to decision-making at earlier stages in the process.[109]

Professional, political, and psychological factors all show why a prosecutor who enters the fray after trial may become wedded to the result and fight to maintain the death sentence. But that's not all. Prosecutors' goal for finality in the criminal process takes on added importance when the ultimate penalty is on the line.

GRAND FINALITY EXPLAINED

Finality is lauded as a core value of our criminal justice system. The concept supports the imposition of obstacles on appellate and post-conviction remedies, among them, preservation doctrines, time limits on filing, and bars on submitting multiple petitions. Prominent observers such as Paul Bator and Judge Henry Friendly have pinpointed the justifications for finality, all premised on the virtues of completion. The arguments go something like this:

Criminal cases must reach an end because otherwise both the system and its participants would grind to halt, worn down by the financial, practical, and psychological burdens of a controversy that remains ever in motion and at risk of reversal. Finality allows victims a measure of psychological closure; prosecutors, defense lawyers, and judges gain an opportunity to turn to more pressing endeavors; and defendants no longer enmeshed in litigating their cases now have a chance to come to terms with their transgressions. Finality yields the benefit of "repose," a moment

---

[107] Medwed, "Prosecution Complex," 128.

[108] See ibid. at 98.

[109] Buried racial biases may emerge when prosecutors inherit a case after trial with the task of defending a death sentence imposed on a person of color. Unconscious favoritism toward whites – victims, judges, jurors – also shades prosecutorial approaches to capital cases in the post-conviction sphere. See supra note 26 and accompanying text.

after which case participants may take comfort that no further proceedings are in the offing. Similar contentions are used to justify statutes of limitations that erect time bars on the capacity to charge crimes at the outset. Whether at the front or the back end of the process, the criminal justice system relies on the idea that the rules of the litigation race must be visible to all – the starting and finishing lines demarcated with clarity and with little chance they can shift.[110] Other rationales for finality include prompting litigants to proceed while the evidence is fresh, incentivizing defense attorneys to prevent errors at the beginning, preserving the integrity of the trial process, and advancing the cultural value of diligence.[111]

At bottom, advocates of finality tend to cite three chief benefits: cost savings, factual accuracy, and systemic legitimacy.[112] Engaging in extensive post-conviction review of a single criminal case takes time and money, burdens shouldered almost exclusively by the public. If a collateral action succeeds, there is often a new trial, signifying the expenditure of ever more resources. This trial would take place years after the original trial; the average time period between the entry of a criminal conviction and the *resolution* of a federal habeas petition by a state court prisoner exceeds seven years.[113] The duration of this review poses challenges to courts in evaluating the underlying accuracy of the outcome. A new trial will occur under the possible cloud of stale evidence, faded memories, and missing witnesses. Money and accuracy alone, however, are not the only costs. Some observers view exhaustive collateral review as a threat to the very legitimacy of the criminal justice system, fearful that public confidence and the deterrent effect of the criminal law may suffer without a clear endpoint to criminal adjudication.[114]

In the death penalty context, many of the arguments in favor of finality take on greater resonance – and assume added complications. The surviving victims of capital offenses and family members of the deceased may need, even more than others, to move on from that chapter of their lives. The system may wish to conserve

---

[110] For the arguments supporting finality, see Medwed, "Up the River," 690–95; Tyler T. Ochoa and Andrew J. Wistrich, "The Puzzling Purposes of Statutes of Limitations," *Pacific Law Journal* 28 (1997): 453; Meghan J. Ryan, "Finality and Rehabilitation," *Wake Forest Journal of Law & Policy* 4 (2014): 121, 123–26; Ryan W. Scott, "In Defense of the Finality of Criminal Sentences on Collateral Review," *Wake Forest Journal of Law & Policy* 4 (2014): 179, 185–88.

[111] Ibid. See also Andrew Chongseh Kim, "Beyond Finality: How Making Criminal Judgments Less Final Can Further the 'Interests of Finality,'" *Utah Law Review* 2013 (2013): 561. As David Wolitz has noted, "[t]he Anglo-American system ... valorizes juries and devalues appeals." David Wolitz, "Innocence Commissions and the Future of Post-Conviction Review," *Arizona Law Review* 52 (2010): 1027, 1034.

[112] Scott, "In Defense of the Finality," 185–88.

[113] Ibid.

[114] Ibid. As Justice Harlan stated: "No one, not criminal defendants, not the judicial system, not society as a whole is benefited by a judgment providing a man shall tentatively go to jail today, but tomorrow and every day thereafter his continued incarceration shall be subject to fresh litigation on issues already resolved." *Mackey v. United States*, 401 U.S. 667, 691 (1971) (Harlan, J., concurring in part and dissenting in part). See also Ryan, "Finality and Rehabilitation," 123–26.

the ample resources deployed to prosecute, defend, and adjudicate death cases. And the integrity of the trial process and the jury's verdict is reinforced when the capital sentence is carried out. The execution of a capital defendant promises to achieve genuine finality; the perpetrator is gone from the earth, unable to mount a defense or keep the case in the limelight by reaching out to the media. As a result, finality has a potent meaning in the capital context, a form of "grand finality" that may prove alluring to prosecutors.

Critics have attacked finality as a justification for limiting review of capital cases, particularly as the use of post-conviction DNA testing in the past quarter century has yielded evidence that actually innocent defendants have faced execution.[115] The lightning rod for many of these attacks is a 1993 U.S. Supreme Court case, *Herrera v. Collins.*[116] In that case, Leonel Torres Herrera was convicted of capital murder. He raised an innocence claim in a federal habeas petition, submitting several witness affidavits asserting that his dead brother had perpetrated the homicide. The lower courts denied Herrera's petition, a decision affirmed by the Supreme Court. In its opinion, the Court trumpeted the virtues of finality:

> [B]ecause of the very disruptive effect that entertaining claims of actual innocence would have on the need for finality in capital cases, and the enormous burden that having to retry cases based on often stale evidence would place on the States, the threshold showing for such an assumed right would necessarily be extraordinarily high. The showing made by petitioner in this case falls far short of any such threshold.[117]

The Court went on to claim that even "a truly persuasive demonstration of 'actual innocence'" would not have altered its decision.[118] The consequences of *Herrera* are that federal courts may now account for innocence in determining whether a petitioner warrants an exception from the procedural limits on habeas corpus, but finality concerns oblige judges to disregard "freestanding" innocence claims – those unaccompanied by claims of constitutional error.[119] *Herrera* represents a triumph for the finality of the process over the potential accuracy of the result.

Herrera and its progeny have provoked the wrath of observers who believe substantive justice for the individual should never bend to procedural expediency and systemic principles. The Death Penalty Information Center reports that more than 150 death row inmates have been exonerated on the grounds of actual innocence since 1973, with the rate of exonerations climbing as DNA technology flourished in the late 1990s and early 2000s.[120] While those prisoners were spared

---

[115] See Death Penalty Information Center, "Innocence and the Death Penalty," available at www
.deathpenaltyinfo.org/innocence-and-death-penalty.

[116] *Herrera* v. *Collins*, 506 U.S. 390 (1993); Ryan, "Finality and Rehabilitation," 123–24.

[117] Herrera, 506 U.S. at 417; Ryan, "Finality and Rehabilitation," 123–24.

[118] Herrera, 506 U.S. at 417.

[119] Ryan, "Finality and Rehabilitation," 123–24.

[120] See Death Penalty Information Center, "Innocence and the Death Penalty."

execution, others have not been so fortunate. Researchers have identified a number of compelling cases in which a person was executed for a crime he almost certainly did not commit. These include the executions of Joe Arridy (Colorado), Carlos de Luna (Texas), William Jackson Marion (Nebraska), and Cameron Todd Willingham (Texas).[121]

Technological advances that increase the ability to prove a defendant's innocence have changed the equation for assessing accuracy. As noted above, finality was traditionally touted as an *aid* to correct results. The trial was the bellwether for airing an innocence claim because, in contrast to post-conviction proceedings, it took place closer in time to the crime when memories were sharper and physical evidence fresher. But that vision of the trial is no longer necessarily the case. Many rape-murders, crimes that not infrequently produce death sentences, contain biological evidence retrieved from the scene that could be subjected to ever-improving DNA tests down the post-conviction road. Preventing a potentially innocent person from litigating in the post-conviction sphere based on the abstract principle of finality harms, rather than protects, the pursuit of truth. As the Supreme Court has declared, "the penalty of death is qualitatively different from a sentence of imprisonment, however long. . . . Because of that qualitative difference, there is a corresponding difference in the need for reliability in the determination that death is the appropriate punishment in a specific case."[122]

On top of the concern about killing an innocent person, there is an evolving cultural understanding about the role that racial bias plays in the administration of the death penalty. In August 2015, the *New York Times* published an article detailing the widespread discriminatory use of peremptory challenges by prosecutors to strike blacks from the jury pool in death penalty cases in Louisiana. These findings dovetail with data from other Southern states.[123] Just a few months later, the Supreme Court heard oral arguments in a Georgia capital case that hinged upon the prosecution's dubious, racially charged use of peremptories. In May 2016, the Supreme Court overturned the conviction.[124] That same month, the Supreme Court refused to lift a stay of execution in the case of Vernon Madison, an African-American man convicted of killing a white police officer in Alabama. The Court cited concerns about Madison's mental competency as the basis for upholding the stay, despite urgings from Alabama prosecutors to implement the sentence. But the back story transcends issues of competency. Madison had three trials, two of

---

[121] *Glossip* v. *Gross*, 135 S.Ct. 2726, 2756 (2015) (Breyer, J., dissenting).

[122] *Woodson* v. *North Carolina*, 428 U.S. 280, 305 (1976). See also *Coleman* v. *Calderon*, 210 F.3d 1047, 1050 (9th Cir. 2000).

[123] Adam Liptak, "Exclusion of Blacks from Juries Raises Renewed Scrutiny," *New York Times*, August 16, 2015.

[124] See *Foster* v. *Chatman*, 578 U.S. ___ (2016), available at www.supremecourt.gov/opinions/15pdf/14-8349_6k47.pdf; Nina Totenberg, "The Supreme Court Takes on Racial Discrimination in Jury Selection," *National Public Radio*, November 2, 2015, available at www.npr.org/2015/11/02/452898470/supreme-court-takes-on-racial-discrimination-in-jury-selection.

which were tainted by allegations of racial bias in jury selection. In the third trial, the jury voted for a life sentence before state court judge Ferrill McRae, who later gained notoriety for racist and sexist comments, overrode the jury determination and installed a capital sentence.[125] Notably, in June 2016, the Supreme Court agreed to review a pair of death penalty cases that implicate the issues of intellectual disability and race.[126]

It is important to view the time-honored justifications for finality through the lens of these contemporary concerns. The legitimacy of the system may hinge less on finalizing results than on making sure those results are both accurate and fair. If the public perceives the system as unjust, then respect for the law and its deterrent effect wanes.[127] Enforcement of criminal codes may be seen as arbitrary and capricious, spurring would-be lawbreakers to take chances based on the impression they might be targeted by authorities regardless of their actions.

Many of the other arguments in favor of finality in capital cases wither in the face of critical examination. In theory, there is merit to the idea that finality spurs defense lawyers to do a better job at trial. If collateral review were limited, defense attorneys might work harder to perform effectively at trial because the system would be less equipped to correct their blunders and prevent their clients' executions; defense counsel would also lack any incentive to make gaffes so as to create issues for future lawyers to litigate. But the suspicion that defense errors occur on purpose in capital cases – that lawyers tactically insert mistakes into the trial to set up an ineffective assistance of counsel claim for appeal – may be more myth than reality. Any lawyer dedicated enough to "fall on the sword" at a post-conviction hearing and confess to major missteps at trial realizes that effective advocacy *during* trial is the best way to

---

[125] See "AL: Repeated Prosecutorial Misconduct the Unseen Backdrop to the State's Push to Execute Vernon Madison," *The Open File*, May 16, 2016, available at www.prosecutorialac countability.com/2016/05/16/al-repeated-prosecutorial-misconduct-the-unseen-backdrop-to-the-states-push-to-execute-vernon-madison/. Recent events outside the capital punishment context have contributed to the growing awareness about the nexus between race and criminal justice. The much-publicized killings of African Americans by law enforcement officers have ignited the "Black Lives Matter" movement and kept the issue of racism on the front-burner of the national consciousness. See, e.g., John Eligon, "One Slogan, Many Methods: Black Lives Matter Enters Politics," *New York Times*, November 18, 2015.

[126] Adam Liptak, "Supreme Court to Hear Death Penalty Cases," *New York Times*, June 6, 2016. As noted earlier in this chapter, there is a growing appreciation for the roles played by gender, class, and mental capacity in the application of the death penalty. See supra note 30 and accompanying text. I. Beverly Lake, the former Chief Justice of the North Carolina Supreme Court, recently voiced his opposition to the death penalty. Among other factors, Lake cited the inability of the law to protect those with intellectual disabilities and mental impairments. I. Beverly Lake, Jr., "Why Protecting the Innocent from a Death Sentence Isn't Enough," *Huffington Post*, May 18, 2016, available at www.huffingtonpost.com/i-beverly-lake-jr/death-penalty_b_10027538.html.

[127] One study of violent offenders in Chicago concluded that people who considered the law less "legitimate" were more likely to violate the law by carrying a gun than others who perceived the system as generally fair. See Chongseh Kim, "Beyond Finality," 565 n. 11.

save the client from execution.[128] Good capital defense attorneys leave no stone unturned when it comes to investigating a case and litigating it during trial. And the bad ones make inadvertent, not strategic, mistakes any way. It is unlikely, then, that restricting post-trial remedies would impact the effectiveness of defense lawyers. If we want to inspire capital defenders to be more diligent at trial, we should focus on boosting funding and training, not cutting back post-conviction relief.[129]

As for concerns about the costs of post-conviction review, it is true that finality saves vast sums of money by forestalling continued litigation in capital cases. The Idaho State Appellate Defenders spends roughly 44 times the hours in a death penalty case than it works in appealing a life sentence, all at taxpayer expense.[130] Yet depriving capital defendants of a thorough process after trial could have significant, and underappreciated, financial costs. For one thing, there is the direct expense of what Andrew Chongseh Kim calls "wrongful incarceration," that is, the imprisonment of factually innocent defendants as well as guilty defendants languishing behind bars due to serious constitutional errors or sentencing mistakes.[131] These direct expenses rise exponentially when the inmate is held on death row rather than in the general population.[132] For another, a questionable execution might beget civil litigation by representatives who claim wrongful death or civil rights violations.

Consider the purported value of "repose" as well. Closure for victims becomes elusive if there is uncertainty about the fundamental accuracy or fairness of the process. Defendants, too, may be hard-pressed to accept their fate if they feel the system treated them unfairly and stymied their efforts to be heard.

The rising disdain for finality in the capital context, premised as it is on newfound concerns about wrongful convictions and racial discrimination, taps into deep-seated objections to the general principle. Oliver Wendell Holmes once asked in the context of statutes of limitations: "[W]hat is the justification for depriving a man of his rights, a pure evil as far as it goes, in consequence of the lapse of time?"[133] To extrapolate from Holmes's comment, does a capital defendant have a right to litigate his case until there is absolutely no question of error? If so, then depriving that person of this right due to finality values is an "evil" that must be redressed. Yet permitting endless re-evaluation would make the death penalty unworkable, the person slated for death never executed unless he waives any right to future claims.

Given the futility of trying to strike the right balance between fairness and finality, is the time ripe for abolition of the death penalty? Support for the death penalty still

[128] Carlos Illescas, "James Holmes Attorney Admits to Mistakes in Previous Murder Case," *Denver Post*, October 24, 2014.
[129] See Chongseh Kim, "Beyond Finality," 583–87.
[130] See Kelly Phillips Erb, "Considering the Death Penalty: Your Tax Dollars at Work," *Forbes*, May 1, 2014.
[131] See Chongseh Kim, "Beyond Finality," 581.
[132] See Beety, "Ethics and Economics in Mississippi," 1454
[133] Oliver W. Holmes, Jr., "The Path of the Law," *Harvard Law Review* 10 (1897): 457, 476.

exists in large doses in pockets of the country. In fact, the United States is one of only two developed democracies to have executed someone in recent years.[134] The first recorded execution occurred in 1608 in the colony of Jamestown, and the penalty has lingered ever since, except for the interlude in the 1970s.[135] Some observers see the death penalty as here to stay, a crucible of a still-fledgling nation built on violence and retribution. Others see abolition as inevitable. What is clear is that race, class, gender, geography, and mental capacity affect the application of the death penalty. It is also clear the process costs exorbitant sums of money.[136] Monetary concerns, perhaps more than those related to the ethics or morality of capital punishment, have driven some states to consider abolition over the past decade.[137]

I am pessimistic about the prospects for abolishing the death penalty in the near term. I do not foresee thirty-one state legislatures, let alone Congress, relinquishing capital punishment as a sentencing option any time soon. The political cards are stacked against it. When the Nebraska legislature dismantled the state's death penalty in 2015, it became the first Republican-controlled lawmaking body to do so since the Nixon administration.[138] In response, a grassroots campaign secured signatures from more than 160,000 Nebraskans eager to reinstate capital punishment. This effort succeeded in putting the issue on the ballot for the 2016 general election, and voters responded by reinstituting the death penalty.[139] Likewise, it is doubtful that state judiciaries will take the bold step of eradicating capital punishment. While some state supreme courts have struck blows against the death penalty, many others have not.[140] Executive officials might declare a moratorium, as

---

[134] Amnesty International, "The World Moves towards Abolition," available at www.amnestyusa .org/our-work/issues/death-penalty/international-death-penalty

[135] Death Penalty Information Center, "Part I: History of the Death Penalty," available at www .deathpenaltyinfo.org/part-i-history-death-penalty#intro.

[136] Estimates put the price tag of the average death penalty trial at roughly $1 million more than a non-capital trial. See Beety, "Ethics and Economics in Mississippi," 1454 n. 90.

[137] Ibid. at 1455–59.

[138] See Krishnadev Calamur, "Nebraska Lawmakers Veto Governor's Override of Death Penalty Appeal," *National Public Radio*, May 27, 2015, available at www.npr.org/sections/thetwo-way/ 2015/05/27/410024375/nebraska-governors-veto-of-death-penalty-repeal-sets-up-override-vote.

[139] Maurice Chammah, "Nebraska's Death Penalty: A Grassroots Effort Aims to Restore What the Legislature Just Ended," *The Marshall Project*, August 28, 2015, available at www.themarshall project.org/2015/07/02/back-on-the-agenda-nebraska-s-death-penalty?ref=tsqr_stream#. eu3JtSZQw. See Aliyah Frumin, "Election 2016: Nebraska, Oklahoma Vote in Favor of Death Penalty," *NBC News*, November 9, 2016, available at www.nbcnews.com/storyline/2016-elec tion-day/election-2016-nebraska-oklahoma-vote-favor-death-penalty-n681301.

[140] See Brakkton Booker, "Connecticut Supreme Court Ruling Bars Execution of 11 Death Row Inmates," *National Public Radio*, August 13, 2015, available at www.npr.org/sections/thetwo- way/2015/08/13/432094536/connecticut-supreme-court-rules-death-penalty-unconstitutional. Individual state judges have taken bold stands against the death penalty, among them, Oliver Diaz of the Mississippi Supreme Court who made an impassioned plea to jettison capital punishment as he stepped down in 2008. Beety, "Ethics and Economics in Mississippi," 1440, 1444–45.

occurred in Pennsylvania,[141] but those actions run the risk of reversal through the legislative process.

That leaves the U.S. Supreme Court as the best bet for comprehensive abolition. Nevertheless, it is far from certain the Court will find capital punishment unconstitutional in the near future, notwithstanding Justice Breyer's impassioned dissent in the 2015 lethal injection decision, *Glossip* v. *Gross*.[142] Until the day of abolition arrives – if it does – perhaps justice can be advanced through more modest reforms aimed at loosening capital prosecutors' grip on grand finality. The most productive reforms are those targeted at the professional, political, and psychological pressures that prosecutors face.

THWARTING GRAND FINALITY

Prosecutorial Culture and Professional Incentives

It is crucial to educate prosecutors about the flaws with using finality to justify an unstinting approach to defending death sentences. Education could be paired with more robust ethical rules. Few ethical rules apply to appellate and post-conviction prosecutors other than some relatively new provisions that oblige prosecutors to take proactive steps when confronted with newly discovered evidence of innocence after trial. Those rules, which derive from the American Bar Association's Model Rule of Professional Conduct 3.8(g)-(h), have gained partial acceptance. As of September 2016, three states have adopted the model rule, 13 states have implemented a variation of it, and five additional states are in the midst of studying whether to adopt it.[143]

Chief prosecutors should supplement educational efforts and revised ethical rules by altering the professional incentives for their employees to obtain and maintain convictions. If people at the top de-emphasize conviction rates, that message would trickle down through the ranks. Chief prosecutors can shift the institutional culture away from a reliance on conviction rates in a variety of ways. Among them are championing the minister-of-justice principle, lauding lawyers who dismiss cases, clamping down on any bragging about conviction rates, formulating promotional criteria beyond "wins," and affording high status to in-house ethicists.[144] State bar associations and political leaders could reinforce this message by advising prosecutors to steer clear of using convictions and affirmances as barometers for success and bases for promotion. But more is required.

---

[141] See, e.g., Williams, "Executions by States Fell in 2015."

[142] *Glossip* v. *Gross*, 135 S.Ct. at 2755–77 (Breyer, J., dissenting).

[143] American Bar Association CPR Implementation Committee, "Variations of the ABA Model Rules of Professional Conduct," available at www.americanbar.org/content/dam/aba/adminis trative/professional_responsibility/mrpc_3_8_g_h.authcheckdam.pdf. Ethical rules that bind prosecutors are traditionally under-enforced by state disciplinary organizations. See, e.g., Medwed, "Prosecution Complex," 31.

[144] See Medwed, "Prosecution Complex," at 83.

Perverse Politics

The model of the elected prosecutor, which dates back to the era of Jacksonian Democracy in the nineteenth century, was intended to promote transparency and accountability. The reality is bleaker. Eclipsed by more prominent political races taking place at the same time, campaigns for county district attorney offices are often simplistic efforts to convince voters of a candidate's tough-on-crime bona fides. Conviction rates and "wins" in high-profile cases serve as surrogates for crime-fighting acumen. Preserving the finality of these outcomes, in turn, becomes essential to the perceived reliability of these claims. For many voters, even those concerned with criminal justice policy, plain tough-on-crime language may be enough to sway their choices.[145]

One suggestion is to hold county district attorney and state attorney general elections on different dates from those of higher-profile races. Put the spotlight on prosecutors for a political season. With this reform in place, the electorate could more easily focus on criminal justice issues and make more informed voting decisions. This could motivate candidates to reach beyond tough-on-crime rhetoric, generating more meaningful policy platforms and engaging in a more substantive dialogue. Turnout would diminish without the pull of a gubernatorial or congressional election to lure voters to the polls. But those who cast their ballots would be those interested in criminal justice policy. Perhaps it is better to have fewer, yet informed, people vote for our country's leading law enforcement officials than to have elections determined largely by party affiliation or name recognition.[146] Studies show that most candidates for chief county prosecutor run unopposed and, even when confronted with an opponent, incumbents prevail 95 percent of the time.[147] This cannot be good for criminal justice policy.

Another idea is to abandon the electoral model and appoint our chief prosecutors as a handful of jurisdictions already do. These posts would look more like those of civil servants, which is the case in much of continental Europe. This would not entirely divorce prosecutors from politics – the process of making the appointment would have political overtones – but it would dilute the role of politics in a prosecutor's career and possibly allow for decisions untethered to concerns for public opinion.[148]

---

[145] Ibid. at 78. The recent electoral losses of notorious tough-on-crime prosecutors in cities such as Chicago and Jacksonville may signal that voters are becoming somewhat more attentive to criminal justice issues and potentially better equipped to evaluate prosecutorial performance. See James Downie, "Is 'Tough on Crime' No Longer Enough for Voters?," *Washington Post*, August 31, 2016, available at www.washingtonpost.com/blogs/post-partisan/wp/2016/08/31/is-tough-on-crime-no-longer-enough-for-voters/?utm_term=.d8197c09a6dd.

[146] Medwed, "Prosecution Complex," at 144.

[147] Ibid. at 143.

[148] Ibid. at 144–45.

With respect to the risk of prosecutors defending a death sentence to shore up their tough-on-crime credentials, some minor tweaks might reap major dividends. Jurisdictions could devise an ethical rule that bans prosecutors on the campaign trail from referring to specific cases they litigated, or that occurred on their watch. As former prosecutor Kenneth Bresler has put it, "[c]apitalizing on capital convictions in campaigns raises the question: Which came first, the decision to pursue the death penalty or the decision to pursue political advantage? The question is hard to answer, and an answer is hard to prove."[149] A rule that prevents "capitalizing on capital convictions" in this way might produce better front-end decisions about whether to charge a case as a capital one or, at least, yield decisions less tainted by long-term political calculations. It could also spawn improved back-end choices about how aggressively to defend death sentences on appeal and post-conviction review. If such a rule seems too incompatible with free speech principles, a prosecutor could instead be banned from ever working on the post-conviction proceedings or re-trial of a case upon which she campaigned.[150]

Psychological Shift: Cognitive Flexibility and A New Vision for Criminal Law Practice

Cognitive bias and a post-conviction prosecutor's commitment to finality may go hand-in-hand. A prosecutor with tunnel vision may be wedded to a death sentence and find the concept of finality attractive. It offers the mirage of a normative principle of litigation: a justification for maintaining the trial result that is distinct from anything peculiar to the individual prosecutor's psychological make-up.

One way to counteract the possible influence of cognitive biases for prosecutors handling a capital case after trial is to put them in separate offices from the charging and trial prosecutors. As noted above, however, many jurisdictions *already* do this, with the county district attorney typically making the charging decision and her assistants trying the case, while another office – normally a unit of the state attorney general's office – is responsible for most subsequent proceedings. This is admirable. But the prospect of a shared affinity between fellow prosecutors and the power of conformity effects are all too real. Something more than formal separation between the various prosecutors in the capital litigation process is in order.

Just as some prosecutors' offices have pretrial capital charging committees that vet cases before seeking the death penalty,[151] appellate and post-conviction prosecutors could hold group reviews of death cases before filing any responses to defense claims. Rather than having the assigned prosecutors determine the course of action alone, it could be a collective endeavor, with multiple people weighing in.

[149] See Bresler, "Seeking Justice," 949.
[150] Ibid. at 953–54; Medwed, "Zeal Deal," 178.
[151] See supra note 13 and accompanying text.

Participants might include experienced lawyers unaffiliated with the office, such as retired prosecutors, judges and defense attorneys, who all agree to abide by rules of confidentiality. One or more people could serve as official "Devil's Advocates" entrusted with the job of presenting the defense side of the case.[152] As Keith Findley has observed, "forcing people to articulate reasons that counter their own position can minimize the 'illusion of validity' that produces confirmation bias."[153] Barbara O'Brien has found that when people are asked to discuss both the evidence for *and* against their hypotheses, they show less bias as compared with those who only discuss the evidence supporting their theories. Her research indicates that people who explicitly entertain the counterevidence reveal no more bias than those who never had a hypothesis at all.[154]

Then there is a much more radical suggestion. We could ditch the concept of an institutional prosecutorial office altogether. Instead of having whole offices of prosecutors and equivalent institutions for public defenders, why not disaggregate the process and just have private criminal lawyers who are assigned cases by contract on a piecemeal basis? Despite the obvious inefficiencies of this structure, it is an idea worth exploring. Under this model, attorneys would self-identify as neither prosecutor nor defense lawyer, but as criminal law specialists capable of playing either role in a given case. Lawyers with no entrenched interest in obtaining or maintaining convictions over time would enter the prosecutorial fold. In the absence of any organizational stake in preserving convictions, and with personal experience on the defense side of the aisle, appellate and post-conviction lawyers handling prosecutorial functions might be less vulnerable to the tug of grand finality in capital cases. Prior to 1985, the United Kingdom utilized this structure for processing criminal law assignments. After the creation of an institutional prosecutor, that country has preserved a rather impressive culture of collegiality and lack of partisanship in its criminal law bar.[155]

Psychological research further suggests that exposure to different roles and tasks can counteract the effect of confirmation bias and enhance "cognitive flexibility," which is the capacity of a person to remain open-minded and optimally creative. The concept has many implications for human behavior. For the narrow purposes of this chapter, the key feature of cognitive flexibility is how it relates to the ability of people to entertain novel theories. People who are "set in their ways" generally have poor cognitive flexibility; they struggle to appreciate, understand, or acknowledge alternative viewpoints. Those with strong cognitive flexibility are able not only to grasp new ideas, but to consider multiple variables or descriptors at once.[156]

---

[152] See Medwed, "Prosecution Complex," 26–27.

[153] Findley, "Tunnel Vision," 317–18.

[154] Ibid. at 318.

[155] See Medwed, "Prosecution Complex," 145. See also George C. Thomas III, *The Supreme Court on Trial: How the American Justice System Sacrifices Innocent Defendants* (Ann Arbor, MI: University of Michigan Press, 2008): 190–92.

[156] See "What Is Cognitive Flexibility?," *Mental Health Blog*, available at http://mentalhealthda ily.com/2015/07/24/what-is-cognitive-flexibility/.

Can a person become more cognitively flexible? It appears so. Scholars link creative thinking to a person's neuroplasticity or, in the vernacular, how one's neural pathways are wired. Exposure to new experiences can alter these pathways, boost neuroplasticity, and spur creativity. For example, researchers have conducted numerous studies on the effect of vacation time on workers. The data suggest that productivity is enhanced by simply taking breaks from work. More to the point, going overseas and absorbing new sights, sounds, and foods bolsters occupational creativity. One study of high-end fashion houses found a powerful correlation between the time a key designer spent abroad and the diversity of the countries that designer experienced with the level of innovation in the company's output.[157]

Encouraging prosecutors to rotate away from the field – to take a "vacation," so to speak, to the foreign land of criminal defense – might encourage cognitive flexibility. As a less drastic measure, prosecutors could take periodic sabbaticals, shift to the civil division of the office if it exists, or otherwise opt out temporarily from the rigors of litigating criminal cases on behalf of the government. With cognitive flexibility comes increased openness to the possibility a miscarriage of justice has occurred in a capital case. And with openness to this possibility by American prosecutors, more judges might spare the lives of capital defendants who are actually innocent or whose convictions hinged on constitutional violations, improper racial or socio-economic considerations, or other injustices.

CONCLUSION

As Peter Fitzpatrick once put it, law in the United States is a blend of "certainty and uncertainty, the determinate and what is beyond determination."[158] Ironically, post-conviction prosecutors' seeming certainty in the wisdom of defending death helps yield the uncertainty that is a hallmark, if not the defining feature, of our death penalty jurisprudence. The uncertainty that characterizes capital punishment in the United States – doubt over whether an inmate will ever be executed and whether an actually innocent person may be facing state-sponsored death – can only fade, short of abolition, if we alter the professional incentives, political realities, and psychological biases that propel prosecutors to hunt for grand finality. This might not be as hard as one would think. Changing the metrics for gauging prosecutorial performance, tinkering with the processes for installing and retaining chief prosecutors, and setting up systems to counteract cognitive biases and promote cognitive flexibility might go far in making prosecutors less wedded to the defense of death after trial. Post-conviction prosecutors might then be better equipped to scrutinize capital cases with the equanimity that those matters deserve and justice demands.

[157] Brent Crane, "For a More Creative Brain, Travel," *The Atlantic*, March 31, 2015.
[158] Peter Fitzpatrick, "'Always More to Do': Capital Punishment and the (De)Composition of Law," in *The Killing State: Capital Punishment in Law, Politics, and Culture*, ed. Austin Sarat (Oxford: Oxford University Press, 1999): 120.

5

Existential Finality

Dark Empathy, Retribution, and the Decline of Capital Punishment in the United States

Daniel LaChance

[W]hile most humans wish to die a painless death, many do not have that good fortune.
Samuel Alito, writing for the majority in *Glossip* v. *Gross*, 2015[1]

INTRODUCTION

It was a moment of life imitating art. During oral arguments for the 1972 case *Aikens* v. *California*, Supreme Court Justice William O. Douglas listened as an attorney for the state of California defended the constitutionality of the death penalty. Arguing against the claim that capital punishment violated the Eighth Amendment, Ronald George told the Court, "there is no cruel and unusual punishment, certainly not under our humane method...In fact, the death that comes to such a prisoner is, perhaps, less cruel than the death by natural causes that comes to us all eventually." At this, Douglas interrupted, "Except nobody knows."[2]

Douglas's remark was not just a retort to an attorney; it was also an echo of an emotionally wrenching moment in a climactic execution scene the Justice had watched fourteen years earlier. In 1958, Douglas had screened Walter Wanger's cinematic salvo against the death penalty, *I Want to Live!*, for himself and colleagues in the conference room at the Supreme Court.[3] In the film's climactic scene, the

---

[1] *Glossip et al.* v. *Gross et al.*, 576 U.S. ___ (Slip Opinion) (2014), 10. Available at www.supreme court.gov/opinions/14pdf/14–7955_aplc.pdf. (Accessed March 1, 2016).

[2] Quoted in Evan J. Mandery, *A Wild Justice: The Death and Resurrection of Capital Punishment in America* (New York: W. W. Norton, 2013), 153.

[3] One contemporary at the time said that he could not remember, save for cases involving copyright infringement, when members of the Court had ever gathered at work to watch a film together. In a letter to Wanger, James V. Bennett, Director of the Bureau of Prisons, told Wanger that three Supreme Court justices, including Douglas, screened the film alongside some lower court judges and other officials in the Court's conference room. "I don't think there has ever been a projection of a picture in the Supreme Court Building," aside from the screening of films embroiled in censorship disputes, Bennett wrote. James Bennett to Walter Wanger, January 16, 1959, Walter Wanger Papers, Box 80, Folder 23, University of Wisconsin,

protagonist Barbara Graham walks blindfolded to her death in the San Quentin gas chamber for a crime she did not commit. As she is strapped into the chair, a well-meaning guard leans in and offers her some advice: "When you hear the pellets drop, count 10. Take a deep breath. It's easier that way." Graham replies, acidly, "How do you know?"[4] Expressing a similar sentiment in a very different context,[5] Douglas called attention to the inability of the living to know what it feels like to be executed and criticized the hubris of those who engaged in self-assured speculation.[6] Yet such speculation has been historically commonplace. Efforts to bridge the chasm between the living and the soon-to-be dead – to inhabit the minds of those undergoing an execution, to wonder about the pain they may or may not feel, to understand how they are managing the psychological pain of imminent death – have a history that deserves contemplation.[7]

At the heart of that history is the emergence of what historian Lynn Hunt has called "empathetic selfhood."[8] Amid a broader western trend toward secularization during the Enlightenment, as a divinely enchanted world gave way to an

---

Madison, Library. Douglas himself wrote to Wanger, telling the producer that he found the film "powerful." William O. Douglas to Walter Wanger, December 11, 1958, Walter Wanger Papers, Box 80, Folder 23, University of Wisconsin, Madison, Library.

4   Walter Wanger, *I Want to Live!*, directed by Robert Wise (1958; Hollywood, CA: MGM, 2002), DVD. The film was based on actual persons and events. Barbara Graham was executed by the state of California in 1955.

5   I have noted this connection between Douglas's remarks and *I Want to Live!* elsewhere. Daniel LaChance, *Executing Freedom: The Cultural Life of Capital Punishment* (Chicago: University of Chicago Press, 2016), 205 (n. 21).

6   Seven years later, in *In Cold Blood* (1965), the famous account of a capital case in Kansas, Truman Capote called critical attention to a similar kind of assertion: "After the execution of one of the two killers, a bystander wonders about the pain of execution, prompting this exchange with a guard: "'They don't feel nothing. Drop, snap, and that's it. They don't feel nothing.' 'Are you sure? I was standing right close. I could hear him gasping for breath.' 'Uh-huh, but he don't feel nothing. Wouldn't be humane if he did.' 'Well. And I suppose they feed them a lot of pills. Sedatives.' 'Hell, no. Against the rules.'" Truman Capote, *In Cold Blood* (New York: Vintage, 1965), 340.

7   It is a history, in turn, not simply of capital punishment but of death in general and, in particular, of how many have managed their anxieties about it. In late modern culture, death, David Garland suggests, has the "cultural status as the last great taboo." The powerlessness we feel in the face of death shapes the appeal of the death penalty: "It can be liberating to talk of death in a positive way and pleasurable to exert some control over its imposition." David Garland, *Peculiar Institution: America's Death Penalty in an Age of Abolition* (Cambridge, MA: Harvard University Press, 2010), 287.

8   Lynn Hunt, *Inventing Human Rights: A History* (New York: W. W. Norton, 2007), 30. For Michel Foucault, the rise of individualism and the empathy for strangers it engenders is a function of changing discourses of knowledge, power, and the body and the new technologies of governance those changes produce. Discourses that individualize persons by encouraging them to think of themselves and others as beings with complex interior lives ultimately "turns individuality into an instrument of domination and subjection," making persons unable to hear the "low hum of a vast machinery that fabricates us as individuals." Michael Clifford, *Political Genealogy after Foucault: Savage Identities* (London: Routledge, 2001): 6, 15.

increasingly knowable and secular one, humans increasingly saw themselves as self-owning, self-disciplining beings capable of governing their world without divine intervention or inspiration. A society rooted in such a premise required persons who could mutually recognize one another as endowed with similar qualities and capacities. Novels tellingly emerged in this context, reflecting and reinforcing the idea that persons beyond one's immediate social world were also autonomous individuals endowed with rich inner lives. Strangers were more readily recognized as possessing a self that resembled, in its depth and complexity and sacredness, one's own.

The rise of empathetic selfhood changed the practice of capital punishment in the western world. A heightened respect for individual self-ownership made bodies inviolable and the mutilation of them, even in the name of repairing a sacred order sundered by crime, immoral. By the late eighteenth century, torture had ended and a never-ending quest for painless and quick execution methods had begun.[9] But empathetic selfhood also added new meanings to executions and their representations in print culture. In a world where God was no longer a given, the last moments of a life could take on a kind of finality – what I call existential finality – that was previously unimaginable. As invocations of divine authority faded, though did not disappear, from execution ceremonies, some executions were memorialized as dramas about the mortal limits placed on humans in a world that increasingly saw people as God-like shapers of their fate. Such executions took on a melodramatic rather than moralistic frame. In such accounts, the condemned was a stand-in for humanity, bravely confronting the inescapable limits to individual existence, limits observers shared with him and that called into question the Enlightenment's faith in human autonomy and agency. Such confrontations with death appear in what I call "empathy-inviting execution narratives," a small, but significant subset of journalistic accounts of executions that invited readers to grapple with what a good departure from this world looked like and whether – and how – individuals might transcend the limits death placed on their own existence.

In what follows, I offer a brief gloss of the history of the desire to inhabit the mind of the condemned before arguing that it is ultimately at the heart of the declining use and popularity of the death penalty in the contemporary United States. In the first section, I describe the rise of empathetic personhood and interpret the move away from torture in the eighteenth century and the desire to make executions painless and instantaneous in the nineteenth and twentieth centuries as a symptom of it. I then turn, in particular, to the chief effect of such changes: written accounts of executions that amplified the inner life of the condemned person and portrayed his final moments in ways that stoked fantasies and managed anxieties about humans' capacity to control the uncontrollable.

---

[9] Hunt, *Inventing Human Rights.*

Finally, I consider the relevance of this history to the declining support for capital punishment in the contemporary United States. I argue that two late twentieth century developments – the widespread adoption of lethal injection as the method of execution in the United States and the dramatic elongation of the amount of time condemned inmates spent on death row – are best understood as the latest effects of the rise of empathetic selfhood and its transformation of executions into existential, as well as punitive, events. In different ways, these developments have divested executions of much of their retributive character, making them increasingly unsatisfying to a public that turns to them for a moral clarity they no longer possess and retributive satisfaction they often fail to deliver.

FROM *AMENDE HONORABLE* TO PRIVATE RECKONING: THE CONDEMNED IN AN AGE OF EMPATHY

The divine nature of law profoundly shaped the meaning of capital punishment in ancient, premodern, and early modern western cultures. In executions, the broken body of the transgressor became the fearsome proof of the vitality of the sacred moral order to which all were subordinate. Studying the Biblical account of Moses giving the Israelites the law in Exodus, philosopher Jacques Derrida considers its depiction of "the birth of law as birth of the death penalty."[10] After giving them the Ten Commandments, Moses invites the Israelites to hear, directly from God, the "judgments" that will be visited upon those who break them. They shrink away, however, preferring instead to hear it through their human intermediary. They

> do not want to hear God anymore. At least they do not want to lend an ear directly to the divine speech; they do not want to listen to God any longer, as if they were expecting the worst, which also awaited them, because they will listen to Moses, whereas the word of God, if they hear it directly, without intermediary, risks bringing about their death, of putting them to death. . .[they] have the presentiment that God is on the verge of inventing not killing but the death penalty – and the Jews, the children of Israel, are terrified by this divine word that elects them, that chooses them by uttering in their direction, addressing them, by getting ready to utter the first threat of the first death penalty in the world, on man's earth.[11]

The reluctance to hear the law directly from the lawgiver was a tacit recognition of the frailties of human beings. Given a world in which authority lay beyond individuals and humans' sinful tendencies made violating the law inevitable, law's overwhelming and mysterious violence was a source of terror.

As divinely authorized executions in early modern western societies would illustrate, this terror was well founded. In *Discipline and Punish: The Birth of the Prison*,

---

[10] Jacques Derrida, *The Death Penalty*, Volume I, Geoffrey Bennington, Marc Crépon, and Thomas Dutoit, eds. (Chicago: University of Chicago Press, 2014), 20.
[11] Ibid., 18–19.

Michel Foucault most memorably captured the awe-inspiring nature of executions in pre-Enlightenment Europe. Foucault recounts the torturous execution of Robert-François Damiens, the eighteenth-century Frenchman who attempted to assassinate King Louis XV. Damiens's execution, the last drawing and quartering in France, was a gruesome affair, one in which the divine judgment that authorized it was foregrounded. Authorities stopped their dreadful acts of torture periodically in order to allow Damiens to repent his sin publically. In between the excruciating pains of a dismembering punishment, Damiens cried out for the Lord's pardon, spoke with confessors, kissed a crucifix that was held out to him, asked his executioners to pray for him, and requested that a priest remember him at the next mass. The evisceration of the condemned man's body expiated the crime while the pleas for forgiveness affirmed the sacred order his criminal act had sundered. In the body of the condemned, the word of the law was made flesh.[12] In Damiens's execution and others, if the spectacle of punishment was successful, onlookers would see a glimpse of what the Israelites shrank from: the terribleness of the violent force that underlay divinely given law.

The Enlightenment brought dramatic changes to the way eighteenth century Americans and Europeans understood themselves and their relationship to others, changing the meaning of executions. In Lynn Hunt's account of the invention of human rights, a capacity for empathy dramatically expanded during this period. New kinds of reading, viewing, and listening experiences encouraged people to see themselves as more distinct from one another as they had in the past, yet also "reinforced the notion of a community based on autonomous, empathetic individuals who could relate beyond their immediate families, religious affiliations, or even nations to greater universal values."[13] Some saw the execution victim differently as a result. For those influenced by newer ways of thinking about pain and punishment, the torture that accompanied an execution moved from signifying the "redemption and reparation of the community" to being a mere "sensation without connection to moral sentiment" that had no capacity to proclaim a society's moral and religious identity.[14] Torture, in other words, lost its sublime qualities, its capacity to induce in the public, through identification with the victim, a sense of "the overwhelming majesty of the law, the state, and ultimately God."[15] An understanding of the condemned shifted as a result: increasingly, observers no longer saw the condemned solely as an expiator of sin, his mangled body the vindication of the divine order,

---

[12] "The law required that its victim should authenticate in some sense the tortures that he had undergone." Michel Foucault, *Discipline and Punish: The Birth of the Prison* (Paris: Editions Gallimard, 1975). Trans. Alan Sheridan (New York: Vintage Books, 1995), 66. Citations refer to the Vintage edition.

[13] Hunt, *Inventing Human Rights*, 32.

[14] Ibid., 101, 94, 101.

[15] Ibid., 94.

but as a discrete individual with an identity that could be valued and understood outside of a reference to God. Hunt explains,

> Once sacred only within a religiously defined order, in which individual bodies could be mutilated or tortured for the greater good, the body became sacred on its own in a secular order that rested on the autonomy and inviolability of individuals. There are two parts to this development. Bodies gained a more positive value as they became more separate, more self-possessed, and more individualized over the course of the eighteenth century, while violations of them increasingly aroused negative reactions.[16]

Under these conditions, the empathy felt at an execution would be for an individualized, autonomous victim, not for a sacrificial lamb. Under such circumstances, torture impermissibly violated an essence that could not be harmed, no matter how bad one's actions were.

While empathetic selfhood aroused feelings that ultimately led to the end of public torture, it did not succeed at ending executions.[17] It did change the practice of state killing dramatically, however. Elites viewed heightened expressions of empathy for the condemned in execution audiences in the same vein as they viewed expressions of heightened antipathy toward the offender: both threatened to undermine the legitimacy of the death penalty altogether.[18] An expanded capacity for empathy on the part of elites may have also underlay a genuine sense that the carnival-like qualities of public executions were vulgar and uncivilized, the mark of a primitive insensitivity to the feelings and comfort of others.[19] As a result, in the nineteenth century, executions in Europe and the United States gradually became private affairs that excluded the public. Public access to lethal punishment was filtered through newspaper accounts. Elites hoped that sober-minded journalists would cultivate the public's respect for the moral order and the state that punished in its name.[20]

---

[16] Ibid., 82.

[17] In enlightenment thought, the torture-less execution was *not* at odds with the dignity of the condemned. Immanuel Kant's late eighteenth-century defense of the death penalty, for instance, came with the caveat that "the death of the criminal must be kept entirely free from any maltreatment that would make an abomination of the humanity residing in the person suffering it." No longer a source of terror, as it was to the Israelites in Exodus, embeddedness in a legal order was a source of dignity. It distinguished humans from other animal life and marked them as reasonable members of a transcendent enterprise. The endurance of the death penalty could instead become a sign that by his membership in the political community, the condemned had elected to rise above the status of animals. Immanuel Kant, *The Metaphysical Elements of Justice*, trans. John Ladd (1797; Indianapolis: Bobbs-Merrill, 1965), 102.

[18] Foucault, *Discipline and Punish.*

[19] See Louis P. Masur, *Rites of Execution: Capital Punishment and the Transformation of American Culture, 1776–1865* (New York: Oxford University Press, 1989); Stuart Banner, *The Death Penalty: An American History* (Cambridge, MA: Harvard University Press, 2002).

[20] Banner, *The Death Penalty.* Some states did not trust the press and passed laws forbidding execution coverage altogether. Such efforts failed miserably. See, e.g., John D. Bessler, *Legacy of Violence: Lynch Mobs and Executions in Minnesota* (Minneapolis: University of Minnesota Press, 2003).

The rise of empathetic selfhood did more than temper the violence of executions and restrict access to them. In a society transformed by the rise of empathetic selfhood, journalists increasingly wrote accounts of executions that purported to give readers access to the meaning that death had for the condemned. They wrote for audiences they imagined in increasingly secular terms, audiences who no longer saw themselves in Damiens, but in men and occasionally women who were, as they someday would be, standing on the verge of nonexistence.[21] Such execution accounts seemed designed to help ordinary persons manage their own anxieties and uncertainties about death in an increasingly secular and individualizing age. They provided an opportunity for the onlooker to grapple with her own mortality, to contemplate whether death meant permanent obliteration and, if it did, what might be done to mitigate the terribleness of such an outcome. "What does a good death entail?" these stories tacitly asked audiences. "What role do pain and fortitude play in achieving it?"

Recognizing this existential function of post-enlightenment executions allows us to see how the abolition of torture-based executions was driven not only by a desire to protect and control the sensibilities of the execution audience, but also by a desire to present the condemned as more than a symbol, as an authentic, autonomous member of a society grounded in empathetic selfhood. The diminution of physical pain enabled the presentation of an authentic self as much as it protected that self from inhumane treatment. Indeed, one of the markers of autonomous personhood is the capacity to speak unscripted. Such capacity is threatened by pain. Intense physical pain, literary scholar Elaine Scarry notes, destroys the torture victim's capacity for language, "bringing about an immediate reversion to a state anterior to language, to the sounds and cries a human being makes before language is learned."[22] By minimizing the physical pain the condemned feels during the execution, reforms to executions maximized access to his consciousness. The

---

[21] Scholars of capital punishment have traditionally presented empathy, by contrast, as a sentiment that thwarts the effectiveness of a punishment. Hunt frames the abolition of torture as a benevolent effect of the rise of empathetic selfhood. Others, meanwhile, treat empathy for the condemned as an emotion that has redounded to their benefit, either by reducing the physical and emotional pain they endured during their executions or by mobilizing the public against punishment (and possibly sparing them from it). But empathy, critical criminologist Michelle Brown notes, "is a modality that is not inevitably prosocial or benevolent in its efforts or effects." Indeed, we might view the kind of empathy that is the focus of this chapter in this light. It is a "dark empathy," one that enables the satisfaction of the empathizer's emotional needs while doing nothing to ameliorate the suffering of the condemned. Michelle Brown, "'Which Question? Which Lie?' Reflections on *Payne* v. *Tennessee* and the 'Quick Glimpse' of Life," in *The Punitive Imagination: Law, Justice, and Responsibility*, ed. Austin Sarat (Tuscaloosa: University of Alabama Press, 2013), 127–57, 131.

[22] Elaine Scarry, *The Body in Pain: the Making and Unmaking of the World*. (Oxford: Oxford University Press, 1985), 4. Qtd. in Robert M. Cover, "Violence and the Word," *Yale Law Journal* 95 (1986): 1601–29, 1603.

condemned, free from the coercive and debilitating grips of pain, could express his inner thoughts and feelings at the moment of execution.

The abolition of torture and the quest for increasingly painless methods of putting offenders to death that would follow, then, should be read not only as efforts to protect a newly discovered dignity that lay within the condemned, but also as efforts to enable the performance of that dignity in displays of authentic, autonomous selfhood by the condemned. Empathy-inviting execution narratives became the vehicle through which that self-presentation – and the broader, existential anxieties and fantasies that accompanied it – reached wide audiences.

PITY AND PUTTY: THE EMPATHY-INVITING EXECUTION NARRATIVE

Empathy-inviting execution narratives have been overshadowed by the attention scholars have paid to discourses about criminality in the nineteenth and twentieth centuries that explicitly discourage empathetic identification with criminals. From the rise of mad killers in mid-nineteenth-century Gothic literature to the "moral alien" with a "criminal brain" in late nineteenth-century eugenics discourse to the psychopathic serial killer of twentieth-century forensic psychology, discourses of human evil in the aftermath of the enlightenment have often reinforced an image of the worst offenders as monstrous others.[23] This construction of the murderer, Karen Halttunen argues, was a significant legacy of the Enlightenment. Before the eighteenth century, accounts of executions in colonial New England presented the worst criminals as embodiments of a sinful humanity. The "universal depravity" ascribed to humanity before the Enlightenment could not survive the age's insistence that humans were good, rational, and capable of self-government.[24] The irrational evil at the heart of the worst crimes became increasingly incompatible with that image of humanity. Thus, Halttunen says, the murderer moved

> from common sinner with whom the larger community of sinners were urged to identify in the service of their own salvation, into moral monster from whom readers were instructed to shrink, with a sense of horror that confirmed their own 'normalcy' in the face of the morally alien, and with a sense of mystery that testified to their own inability even to conceive such an aberrant act. The new Gothic monster – like the villain in Gothic fiction – was first and last a moral monster, between whom and the normal majority yawned an impassable gulf.[25]

---

[23] Karen Halttunen, *Murder Most Foul: The Killer and the American Gothic Imagination* (Cambridge, MA: Harvard University Press, 2002), Nicole Rafter, *The Criminal Brain: Understanding Biological Theories of Crime* (New York: NYU Press, 2008), and Robert Weisberg, "The Unlucky Psychopath as Death Penalty Prototype," in *Who Deserves to Die: Constructing the Executable Subject*, ed. Austin Sarat and Karl Shoemaker (Amherst: University of Massachusetts Press, 2011).

[24] Halttunen, *Murder Most Foul*, 4.

[25] Ibid., 4–5.

Disidentification, rather than empathy, was the response of many to condemned criminals.

Halttunen's broader story of change over time captures the dominant trend in discourse about the worst criminals. Nonetheless, a significant minority of condemned inmates continued to be portrayed in ways that did encourage audiences to identify with them, yet in terms that were more secular. Execution practices, after all, had changed in ways that reflected the rise of a society grounded in empathetic selfhood. Journalists, in turn, sometimes wrote accounts of executions that were less concerned with upholding enlightenment principles – like the notion that humans were innately rational and virtuous – and more concerned with grappling with what those principles often did not account for: human vulnerability and mortality.

In widely publicized cases of the executions of young white men, journalists often took advantage of the public's expanded capacity to empathize with those from different social worlds by portraying the condemned as both guilty *and* loved.[26] Stripped of lurid references to the crime or its impact on the victims, execution coverage would invite readers to connect with the condemned as mortal persons with rich interior lives who were undergoing what they, too, would someday undergo, albeit in a different context: a coming to terms with what their lives had meant as death rapidly approached. As a result, in some special cases, the punitive meaning generated by executions became wrapped up in a broader display of self-management in the face of death. In these cases, the condemned modelled for the living how to die with dignity.

---

[26] The case of John Dutton that I discuss below is representative of broader themes that emerged in a survey of exceptionally melodramatic accounts of executions found in a comprehensive analysis of newspaper coverage of 941 executions in eight jurisdictions from 1915–1940. (Dutton's case is from 1893, but I have not yet systematically examined data from newspapers prior to 1915). In all, ten research assistants and I comprehensively searched for execution coverage from 1915 to 1940, inclusive: *The Atlanta Constitution*, *The Baltimore Sun*, *The Chicago Tribune*, *The Boston Globe*, *The New York Tribune/New York Herald-Tribune*, *The New York Times*, *The Los Angeles Times*, *The San Francisco Chronicle*, *The Washington Post*, and *The New Orleans Times-Picayune*. We searched for coverage of all 1,182 executions in the states (or district) these newspapers served and found coverage of 941 (some executions were covered in multiple, same-day stories; conversely, in states that put multiple men to death on the same day, multiple executions were often covered in one story). Empathy-inviting execution narratives constituted a minority of the coverage we found. The average length of execution stories across the ten newspapers we surveyed was 11.2 paragraphs. Empathy-inviting narratives were found exclusively, though not by default, in the longest articles printed by newspapers: 21 percent of the coverage was longer than 15 paragraphs, and 10.2 percent of the coverage was longer than 25 paragraphs. (These data include articles covering single and multiple executions. For single executions only, 11 percent were longer than 15 paragraphs and only 4.6 percent were longer than 25 paragraphs.) The protagonists of empathetic execution narratives were almost always white men. I write more fully about melodramatic execution narratives in newspaper and film elsewhere. Daniel LaChance, "Executing Humanity: Legal Consciousness and Capital Punishment in the United States, 1915–1940," *Law and History Review*, forthcoming.

An illustrative example of one such case is the public execution of John W. Dutton in Cartersville, Georgia, on October 20, 1893. Dutton was convicted and sentenced to death for stabbing and killing Sallie Mobbs on a road on the outskirts of Stilesboro, Georgia. Mobbs, a married woman whose husband was frequently away traveling, was attacked while on the way to deliver an evening meal to local cotton pickers. Dutton had attacked her, the papers implied, for resisting his earlier advances.[27] Three years later, still proclaiming his innocence, Dutton was executed in front of a crowd of 3,000.[28]

In its initial coverage of the crime, *The Atlanta Constitution* had described the murderer as a "fiendish assassin" who had "horribly butchered" the woman.[29] Nevertheless, in its coverage of Dutton's execution, the newspaper portrayed his experience on the gallows not as an opportunity for atonement but as an invitation to readers to contemplate what it would be like to say goodbye to the world forever.

Throughout its 119-paragraph-long account of the eve and day of his execution, the paper depicted a Dutton steadfastly committed to maintaining his image as an innocent man in the face of immense pressure to confess to the crime. The paper described the degree to which Dutton had been pressured by his jailers to unburden himself of his pride and confess to the crime. "If you haven't, John, your coffin will make you change your tune," the guards told Dutton on the evening before his execution. "That coffin has been made and when you see it tomorrow at the gallows you'll tell the truth." But Dutton refused to confess, slept soundly that night, and resisted similar urgings by his minister, the doctor attending the execution, and even Sheriff Puckett. The sheriff "is one of the largest men in that section of the state," the paper told readers. Yet "in his big chest there is a heart as tender as a woman's…Tears ran down the big man's cheeks as he spoke."[30] Despite this unusual display of feminine emotion from the sheriff, readers learned, Dutton refused to confess.

Rather than describing Dutton's presence in the jail in ways that reinforced him as a moral monster, the paper described Dutton as occupying an equal social footing with the men who guarded and ministered to him. After praying with a minister in his cell, the paper told readers,

> Dutton came back into the hallway and was free as any man in the corridor. He talked pleasantly to all and answered such questions readily as were asked of him. He was not at all surly, but seemed to think that he was the one of the party to be admired. He was constantly looking at himself as though he wanted to be considered fair looking.[31]

---

[27] "Bill Dutton's Crime," *Atlanta Constitution*, March 25, 1892.
[28] "Choked to Death," *Atlanta Constitution*, October 21, 1893.
[29] "Bill Dutton's Crime."
[30] "Choked to Death."
[31] Ibid.

The jail figures, here, not as a place that reinforced "impassable barriers between the normal and the abnormal"[32] but as a site in which the ego of a man about to be put to death is meticulously studied by interested parties who want to know him and experience, as much as possible, his internal preparations for his impending death.

Dutton's desire to die "game" – to face his death with bravery and a hint of defiance – was detailed by the paper. The *Constitution* reported that "Dutton's approaching death did not cause him to lose any of the enjoyments of life during the last twenty-four hours he was alive." He ordered and ate his final meal eagerly. He slept soundly. On the day of his execution, he went about bathing himself, with water brought to his cell, "with a careless abandon that was almost horrifying to those about him. He was as cool and calm as a man could possibly be and no one who did not know that he was about to hang would ever have imagined it by looking at him as he was taking his last bath." Dutton elicits horror not because his crime is so repulsive but because his appreciation of the finality of what was about to befall him seemed absent. As the carriage that took him to the execution site approached its destination, Dutton "settled himself to his smoke and again he seemed to enjoy that smoke. . . .He referred to his coming doom with the same nonchalant air that he had manifested all during last evening and this morning before leaving the jail. He either did not appreciate his situation or he was a man of the most remarkable nerve."[33]

Once at the execution site, the doctor announced to the crowd that "Mr. Dutton has here a book of his life written by himself, and Sheriff Burroughs has been kind enough to allow him time to sell it. He wants the proceeds to go to his wife and children in Alabama. Those who want a book can buy it from Mr. Dutton." After fifteen minutes of brisk sales, a lull occurred. Sales were revived briefly by Mr. Hutchison, a tall fellow who "mounted the scaffold and made a plea to the crowd to buy the book." Dutton himself eventually mounted the scaffold ("with a firmer and steadier tread than any of those about him") where he

> gave another of those searching glances of his and seemed to be pleased with the throng he had brought out. The deputy sheriff asked him if he would like to have the cuff removed and he replied that he would. The cuff was taken from the right arm and Dutton stood upon the gallows as free as any man upon it. A single leap would have put him over the rail and then it would have been a chase and death at the hands of one of the guards or an escape. But Dutton had no idea of attempting it. . .He appeared to think that he was the hero of the occasion and wanted to play his part out.

The paper noted only one moment in which Dutton's cool veneer seemed to falter and he showed emotion. During the doctor's prayer,

---

[32] Halttunen, *Murder Most Foul*, 6.
[33] "Choked to Death."

He was kneeling and had his face covered with his hands, but he was constantly peeping between his fingers about him. At one stage of the prayer he was certainly moved and showed it by the nervous twitching of his chin. But he had decided to die game, and with a terrible effort he pulled himself together and before the prayer was over, he was as calm as ever.

Sales of the book resumed after these prayers when an individual approached the scaffold asking for one. When Dutton signed it, all those who had bought copies rushed forward, and he spent many more minutes signing the copies he had sold.[34]

The sheriff finally stopped the sales a full hour and seventeen minutes after the carriage had arrived at the scaffold. At that point, the sheriff invited Dutton to go to the end of the scaffold to say goodbye to his friends, and "without being in any way bound [he] shook hands with quite a number. He then turned to the crowd and said 'Friends, this seems to me like going to meeting; it don't seem like it is going to death, but it is death, but I am prepared for this day and hour.'" Brought to the trap, attached to the noose, and masked, Dutton finally seemed poised to die. As the sheriff approached the lever that would release the trap, though, Dutton called out from beneath the mask, asking for the opportunity to pray. The sheriff acquiesced. After a minute passed, the sheriff once again approached the trigger "and was trying to slip it out noiselessly, but the pin creaked, and as quick as a flash Dutton turned his head. He had heard it and seemed to know what it meant. The sheriff gave a quick jerk, the drop fell and Dutton went down like a flash."[35]

Coverage of Dutton's death on the north Georgia gallows was one of several variants of the empathy-inviting execution narrative. In these narratives, the monstrosity of the inmate is minimized and he is presented quasi-heroically as maintaining a freedom and a composure that invites readers to fantasize that it is possible, though very difficult, to maintain a coherent self-presentation in face of one's immediate annihilation. In these narratives, the drama of punishment is overshadowed by the drama of preparing for and then submitting to death. Dutton, for instance, is treated by the authorities, and presented by the journalist, as a free person who, like all free people, cannot evade, in the end, death. He is trusted to hawk his books, wander into the crowd and around the execution platform, shake hands with his friends. He requests and receives extra time to pray. His freedom, his lack of monstrosity, makes him relatable, inviting readers to take up the challenge of reconciling their own freedom with their own inability to avoid death.

Indeed, Dutton spends his last hours managing his legacy. His behavior bespeaks a broader desire to exert control over a future from which he will be absent. The autobiographical book becomes an extension of the self that will survive in the world after Dutton himself has left it. It also provides a mechanism for managing the helplessness any dying man might feel at the prospect of not being able to care for a

---

[34] Ibid.
[35] Ibid.

vulnerable child. Dutton, the crowd is told, is selling his book to raise funds for his little girl, a way of conquering the economic incapacity to care for her that death would impose and crystallizing a final impression of himself as honorable. His steadfast insistence on his innocence, despite multiple pleas for him to confess, reveals the coherence of the self under immense pressure. Dutton had, readers learned, even figured out a way to minimize the ignominious aftermath of his execution. As the noose is placed around his neck, he cries out to the sheriff, "Burroughs you won't let this rope stay around my neck will you? Remember you have promised to take it off as soon as I am dead." The sheriff gives reassurance and, in so doing, helps create the impression that the condemned man is successfully protecting his post-mortem image, influencing a future in which he would not partake.[36]

Religion and religiosity are often present in these and other empathy-inviting execution narratives, but crowds or newspaper readers are invited to see the condemned not as objects being sacrificed to a holy or secular collective conscience but persons on the verge of death trying to hold themselves together and find meaning in their final moments. The mind that execution audiences are invited to inhabit is not necessarily that of the penitent sinner but of the anxious, self-managing mortal. God, when he is invoked, is not the center of a theological universe, but one of many profound sources of meaning that a condemned prisoner may – or may not – draw upon to find existential closure.

Of course, acts of self-management in the face of death are not guaranteed to work, and journalists made these narratives more powerful by recognizing the possibility that the dying may at any moment unravel psychologically, even as they ultimately upheld the fantasy of self- coherence. Dutton's bravado – his desire to die "game" – cracks at certain points, only to be reasserted. At one point, the paper reported, after the noose was lowered but before it was placed around his neck, Dutton's

> face flushed, and straightening up, he asked: 'Brother Mashburn, ain't that my little girl over there?' As he spoke he pointed to a group. Mr. Mashburn looked and assured him that it was not his little girl. 'Yes, it is,' he said, 'and her mother is with her. I believe it is them.' For a second or two he appeared unstrung, but upon being assured that it was not his wife and child he became himself again.

Wives, children, mothers – these vulnerable loved ones figure prominently in moments on the gallows (or, later in the gas chamber or the electric chair) – when men do let out a few sobs. But these emotional cracks are most often quickly sealed with a spiritual resolve.[37] The texts engineer the fantasy of self-control by raising – in order to vanquish – the possibility of the self unraveling in the face of death.

[36] Ibid.
[37] Ibid.

In another Georgia case three decades later, for instance, James Satterfield's "mighty frame [shook] with a few sobs" as he spoke about his daughter in his very last moments on the gallows platform. Yet he was nonetheless still able to meet death "unflinchingly without the slightest tremor." In the end, Pierre van Passen, the journalist who covered his case, seemed to want to fulfill a desire, in readers, to triumph over death, to conquer the unconquerable. "Satterfield died not below the scaffold," Passen began the concluding sentences of his empathy-inviting execution narrative. "He died on top there. The law did not kill him. He willed his own death. In that moment when he said 'I am ready,' the spirit was already taking flight from his body."[38]

John Dutton's execution in Georgia offers a case study in the way that executions in a world reshaped by empathetic selfhood could serve as the occasions for grappling with existential anxieties. Coverage of the 1922 execution of Harvey Church in Chicago offers a different kind of case study, one in which the existential dimensions of executions become apparent in a condemned man's failure to respond at all to the execution ceremony. To many, the execution lost its meaning when its victim arrived in the execution chamber in a comatose state.

In the fall of 1921, the twenty-three year old Church murdered two car salesmen in order to steal a luxury automobile. The crime was poorly planned and authorities quickly apprehended Church. He confessed his crimes to the police officers who interrogated him and led them to one of the bodies, which he had buried in the basement of his mother's home (he had thrown the other in a river). At trial, however, Church appeared increasingly unresponsive to the events happening around him. To skeptics, it seemed more than a little convenient that this dramatic change overcame Church after his legal team had decided to claim that he was insane. Prosecutors strongly disputed Church's insanity claim.[39] He was, they argued, clearly feigning insanity to avoid responsibility for his crime.

On the day before Christmas Eve, a Chicago jury listened to the prosecutor's final arguments on the case – an extended plea to them not to give into the Christmas spirit and buy the insanity plea the defense was peddling to save Church from death. After a day's deliberation, jurors reached their verdict: guilty, with no recommendation for mercy. Church was to die.

Spectators made an intensive effort to discern Church's response to the verdict. But *The Chicago Evening Post* reported that they "could not tell whether his face twitched for a moment at the word 'death,' or whether their eyes deceived them." Even the bailiffs who had placed their hands on Church's shoulders when the

[38] Pierre van Passen, "Satterfield, on Gallows, Smiles Welcome to Death," *Atlanta Constitution*, May 24, 1924. Qtd. in LaChance, "Executing Humanity."

[39] Its expert witness, a former state alienist, asserted that the mentally deranged exhibited involuntary tension in their muscles and that he found no such involuntary tension in his examination of Church. "Church Faking Insanity, Says Dr. Singer," *Chicago American*, December 20, 1921.

verdict was being read "could not say whether their own tenseness made them seem to feel a slight shudder pass thru the condemned man" or whether Church had, indeed, responded to the decision that he must die.[40] *The Chicago American* reported that Church's response was stoic: "He sat in the courtroom in his accustomed posture, his tousled head bowed and his eyes on the floor. As the foreman of the jury…announced the finding of that body, the muscles in Church's jaw tightened annd [*sic*] a slight shiver seemed to shake his frame. But he never looked up." That paper had a decidedly more skeptical view of Church's behavior, calling his courtroom demeanor a "pose."[41] It was the perspective the jury adopted as well. The alienists for the defense had proven Church peculiar, the foreman explained to the newspapers, but not insane. "We made our own observations day by day and noticed that his position varied," he said. This was evidence, in their minds, that Church was not as psychologically insensitive to the world as his lawyers had insisted.[42]

Whether through mental illness or a concerted effort to feign it, Church deteriorated markedly after the trial, refusing to shave, bathe, or eat. He had become, *The Chicago American* told its readers, known as "the 'hermit of the jail' because he has grown a heavy beard and has been on a hunger strike for thirty days. His eyes are glassy and sunken, his cheeks a greenish yellow in their pallor."[43] The change was dramatic enough that Church's counsel finally persuaded a judge to convene a new jury to decide whether Church was insane.

The week the insanity hearing was held a physician at the County Jail told reporters that Church's state was dismal: "There has been a complete mental, moral, and physical disintegration. One cannot think of him in terms of humankind. What lies here is merely a lump of flesh. Only the fundamental organic processes are functioning," he said.[44] A psychiatrist speculated that Church had become paralyzed, and ultimately mentally destroyed, by his death sentence. The terror of

> confronting an implacable, inexorable fact had taken possession of him. His obsession was the gallows. It had not loomed as that kind of a fact at first…But this fact kept recurring. With relentless regularity each of his [coping mechanisms] was eliminated. Every minute of every hour of the twenty-four there would impinge against his consciousness – "the gallows." It was inescapable…Gradually the mental, moral, and physical disintegration progressed…He began to sit with head down, chin on breast, eyes closed. He forgot to shave, to wash, to dress." He then stopped eating and talking.[45]

[40] "Harvey Church Found Guilty by Jury; Must Hang," *Chicago Evening Post*, December 24, 1921.
[41] "Find Church Guilty, to Be Hanged," *Chicago American*, December 23, 1921.
[42] "Harvey Church Found Guilty by Jury; Must Hang."
[43] "Feed Church by Force to Hang Him," *Chicago American*, February 12, 1922.
[44] "Church Total Human Wreck, Doctor Says," *Chicago Tribune*, February 21, 1922.
[45] Ibid.

At the hearing, doctors testified that they had stubbed lit cigars out on Church's nose, hit him with rubber hammers, and inserted pins into his arms and eyeballs in order to elicit a pain response, all to no avail.[46] The *Tribune* reporter called Church "exhibit A," referring to the defense attorney's request, denied by the Court, that the comatose Church be brought into the courtroom during the insanity hearing as proof of his state of mind. "Exhibit A resembled nothing so much as an amoeba molded into human form," readers learned. "The organic forces were there – that was all."[47] While they agreed that Church's state was unusual, however, two of the three physicians who testified did not declare him insane, and the prosecution ultimately persuaded the jury to find Church sane and thus eligible for execution. On February 21st, the judge promptly set a new execution date of March 3rd.

In the press, however, the impending execution provoked hand wringing. "Hanging will extinguish the physical spark of life," one of the alienists who testified was quoted in *The Tribune*, but not the metaphysical person of Church. "[T]he other side is gone now," the newspaper explained.[48] Some medical professionals speculated that the execution would reveal Church's coma to be an act of fraud. "When he is on the gallows and knows escape is impossible," they opined to *The Tribune*, "he will be betrayed by fright into manifesting consciousness."[49] To most, though, that seemed unlikely. On the eve of his execution, the newspaper was palpably amazed at what was unfolding. It told readers that physicians had performed a new series of tests designed to expose those feigning comas or insanity. They checked under his eyelids and found only the whites of his eyes. They lifted and let go of his limbs, watching them fall downwards lifelessly like lumps of "putty." They tried to shame him into awareness – "Don't you want forgiveness? Aren't you ashamed for your old mother's sake?" Finally, they turned to a more sophisticated and "infallible" test, one that *The Tribune* said would have woken the seven sleepers of Ephesus. "But it didn't awaken Church." "No matter what his original motive may have been, Church is now incapable of a volitional act," said H. L. Davis, professor of mental disease at the University of Illinois and one of Church's examiners. His colleague, Clarence A. Neymann, superintendent of the state's psychopathic hospital, concurred. Church was, Neymann added, "stuporous. He is incapable of receiving any

---

[46] "Church Found Sane by Jury," *Chicago Tribune*, February 22, 1922; *Chicago Evening Post*, February 21, 1922.

[47] "Church Total Human Wreck." Church was, by several accounts, catatonic, and the judge refused his attorneys' request to have Church brought in front of his post-conviction jury so that they could see his deteriorated state. "We are trying his mental condition," the judge sternly admonished defense counsel. "His physical condition has nothing to do with this insanity hearing. Church's physical condition is conceded. You admit that the defendant cannot talk....What purpose can he serve here?" "Judge Rules Slayer Out of Court," *Chicago American*, February 21, 1922.

[48] "Church Found Sane by Jury."

[49] "One Last Appeal for Church," *Chicago Tribune*, March 3, 1922.

impression, any communication, from the external world. His sensorium is void of outside contact."[50]

As the execution approached, even *The Chicago American*, which had been adamant that Church's catatonic state was all a calculated rouse to avoid execution, pronounced Church's condition that of a "mental suicide:"

> [T]hrough exertion of the most marvelous will power that ever has come under observation of Cook County criminal authorities, he has cheated the law of its objective in inflicting capital punishment... According to physicians and psychologists, Church is mentally dead – not insane. They say he will have no consciousness of what is transpiring, and will suffer no pain when the trap is sprung on the gallows Friday..."Church," they say, "by use of his will has brought about a state of self-hypnosis which will end only with the close of his physical life. His hunger strike was secondary rather than primary, as a result of this self-hypnosis. When he had induced this mental state his mind became an absolute blank...The state may exact the supreme penalty for his crimes on his body, but he has cheated it of its real objective."[51]

The newspaper still ascribed to Church a blameworthiness for the state into which he had descended, but it clarified, for readers, that he was now hopelessly gone, psychologically speaking. As the jail's physician, F. W. McNamara, put it, sounding somewhat disappointed, "There is no sign of life except for pulse or respiration. I'm convinced that Church will neither talk nor walk before he is hanged. He will go to the noose in his present condition."[52]

From here, the record offers wildly divergent accounts of Church's last day and execution in the Cook County Jail, one which reflects the degree to which the execution of a catatonic man was an intrinsic source of curiosity and confusion. On the morning of Church's execution day, *The Chicago American* excitedly told readers that a visit to Church by his family had stirred something within him. Within hours of the visit, the newspaper triumphantly proclaimed, Church awoke and made a full confession to his doctor: "I am sorry for what I done – I want to be forgiven," the doctor said Church mumbled. He added,

> "He was conscious and wept copiously...The tears actually poured from his eyes and I wiped them off his cheek. He said that he was sorry for what he had done – said that he hoped he would be forgiven and asked that prayers be said for him...I am absolutely convinced that when Church went to the gallows he was sane and cognizant of everything that was happening to him."[53]

But other newspapers vehemently disputed that claim. Efforts to rouse Church had "failed," the *Chicago Herald and Examiner* reported. "There had been reports from

---

[50] "Last Plea for Church Today as Noose Awaits," *Chicago Tribune*, March 2, 1922.
[51] "Church Past Crisis; Lives to Hang," *Chicago American*, February 27, 1922.
[52] "Will Decide Today in Last Fight to Halt Hanging," *Chicago American*, March 2, 1922.
[53] "Gallows Is Ready," *Chicago American*, March 3, 1922.

the death chamber that Church had 'come to': that he had prayed, reiterated his early confession, asked forgiveness; that he had proposed to die with opened eyes and a touch of gameness. But all these rumors had originated in simple fancy."[54] The change in Church was much more modest. Church was "verging toward consciousness," physicians who observed him in the day before had suggested. As his family surrounded his bed, weeping, "His mother placed her arms about him. 'My boy, my boy,' she sobbed. For a full moment Church lay inert. Only his eyelids continued their ceaseless twitching. Then, as a gurgle rather than an articulation, came the words, 'Mother,' 'Father,' 'Sister.'" Fifteen minutes before his execution, the paper added, Church appeared to try to repeat the "Our Father" that had been prayed aloud at his bedside before his execution.

In the end, the execution itself offered little evidence of a Church capable of consciousness. "From the beginning of the death march to the end, so far as cognition of external events was manifested, Church's skull might have been a sealed crypt, insulating his brain from all outside contact, all communication," *The Tribune* reported in an article headlined "Slayer Still in Coma as He Meets Death."[55] *The Herald and Examiner* offered a similar assessment: "A senseless, though breathing thing that had been Harvey W. Church strangled to death at the end of a rope in the county jail yesterday afternoon. Officially the state had avenged the murder of Carl Ausmus and Bernard Daugherty. But practically the 23-year-old murderer…beat the noose because he was oblivious during the last hours of his life."[56] Church remained comatose until the end, *The Tribune* reported. Jail personnel removed him from his bed and tied him to a kitchen chair with no arms that they used to carry him, head slumped against his chest, to the gallows. When they reached the gallows, a "white percale slip" that resembled a barber shop apron, enveloped his seated body, making only his head visible. He was carried up the stairs in the chair, and the noose set around his neck. The sheriff dutifully asked, "Harvey W. Church, have you anything to say," but the "form in the chair remained inert." The trap was sprung, and Church "plunged into space."[57]

The Herald and Examiner asserted that had Church been simulating a coma, he would have broken at the end:

[S]urely, if Church were the master "faker," if his were the wonder will which could lash the body into emaciation by way of stimulating insanity – now would be the moment when he could be expected to raise the sunken chin, open the bloodless lips and speak. The chair in which the body slumped was as animate as the youth.[58]

[54] "Slayer Dies Strapped in Chair," *Chicago Herald and Examiner*," March 4, 1922.
[55] "Slayer Still in Coma as He Meets Death," *Chicago Tribune*, March 4, 1922.
[56] "Slayer Dies Strapped in Chair," *Chicago Herald and Examiner*, March 4, 1922.
[57] "Slayer Still in Coma."
[58] "Slayer Dies Strapped in Chair."

The paper further observed Church's body's response to the hanging when the trap was sprung to confirm that the brain inside it had died before the heart had stopped beating and the lungs ceased respiring:

> It is customary for one who is strangling under the direction of the state to strain at his lashings, to writhe, to twist to enter a useless struggle to final breath for his shrinking lungs. But Church did not attempt the futile fight for air. Not a quiver crossed his frame…The fact that Church's body made absolutely no movement after dropping through the trap puzzled physicians who attended the hanging. None could recall a case of strangulation where the shoulders of the victim failed to twitch convulsively until death.[59]

The journalistic disputes over Church's state in the twenty-four hours leading up to his execution reveal how a lack of clarity about the ontological status of the condemned inmate could profoundly unsettle the meaning of an execution. *The Chicago Herald and Examiner* offered a meta-analysis of the journalistic desire for Church to demonstrate his humanity before dying. Drawing upon the clichés of execution coverage that appeared frequently in newspapers and fictional films – a careful study of the posture and eye movements of the condemned, an analysis of external light in the execution chamber that was a proxy for an adjacent, yet metaphorically far off land of the living – the newspaper's reporter turned his gaze on his fellow reporters. When Church arrived in the execution chamber, he said, "The witnesses – newspapermen, physicians and jail officials – craned forward with some eagerness," hopeful that Church would respond to what was happening to him. They got nothing:

> The boy was positively unconscious. His face, freshly shaven, was white or almost blue. The weak rays from the late afternoon sun, let in through the high narrow windows, were not strong enough to tone away the bluish tracings in the sunken cheeks. His chin had fallen upon his chest. His eyes were closed. The straggling black hair fell across half the forehead. Not a tremor showed.[60]

But what did it mean to execute a man who seemed utterly unresponsive to the imminence of his death? For the *Herald Examiner*, "a sack of flour might have been dropped with as much evidence of physical result."[61] And, it might have added, with as much evidence of an emotional result as well.

THE LEGACY OF EMPATHETIC SELFHOOD

I have argued thus far that the rise of empathetic selfhood in the eighteenth century fundamentally changed the practice of state killing. Newfound sensitivity to the feelings and thoughts of the condemned, a desire to understand how he faced death

[59] Ibid.
[60] Ibid.
[61] Ibid.

as a distinct individual in a world that no longer saw his suffering solely as the expiation of sin – both of these forces underlay the decline of torturous executions. The desire to eliminate gratuitous suffering did not end with the abolition of torture, however. Concern with the pain of the executed continued to generate changes to how Americans were put to death throughout the nineteenth and twentieth centuries. Beginning in the 1830s, states gradually abolished public executions and the assault on human dignity their carnival-like qualities could sometimes encourage. New technologies, moreover, were developed to minimize the pain and gruesomeness of hanging and, eventually, to replace the gallows with methods of killing that would be faster, cleaner, and less painful.

For most of the nineteenth and twentieth centuries, the changes introduced by new protocols and methods did not threaten the dominant retributive function of executions. With the abolition of torture, executions became less gratuitously violent. But while it was shortened in duration and intensity, the violence of state killing still remained unmistakably punitive in character. No one would mistake a decapitation or a hanging or a firing squad shooting as anything other than a punitive kind of violence. Executions may have disappeared into the bowels of prisons, but representations of them exploded into new media – like celluloid (1890s) – and were readily depicted on the pages of an ever-growing number of newspapers available for Americans to read. Even as Americans embarked on a quest to make executions less painful and mutilating, the devices they initially came up with to kill more humanely – the electric chair (1890) and the gas chamber (1925) – were clearly fearsome and unmistakably punitive in appearance – devised specifically to dispatch the worst of the worst. In short, changes made in the name of protecting human dignity or civilized decorum[62] were never so dramatic that they rendered invisible the punitive character of the execution.

Until the 1970s. At the end of the twentieth century, two developments finally, and perhaps permanently, disrupted the balance between the retributive function and humanistic qualities of capital punishment. The first was the development of a new kind of killing technology – lethal injection. The second was the growth to unprecedented levels of the time between the imposition of a death sentence by a

---

[62] Others have read these changes as a consequence of the evolving forms and functions of state power. As bureaucracies proliferated, the western state became increasingly disembodied. Its power, moreover, became more insidiously and effectively exercised through discipline. In late modern statecraft, a "technically perfect" execution, as political theorist Timothy V. Kaufman-Osborn describes it, is "defined by the certainty of its results and, more specifically, its accomplishment of an instantaneous and so painless death." To make the violence of an execution law-like, three ingredients of the execution must operate harmoniously: a specialized discourse that pronounces death as a legal penalty, technology that mediates "between the law's pronouncements and the bodies they speak of and to," and the body of the condemned. Kaufman-Osborn's theory describes a world in which an execution has become "an end in itself in the sense that its telos is nothing other than the efficient accomplishment of life's termination." Timothy V. Kaufman-Osborn, "The Metaphysics of the Hangman," *Studies in Law, Politics, and Society* 20 (2000), 35–70, 57, 48.

jury and the execution of it by the state. Both of these developments have their origins in the rise of empathetic selfhood and the dignity discourse it inspired. And they have each transformed capital punishment in the contemporary period into an act that has become progressively sapped of its punitive character.

Lethal Injection

By the end of the twentieth century, the quest for humane executions ultimately led states to adopt lethal injection as their method of execution. Oklahoma and Texas first developed the method, which eventually spread to every state with a death penalty. In the protocol developed by those first states, lethal injection consists of the introduction of three drugs, in a prescribed sequence, into the condemned person's bloodstream. The first drug, sodium thiopental, puts her to sleep, while the second and third drugs, pancuronium bromide and potassium chloride, shuts down her nervous and circulatory systems, respectively.

Like its predecessors, lethal injection was a response to the humanistic desire to protect the dignity of the offender. Unlike its predecessors, however, it eroded the retributive character of the execution ceremony. The legal wrangling over pancuronium bromide, the paralytic in the lethal injection cocktail, illustrates how.

Pancuronium bromide proved a controversial drug because it blocked movement of the body. Challenging the constitutionality of the drug, capital defendants argued that if the first drug, sodium thiopental, was insufficiently administered, the inmate might still be conscious, or quasi-conscious, when the potassium chloride, a drug known to cause excruciating, burning pain in conscious persons, was administered. Paralyzed by the pancuronium bromide, though, the inmate would be unable to express her agony. In 2008, the Court refused to order states to eliminate pancuronium bromide from their protocols, noting that the "Commonwealth has an interest in preserving the dignity of the procedure, especially where convulsions or seizures could be misperceived as signs of consciousness or distress."[63]

It is tempting to interpret the execution protocol that the Court upheld as disingenuous in its efforts to protect the dignity of the condemned; the use of the paralytic reveals a superficial attention to the appearance of dignity that comes at the cost of being able to ensure that gratuitous pain will not be inflicted on condemned

---

[63] *Baze v. Rees*, 128 S.Ct. 1520 (2008) at 1535. Justice Stevens disagreed, noting that the "drug's primary use is to prevent involuntary muscle movements, and its secondary use is to stop respiration. In my view, neither of these purposes is sufficient to justify the risk inherent in the use of the drug." The plurality's claim that the state has an interest in making the procedure dignified, he argued, was "woefully inadequate. . . . Whatever minimal interest there may be in ensuring that a condemned inmate dies a dignified death, and that witnesses to the execution are not made uncomfortable by an incorrect belief (which could easily be corrected) that the inmate is in pain, is vastly outweighed by the risk that the inmate is actually experiencing excruciating pain that no one can detect. *Baze v. Rees* 128 S.Ct. 1520 (2008) at 1544 (Stevens, Dissenting).

inmates. But the desire to use pancuronium bromide does more than simply protect witnesses from the unpleasant sight of false indications of bodily pain. It protects the integrity of the metaphysical self of the condemned person. The state's use of the paralytic makes the offender's final volitional activities, rather than involuntary movements, the last impression he leaves on the world. Because it silences the involuntary movements of the body, pancuronium bromide confers an existential finality on the words the condemned speaks and the gestures she makes prior to the injection of the sodium thiopental. The drug ensures that the final, consciously constituted impression of himself the condemned leaves on the world will not be undone by involuntary body movements.[64] Thus, while pancuronium bromide is rightly criticized as increasing the risk of a torturous execution experience for the condemned, it is important to recognize that it serves more than just a cosmetic function. By conferring a certain degree of finality onto the condemned inmate's final utterance, the drug protects the integrity of the condemned person's final moments, reflecting the broader desire, rooted in empathetic selfhood, to treat the condemned as a sacred, autonomous self.

History helps to demonstrate the dignity-protecting effects of this sort of finality. Writing about the lynching of African Americans in the late nineteenth and early twentieth centuries, Timothy V. Kaufman-Osborn notes that mobs would some-times display the mutilated corpses of lynching victims and hang signs on them, thus compelling "the body to signify long after its capacity to speak has been destroyed."[65] The severing of a person's voice from his will denies his autonomy, perversely transforming him into an expression of his own lack of self-ownership. What could negate a person's dignity more than coercing his corpse to proclaim self-mockingly that he never had it? In the lethal injection procedure developed in the late twentieth century, a diametrically opposed set of values operated. The state became invested in compelling the body to stay silent after the person's capacity to speak has been destroyed. Preventing the involuntary movements of the body, then, amplifies,

---

[64] The persistence of journalists' reports of the final meals that inmates select and the final words they speak in contemporary execution reporting is a testament to the desire that many have to relate to the condemned as a fellow human being – one who, like them, engages in both mundane activities (like eating) and sublime ones (like making meaning out of lived experi-ence). On the empathy-generating function of these rituals, see Linda Ross Meyer, "The Meaning of Death: Last Words, Last Meals," in *Who Deserves to Die: Constructing the Executable Subject*, ed. Austin Sarat and Karl Shoemaker (Amherst: University of Massachu-setts Press, 2011). The Supreme Court's insistence, in its contemporary jurisprudence, that offenders be aware of the punishment they are undergoing in order to be eligible for execution is likewise the product of a broader humanistic imperative that executions be occasions for existential reckoning. "[I]t might be said that capital punishment is imposed," Justice Anthony Kennedy wrote in a 2007 majority opinion, "because it has the potential to make the offender recognize at last the gravity of his crime." *Panetti* v. *Quarterman* 551 U.S. 930 (2007) at 958.

[65] Timothy V. Kaufman-Osborn, "Capital Punishment as Legal Lynching?" in Charles Ogletree, Jr., and Austin Sarat, *From Lynch Mobs to the Killing State: Race and the Death Penalty in America* (New York: NYU Press, 2006), 21–54, 30.

as much as possible, the ego that lies within that body, protecting its capacity to make a final statement that is, indeed, final.

Ironically, though, in its efforts to safeguard the dignity of the condemned, lethal injection ultimately upended the balance between the humanistic and the retributive functions of capital punishment. Rather than amplifying the metaphysical subject or "inner person" as the object of attention, efforts to excise the body from execution and end life as quickly as possible have produced an opposite sort of effect. The changing bodily position of the condemned at an execution over the past century offers a brief glimpse at this change: over time, inmates facing imminent death have gone from standing (hanging), to sitting (electrocution and lethal gas), to lying down (lethal injection).[66] In the name of increasing his comfort, the condemned was placed in positions that increasingly undermined a perception of him as a unique moral agent. He became, rather, a specimen or a patient. By masking the physical effects of the punitive violence visited upon the condemned person, pancuronium bromide makes it harder for onlookers to see that what is happening is punishment. Lethal injection has transformed executions into acts that resemble medical procedures. In an opinion piece protesting the hospital-like scene that surrounds the condemned being punished, for instance, legal scholar Robert Blecker writes of the disappearance of retribution in executions that follows such a transformation. Lethal injection, he argues, "conflates punishment with medicine. The condemned dies in a gurney, wrapped in white sheets with an IV in his veins, surrounded by his closest kin, monitored by sophisticated medical devices." Such symbolism is confusing, he argues: "How we kill those we rightly detest should in no way resemble how we end the suffering of those we love."[67] For death penalty advocates in the contemporary era, the eradication of pain altogether has diminished the moral clarity that had been one of the greatest virtues of capital punishment.

The discourse of pain alleviation has more subtly – yet more powerfully – diminished the retributive value of the death penalty in a different way: by silently enabling the unprecedented delays between sentencing and execution that are the most historically distinctive feature of contemporary capital punishment.

Delay

The average time between sentencing and execution began growing much longer in the 1970s. In that decade, the Supreme Court suspended executions and then oversaw an elaborate overhaul of states' sentencing procedures. As a result, federal

---

[66] Banner, *The Death Penalty*. Contemplating lethal injection in the 1950s, the British Royal Commission found hanging, in which the condemned stands, more dignified. Timothy V. Kaufman-Osborn, "The Death of Dignity," in *Is the Death Penalty Dying? European and American Perspectives*, ed. Austin Sarat and Jürgen Martschukat (Cambridge: Cambridge University Press, 2011).

[67] Robert Blecker, "With Death Penalty, Let Punishment Truly Fit the Crime," *CNN.com*, August 22, 2013, online at www.cnn.com/2013/08/22/opinion/blecker-death-penalty/ (accessed March 1, 2016).

courts became much more deeply involved in state capital cases after executions resumed in 1977. A much more rigorous, and time-consuming, process followed a capital sentence. Offenders executed in 2013, the latest year for which data are available, had spent an average of fifteen and a half years on death row.[68] In the contemporary era, delay is inevitable, but execution is not. The vast majority of those sentenced to death since the 1970s have not been executed; their convictions or sentences have been overturned in response to appellate scrutiny, they have died on death row of other causes, or they are still waiting for their execution dates to be set.[69]

The delays that developed in appellate reviews of capital cases have their ultimate origin in the rise of empathetic selfhood. Seeking to create greater consistency in juries' determinations of which capital defendants deserve to die, the Court nonetheless rejected sentencing statutes that made the death penalty automatic upon conviction of a capital crime.[70] Juries, the Court insisted, needed to be able to judge each defendant individually. It was only after empathetically considering the potentially mitigating experiences the defendant has had in life and their effect on his psyche, the Court held, that the ascription of moral blameworthiness that a death sentence requires could be reliable and the sentence just.[71] A body could be subjected to punishment not just for the damage it had caused, but for the nature of the inner person who inhabited it. That the nature of that person could be excavated through courtroom testimony and then evaluated by a jury was a premise made possible by the emergence of empathetic selfhood.

This new set of legal regulations, developed in the Court's 1970s jurisprudence, enabled the delays that now followed a death sentence. Whereas the decision to sentence a defendant to death was left to the unfettered and unreviewable discretion of juries before that decade, it was now the subject of statutory regulation, greatly multiplying the issues appellate attorneys could raise on behalf of their clients. The slow-moving nature of this brave new world quickly became apparent after the resumption of executions in 1977. In 1981, Supreme Court Justice William Rehnquist wrote with disgust of the fact that, five years after the Supreme Court had reauthorized the use of capital punishment in the United States, delays at the appellate level had created a situation in which "the existence of the death penalty is virtually an illusion."[72] Only one involuntary execution had been carried out, Rehnquist noted. "Perhaps out of a desire to avoid even the possibility of a 'Bloody Assizes,' this Court and the lower federal courts have converted the constitutional

---

[68] "Capital Punishment, 2013 – Statistical Tables," Bureau of Justice Statistics, U.S. Department of Justice (Washington, D.C.), 2014. Online at www.bjs.gov/content/pub/pdf/cp13st.pdf (accessed June 3, 2016).

[69] "Capital Punishment 2013."

[70] *Woodson et al.* v. *North Carolina* 428 U.S. 280 (1976).

[71] *Gregg* v. *Georgia* 428 U.S. 153 (1976).

[72] *Coleman* v. *Balkcom*, 451 U.S. 949 at 958 (Rehnquist, Dissenting).

limits upon imposition of the death penalty by the States and the Federal Government into arcane niceties which parallel the equity court practices described in
Charles Dickens' 'Bleak House.'"[73] Rehnquist described the consequences of delay.
The constitutionally recognized purposes of retribution and deterrence were diminished as jurists had "lost sight of the equally important objective of enabling the
government to control the governed."[74]

Delay, both opponents and proponents of the death penalty seem to agree,
diminishes, if not destroys, the retributive effect of an execution. In a 2014 federal
court ruling in California, later overturned, a federal judge found that the delays in
California had become so inordinate that the death penalty had lost all penological
purpose and become unconstitutional. In *Jones* v. *Chappell*, Federal District Court
Judge Cormac J. Carney held that given the state's failure to execute anyone in
nearly a decade, a death sentence in California had become, effectively, a sentence
of "life imprisonment with the remote possibility of death."[75] The death penalty, he
found, could no longer be justified as a retributive sanction. Carney wrote,

> In California, a Death Row inmate will likely wait at least 25 years before his
> execution becomes even a realistic possibility. Were such lengthy delay an isolated,
> or even necessary, circumstance of a system that otherwise acts purposefully to give
> meaning to society's moral outrage, the retributive purpose of the death penalty
> might continue to be served. Here, however, the delay is systemic, and the State
> itself is to blame. The State has allowed such dysfunction to creep into its death
> penalty system that the few executions it does carry out are arbitrary. Whereas few
> have been or will eventually be executed by California, the vast majority of
> individuals sentenced to death – each of whom, in the State's view, committed
> crimes sufficiently reprehensible to warrant death – will effectively serve out terms
> of life imprisonment.[76]

While Carney's ruling was ultimately overturned on procedural grounds by the
United States Court of Appeals for the Ninth Circuit, the ruling called attention to
the systemic failure of the death penalty to deliver finality, or "closure" in the
nomenclature of the victims' rights movement, in capital cases.

Judge Carney's decision overturning the death penalty in California was not the
first effort made by defense attorneys to argue that delay rendered the punishment of
death unconstitutional. Prior to *Jones*, courts had failed to recognize the psychological anxiety of waiting for one's sentence to be carried out as a legally cognizable
form of punitive pain. In 1995, lawyers in Texas launched the first major, albeit
unsuccessful challenge to the constitutionality of capital punishment based on the
psychological pain of delay. Attorneys for Clarence Lackey argued that he had been

[73] Ibid.
[74] Ibid. at 962.
[75] *Jones v. Chappell*, 31 F.Supp.3d 1050 (2014) at 1053.
[76] Ibid. at 1065.

on death row for nearly two decades and that such a delay, because it was largely attributable to the dilatory behavior of the state, made death a cruel and unusual punishment. The briefs filed in the case were consumed with how to properly cognize the anxiety of waiting. Without conceding that the suffering of living under a sentence of death was part of his punishment, the state carefully parsed Lackey's time on death row. State attorneys disagreed with defense counsel's contention that Lackey's psychological pain should be calculated (if it had to be calculated at all) from the time of the imposition of his first death sentence in 1978. "[H]is first conviction and death sentence was reversed, resulting in a new trial at which Lackey was presumed [innocent] of the crime and not under any sentence. His current death sentence was not assessed until April of 1983," prosecutors argued to the Court.[77] It then added that the formalized setting of the execution date, not the date of sentencing, was relevant in determining the time Lackey had spent under the stress of awaiting execution. "[N]o execution date was set until after Lackey's second conviction was affirmed in April of 1992...therefore Lackey has spent less than three years with a pending execution," the state argued.[78] In Lackey's case, and in others like it, courts have sided with the state, refusing to recognize the pain of awaiting death as a cruel or unusual form of punishment. Indeed, aside from *Jones*, which was subsequently overturned, claims rooted in undue delay have gotten little traction in federal and state Courts, despite some notable and potentially promising language in dissents old and recent.[79]

Why have courts not seen the psychological pain resulting from long stays on death row a disproportionately harsh punishment banned by the Eighth Amendment? The legalistic idea that the suffering of awaiting execution was not holistic but turned "on" and "off" or "reset" at various points in Lackey's decades of trials and appeals,

---

[77] Respondent's Brief in Opposition and Opposition to Motion for Stay of Execution, *Lackey* v. *Texas*, WL 17904099 (1995) at 18.

[78] Ibid.

[79] In *Coleman* v. *Balkcom* (1981), Justice John Paul Stevens argued that the Court failed to take seriously the period of waiting as a constitutive part of the punishment. He wrote, "The deterrent value of any punishment is, of course, related to the promptness with which it is inflicted. In capital cases, however, the punishment is inflicted in two stages. Imprisonment follows immediately after conviction; but the execution normally does not take place until after the conclusion of post-trial proceedings...However critical one may be of these protracted post-trial procedures, it seems inevitable that there must be a significant period of incarceration on death row during the interval between sentencing and execution. If the death sentence is ultimately set aside or its execution delayed for a prolonged period, the imprisonment during that period is nevertheless a significant form of punishment. Indeed, the deterrent value of incarceration during that period of uncertainty may well be comparable to the consequences of the ultimate step itself." *Coleman* v. *Balkcom*, 451 U.S. 949 at 952 (Stevens, Concurring). More recently, the issue has been raised in the dissents of Justices Breyer and Stevens in *Thompson* v. *McNeil*, 129 S. Ct. 1299 and the questions of Justice Kennedy in the oral arguments of *Hall* v. *Florida*, available at www.oyez.org/cases/2013/12-10882 (Accessed March 1, 2016). Cited in "Time on Death Row," The Death Penalty Information Center. Available at http://www.deathpenaltyinfo.org/time-death-row (Accessed March 1, 2016).

we have seen, is one rather arcane reason. Animus toward capital defendants is another. In some rhetoric against Lackey claims, defendants are portrayed as cunning manipulators who create delays in an effort to "run down the clock," claiming – after having wasted so much time with frivolous appeals – to have suffered from waiting.[80]

But the rise of empathetic selfhood and its transformation of executions into occasions for the collective contemplation of the psyche of the condemned offer crucial context for Courts' refusals to hear *Lackey* claims. At first glance, it is easy to miss the role that empathy for the condemned has played in the failure of these claims. Our conventional understandings of empathy push us to think of it as an emotion that would *help* defendants making such claims; just as the movement against solitary confinement has been galvanized by members of the public (and, increasingly, penal elites[81]) who shudder as they imagine being locked in a small box without human contact for a small period of time, we might expect a similar response to the news that death row inmates wait for decades with death sentences hanging over their heads. And no doubt, empathy does have this effect for many potential abolitionists on or off the bench. But if we adopt a more critical understanding of empathy, as an emotion that can exploit its object as well as benefit it – we can see how empathetic selfhood is also a culprit in the devaluation of psychological pain, allowing capital defendants to languish on death row in legal limbo for decades.

As we have seen, one of the legacies of the rise of empathetic selfhood was the expectation that the condemned, free from physical pain, could take observers with them to the brink of death. The desire to inhabit the psyche of the condemned in "eternity's reception hall," as one reporter from *The Atlanta Constitution* memorably described the execution chamber in the melodramatic coverage of the 1920s,[82] helped to limit how we perceive the mental suffering of the condemned. The fantasy of meeting death courageously required a physically painless execution. But it has also required a willful refusal to see the psychological pain of awaiting death as crippling; mental pain cannot be understood to have the equivalence to intense physical pain, to be overwhelmingly debilitating, paralyzing, and consciousness-occupying. The public's capacity to connect with the condemned, to vicariously inhabit his confrontation with mortality or witness a kind of self-reckoning, would be endangered if we accepted that the mental anxiety of awaiting execution produces, as some studies suggest, a dissolution of the self. The intensity of our efforts to reduce physical pain has inflated not only our focus on the psyche of

---

[80] See, e.g., *Thompson v. McNeil*, 556 U.S. 1114 (2009) (Thomas, concurring in denial of certiorari).

[81] See Rick Raemisch, "My Night in Solitary," *New York Times*, February 20, 2014.

[82] Whitner Cary, "With Plea for Life of Wife, Thompson Goes to His Death," *Atlanta Constitution*, August 4, 1928.

the condemned, but also our estimation of his mental strength and integrity under extreme circumstances.

Had they been successful, *Lackey* claims might have rendered unconstitutional the immense delays which now characterize the appellate reviews of capital cases in the United States, potentially striking a fatal blow to the constitutionality of the death penalty. But they were made in a culture that has long conflated protecting the integrity of the body with safeguarding the autonomy of the metaphysical person who resided within that body. Thus, lengthy delays between sentencing and execution, which involve little pain to the body but much psychological pain, have evaded judicial scrutiny. This blindness to mental suffering is ironically the legacy of the rise of empathetic selfhood. Extended appellate reviews express a greater sensitivity to the importance of the individual psyche of the condemned inmate, yet they impute an integrity onto that psyche that is ultimately devastating to it. An assumption that the condemned is an autonomous self – celebrated, as we have seen, in empathy-inviting execution narratives – contributes to an unfounded faith in his capacity to resist the debilitating effects of living under a death sentence.

The delays that now characterize the administration of death in the United States have sapped the punishment of its retributive character. The vast minority of condemned inmates who are executed today receive their punishment over a decade – and sometimes over two decades – after they committed their crime.[83] For those not related to the victims, the memory of the crime has faded, and the retributive impact of the punishment is consequently tempered by the emotional distance time has created between the crime and the punishment. For relatives and friends of the victims of capital murder, meanwhile, the long wait for an execution hinders the healing process.[84] Those whose loved ones' killers received death sentences become caught in purgatory as Courts review the sentence, making it difficult to find the closure that proponents of the death penalty have argued can only be delivered by the death of the offender. For both the public and those directly impacted by a capital crime, the retributive promise of the death penalty has lost its credibility.

CONCLUSION

I have argued that the rise of empathetic selfhood during the Enlightenment introduced a new, humanistic function to capital punishment. In addition to fulfilling their long-standing, retributive function as occasions for reasserting the vitality of a society's dominant collective conscience, executions became occasions

[83] "Capital Punishment 2013."

[84] A study of the family members of homicide victims in Texas found that the appeals process generated "layers of injustice, powerlessness, and in some instances, despair." Marilyn Peterson Armour and Mark S. Umbreit, "Assessing the Impact of the Ultimate Penal Sanction on Homicide Survivors: A Two State Comparison," *Marquette Law Review* 96 (2012), 1–131, 98.

for the collective contemplation of how individuals face death in a secularizing age. For the better part of the past two hundred and fifty years, the changes wrought by empathy – the development of new kinds of killing technologies like the electric chair or the gas chamber, the production of empathy-inviting narratives about some of the more "relatable" victims of state killing – did not pose a threat to the fundamentally retributive character of most executions. In the late twentieth century, however, innovations ultimately derived from the rise of empathetic selfhood and its discourse of human rights began to undermine the retributive function of the American death penalty: the medicalization of the execution method and the unprecedented growth of the average amount of time a condemned inmate spends on death row.

Indeed, one of the more compelling theories explaining the tendency toward moderation in penal harshness in recent years is a story of failed returns: a strong will to degrade consigned massive quantities of people to a technocratic penal system charged with warehousing them, often for the rest of their lives. Punishment, as a result, became so consumed with managing risk that it lost its symbolic and expressive functions. Invoking Erving Goffman's concept of "mortification," the loss of an autonomous self that happens in institutions like mental hospitals, Patricia Ewick has argued that the proliferation of life without parole sentences has mortified the subjects of punishment in Americans' punitive imagination.[85] While in previous eras, mortification was a necessary prelude to a personal transformation that marked the violence of the state as regenerative in a way that lawless violence was not,[86] "[i]n a regime of total incapacitation," Ewick argues, "where there is no possibility of redemption or rehabilitation and, increasingly, no possibility of release, there is simply no way to end this story of punishment. The harsh logic of contemporary punishment denies itself the possibility of moral closure and thus, the possibility of meaning."[87] Meaninglessness, she argues, has become the by-product of the expansion of life without parole sentences over the course of the last forty years, and it may explain why Americans have, at least to a certain extent, fallen out of love with harsh punishment over the past few years. Ewick's broader explanation for the recent decline in penal harshness is particularly apt in explaining the flagging support for capital punishment. The thoroughness of appellate reviews and the delays that the modern system of super due process creates in capital cases have blunted the retributive impact of executions. Anger about a particular crime fades over the years. If and when they do appear in the execution chamber over a decade after their sentence, offenders rarely resemble the loathed folk devils who had

---

[85] Erving Goffman, *Asylums: Essays on the Social Situation of Mental Patients and Other Inmates* (Garden City, N: Anchor, 1961).

[86] Caleb Smith, *The Prison and the American Imagination* (New Haven, CT: Yale University Press, 2009).

[87] Patricia Ewick, "The Return of Restraint: Limits to the Punishing State," *Quinnipiac Law Review* 31 (2013), 577–597, 579.

originally been sentenced to death. And the consequence they receive there, an injection that appears to put them to sleep, makes it harder to see that what is happening to them is punishment.

Capital punishment, as Corinna Lain has written elsewhere in this volume, is indeed collapsing under its own weight. That weight, importantly, is not only an artifact of the Court's contemporary jurisprudence. Its cultural roots are much deeper, reaching ultimately into the very foundations of modern ways of living – and dying.

Afterword

Death and the State

Jenny Carroll

INTRODUCTION

The contributions in this book lend a multifaceted analysis to a topic that long has been a darling and a conundrum of legal scholars and practitioners alike:[1] where precisely does the death penalty fit into the larger jurisprudence of justice and punishment? The question might be asked in different ways: What role does the death penalty play in shaping both our system and our concepts of punishment or justice? Is that role still valuable? Or has the pursuit of this ultimate punishment left us, as a society, perpetually strung up between the possibilities of getting it wrong – meting out the punishment unjustly, arbitrarily, unconstitutionally, or to the innocent – and failing to punish enough to deter crime and to restore social order?

Contributors offer different perspectives on these questions. Professor Medwed argues that like many hard-won prizes, prosecutors who have obtained a death penalty in cases continue to advocate for and to justify that sentence even in the face of post-conviction evidence of innocence.[2] Professor Hessick notes in her contribution that while the Supreme Court has suggested the possibility of review in some juvenile cases for life without parole sentences, no such proposal has surfaced for adult death penalty cases.[3] Both contributions acknowledge that there is a sort of special finality in death that renders this type of reconsideration abhorrent and contrary to the ethos of the sentence itself. The death penalty's purposes of

---

[1] A Westlaw search of Law Reviews and Journals for the phrase "death penalty" yields nearly 10,000 results. A similar search of the Library of Congress online index for the phrase "death penalty united states" yields over 5,000 results.

[2] Daniel Medwed, "Grand Finality: Post Conviction Prosecutors and the Defense of Death," in *Final Judgments: The Death Penalty and American Law*, ed. Austin D. Sarat (Cambridge: Cambridge University Press, 2016).

[3] Carissa Byrne Hessick, "Finality and the Capital/Non-Capital Punishment Divide," in *Final Judgments: The Death Penalty and American Law*, ed. Austin D. Sarat (Cambridge: Cambridge University Press, 2016).

maintaining social order by deterring crime and punishing the most wicked would seem to be undone by the possibility that the death penalty might have been imposed improperly or be overturned years after its imposition. Professor Lain concludes that while the cost of allegiance to the death penalty is astronomical, states seem reluctant to abandon this ultimate punishment.[4] This allegiance is not new, as Professor LaChance explains – citizens have long gathered to witness the horrible spectacle of the punishment[5] – suggesting as Professors Lain and Medwed note that there is some value or vindication that a community grounds in the death penalty regardless of the cost – monetary or otherwise.[6] Professor Culbert concludes that such an assessment of value is consistent with our calculation of punishment as time, with the death penalty providing the end of that calculation literally and figuratively.[7]

Each of these contributions, in their nuance and difference, focus on facets of the underlying premise that the death penalty in all its finality is different than all other forms of punishment or even State action.[8] In reviewing the contributions I am left to wonder about that difference itself. This essay seeks to explore, and at times to push back on, this notion that death, or more accurately the death penalty, is in fact "different." I do not mean to suggest that the legal system and citizens alike do not treat this punishment as "different" or that such treatment is improper.[9] But I do mean to question whether, in our efforts to distinguish, differentiate, and justify this punishment, we have overlooked a much starker reality – that the death penalty is different not for its finality or its status as a state-sanctioned homicide, but that it is different because it is afforded far more attention and procedural protections than other state-sanctioned deaths. Citizens die when they are shot by police officers, or as a result of losing health or nutrition assistance. Citizens die in car accidents that would have been preventable with lower speed limits, or in prisons because they

[4] Corinna Lain, "Following Finality: Why Capital Punishment is Collapsing under Its Own Weight," in *Final Judgments: The Death Penalty and American Law*, ed. Austin D. Sarat (Cambridge: Cambridge University Press, 2016).

[5] Daniel LaChance, "'They Do Not Move': Capital Punishment in an Age of Super Due Process," in *Final Judgments: The Death Penalty and American Law*, ed. Austin D. Sarat (Cambridge: Cambridge University Press, 2016).

[6] Lain, "Following Finality" and Medwed, "Grand Finality."

[7] Jennifer Culbert "Final Judgments," in *Final Judgments: The Death Penalty and American Law*, ed. Austin D. Sarat (Cambridge: Cambridge University Press, 2016).

[8] The notion that "Death is different" has permeated modern death penalty debate. Justice Brennan is credited with first using the phrase in his concurrence in *Furman v. Georgia*. 408 U.S. 238, 286 (1972) (Brennan, J. concurring) ("Death is a unique punishment in the United States."). *See also* Carol S. Steiker and Jordan M. Steiker, "Sober Second Thoughts: Reflections on Two Decades of Constitutional Regulation of Capital Punishment," 109 *Harvard Law Review* 355 (1995): 370.

[9] Professor Steiker explains that the importance of continuing to differentiate the death penalty from other types of murders or deaths. Carol S. Steiker, "No, Capital Punishment Is Not Morally Required: Deterrence, Deontology, and the Death Penalty," 55 *Stanford Law Review* 751 (2005): 751.

could not get access to their medication. Citizens die at the hands and in the hands of State actors with regularity,[10] but only a select few seem to have captured and held our collective attention like the death penalty.[11] Only capital punishment has suffered the elaborate procedural and substantive legal constructs designed to ensure an ever-illusive fairness[12] and to preserve our collective humanity as we deny the humanity of the condemned.[13] Why?

Perhaps – as the contributors to this book suggest – the death penalty matters and deserves our attention not just because it produces a death, but also because the very death it produces holds layers of purpose and meaning. As a punishment, the death penalty signals our collective condemnation of the convicted,[14] but as a policy it speaks to our aspirations for our own crime-free future.[15] It looks forwards and backwards at the same time, imagining both what was – the murder, trial, and sentence – and what could be – a world with fewer crimes and victims. There is surely something to this.

Scholars, courts, legislators, and citizens have long described capital punishment as the ultimate deterrent and punishment rolled into one neat package.[16] It is a

---

[10] It is difficult to gather exact numbers for individuals killed by state actors or who die while in the custody of state actors, but some limited data are available. In 2015, the *Washington Post* created a national database to track fatal police shootings. Based on the information they gathered on December 24, 2015, they estimated there were 965 fatal shootings by police in 2015. Of those victims, 564 were armed with a gun, 281 were armed with another weapon, and 90 were unarmed. *See* Kimberly Kindy, Marc Fisher, Julie Tate, and Jennifer Jenkins, "A Year of Reckoning: Police Fatally Shoot Nearly 1,000," *Washington Post*, December 24, 2015. Other sources place the fatal police shootings slightly higher. *See, e.g.*, Jon Swaine and Oliver Laughland, "Number of People Killed by U.S. Police in 2015 at 1,000 after Oakland Shooting," *The Guardian*, November 16, 2015 (estimating the rate of fatal police shootings to be 3.1 per day in 2015). The Department of Justice tracks data for deaths in custody, but the latest data available online were for 2013 and not all categories were so up to date (for example, data on deaths while in custody at juvenile facilities were only available through 2007). *See* www.bjs.gov/index.cfm?ty=dcdetail&iid=243.
[11] In contrast, only 28 people were executed in 2015. *See* www.deathpenaltyinfo.org/executions-year.
[12] As Justice Blackmun noted in his dissent in the denial of certiorari in *Callins v. Collins*, the death penalty was irredeemable. He wrote: "It is virtually self evident to me that no combination of procedural rules or substantive regulations ever can save the death penalty from its inherent constitutional deficiencies." 501 U.S. 1141, 1145 (1994) (Blackmun, J. dissenting).
[13] J. Brennan, *Furman v. Georgia*, 408 U.S. 238, 290 (1972). Justice Brennan noted that "[t]he calculated killing of a human being by the State involves, by its very nature, a denial of the executed persons' humanity...the finality of death precludes relief. An executed person has indeed 'lost the right to have rights.'"
[14] Alice Ristroph, "Desert, Democracy, and Sentencing Reform," 96 *Journal of Criminal Law and Criminology* 1293 (2006): 1306 (noting that the death penalty is commonly justified by linking culpability with the punishment).
[15] Sara Colón, "Capital Crime: How California's Administration of the Death Penalty Violates the Eighth Amendment," 96 *California Law Review* 1377 (2009): 1377 (noting that theories of deterrence and incapacitation are widely used to justify the death penalty).
[16] For a variety of views on this issue *see* Michael L. Radelet and Traci L. Lacock, "Do Executions Lower Homicide Rates?: The Views of Leading Criminologists," 99 *Journal of Criminal Law*

promise to rid the whole of the worst of the worst while discouraging future actors from following a similar, diabolical path.[17] Whatever controversy may attach to this description, it seems to persist and survive, suggesting some fidelity of belief that sustains it.[18] This allegiance, or faith, that the death penalty both deters and properly punishes allows it to survive and even to remain popular in certain quarters despite death row exonerations and evidence of bias or rehabilitation.[19]

While this perspective has been long visited, the contributions in this book stretch beyond a new exploration of this "old" ideal of the death penalty. It seems there is a larger message at play, present just beneath the surface of the chapters of this book. In this final essay, I suggest that we need to take a metaphorical step back and look not only at the death penalty but at all death imposed by the State, and thereby to question the boundaries of when we as a community allow the State to take mortal action in our collective name. In this it is not the death penalty that is different; it is state-imposed death that is different.

The death penalty has long been labelled as different, but this identification obscures the underlying and, because we are talking about law, infinitely more complex, reality that death is different when imposed as a punishment.[20] Death itself is, after all, one of the few inevitabilities we can count on (the other apparently being

---

    and Criminology 489 (2009): 489 (questioning the deterrent value of the death penalty) and Cass Sunstein and Adrian Vermeule, "Is Capital Punsihment Morally Required? Acts, Omissions, and Life-Life Trade Offs," 58 *Stanford Law Review* 703 (2005): 705 and 711 (arguing that the deterrent effect of the death penalty not only justifies the punishment but renders the punishment a moral necessity).

[17] *Gregg* v. *Georgia*, 428 U.S. 153, 185–86 (1976) (noting that deterrent effect of the death penalty as a justification for the punishment); Paul Robinson and John Darley, "The Utility of Desert," 91 *Northwestern Law Review* 453 (1997): 454–55 (discussing deterrence as a utilitarian justification for the death penalty).

[18] While many argue that the death penalty in fact accomplishes its deterrent goals, *see, e.g.,* H. Naci Mocan and R. Kaj Gittings, "Getting Off Death Row: Commuted Sentences and the Deterrent Effect of Capital Punishment," 46 *Journal of Law and Economics* 456 (2003): 474 (stating that "[e]ach additional execution decreases homicides by about 5, and each additional commutation increases homicides by the same amount."); Paul H. Rubin, "Death Penalty Deters Scores of Killings," *Atlanta Journal Constitution* (2002): 22A (claiming that the death penalty deters 18 homicides annually); William J. Bowers and Glenn L. Pierce, "Deterrence or Brutalization: What Is the Effect of Executions?," 26 *Crime and Delinquency* 453 (1980): 481–84 (finding an increase in homicides in New York state in months following executions), others criticize such studies as failing to accurately such deterrent claims, while acknowledging that the deterrent narrative remains strong among death penalty proponents, *see, e.g.,* Radelet and Lacock, "Do Executions Lower Homicide Rates?" at 490–92 (2009) (criticizing previous studies that claim a deterrent effect, but acknowledging that deterrence remains a strong basis of support for the death penalty among citizens) and John J. Donohue and Justin Wolfers, "Uses and Abuses of Empirical Evidence in the Death Penalty Debate," 58 *Stanford Law Review* 791 (2005).

[19] Sunstein and Vermeule go so far as to argue that it is a moral imperative. *See* Sunstein and Vermeule, "Is Capital Punishment Morally Required?," at 711 and Cass R. Sunstein and Adrian Vermeule, "Deterring Murder: A Reply," 58 *Stanford Law Review* (2005): 847.

[20] *See* Steiker, "No, Capital Punishment Is Not Morally Required" at 756–63.

taxes).[21] As E. B. White's iconic character Charlotte notes, "[a]fterall what is life? We're born, we live a little while, and we die."[22] But when the State, in the name of justice or retribution or morality, claims a life, the moment is noted and observed in ways different from the ordinary and inevitable end of life. There is a machinery and process to a death imposed by the State at a designated hour that eludes other more spontaneous passings. In this, the death penalty claims a significance that eludes other deaths, including those caused or furthered by State actions. The imposition of the death penalty is, at least in its modern incarnation, a reasoned and reviewed decision with layer after layer of review.[23] This review is subject to advocacy, is often broad in its scope,[24] and is costly in its slow, winding toward punishment.[25] As such the decision to execute is not the impulsive or quick decision of a single actor or the product of a natural demise. It is not based on one individual's sense of justice or morality or proper procedure. Rather it is a product of many views and voices, all of which come to a single and final conclusion – this crime, this person, deserves the ultimate punishment, and we as a society benefit from that decision.

In this essay I want to suggest that this view, while not wholly wrong, is also not wholly "right." It too easily cabins the penalty as unique from all other State actions that produce a death. It shrouds the death penalty with a rarefied status while overlooking other systematic decisions that result in State-sanctioned and -imposed death. Each such death – whether resulting from the death penalty or by other state action – carries a weight that deserves our attention and process. Our system produces death in a variety of ways as it seeks to define justice and order; the death penalty is only one such way.

WHY SO MUCH PROCESS FOR THE DEATH PENALTY?

As a practical matter the death of any citizen at the hands of the State is constant in its biological determinism. Life ceases often as result of a variety of factors culminating in the body's failure. No matter who we are or how virtuous a life we lead, in the

---

[21] This quote is often attributed to Benjamin Franklin who wrote in a 1789 letter "Our new Constitution is now established, and has an appearance that promises permanency; but in this world nothing can be said to be certain, except death and taxes," but it seems this was a popular sentiment at the time as the *Yale Book of Quotations* attributes it to both Christopher Bullock in *The Cobler of Preston* (1716) ("It is impossible to be sure of anything but Death and Taxes.") and Edward Ward in *The Dancing Devils* (1724) ("Death and taxes, they are certain."). Fred R. Shapiro, ed. *The Yale Book of Quotations* (New Haven: Yale University Press, 2006).

[22] E. B. White, *Charlotte's Web* (New York: Harper Collins, 1952) at 258.

[23] Steiker, "No, Capital Punishment Is Not Morally Required" at 757 and Rachel E. Barkow, "The Court of Life and Death: Two Tracks of Constitutional Sentencing Law and the Case for Uniformity," 107 *Michigan Law Review* 1145 (2009): 1145–46.

[24] Though as Professors Medwed and Hessick note frequently the review is neither broad nor thorough enough. Medwed, "Grand Finality" at 90 and Hessick "Finality and the Capital/Non-Capital Divide" at 9.

[25] *See* Culbert, "Final Judgments" at 157 (noting the temporal aspect to this sentencing and review process) and Lain, "Following Finality" (noting the monetary costs of such review processes).

end, Charlotte is right. We die. Within this broad reality of death, a sub-category of deaths exists – those that are the product of State decisions. Sub-grade steel is bought to save money on bridge construction or repair; when it collapses, people die.[26] Funding for social welfare programs are cut to balance the budget; people who lose their food, housing, or health care die.[27] A treaty is negotiated that redraws a boundary or ensconces a government, and in the unrest that follows people die. Arguably any decision imaginable contemplates the harm it might produce. Just as death is inevitable, therefore, so is death by State fiat.

But on some level the death penalty *is* different. Unlike its brethren State-promulgated demises, it is not the product of a split-second, them-or-me style decision or a weighing of long-term benefit and harm. It is the product of overlapping layers of discretion and review by fellow citizens, each occupying unique spaces that converge only around the decision of whether or not some particular individual deserves to die as a function of law.

Discretion and the Penalty

All decisions regarding whether or not to impose and carry out the death penalty rely on some degree of discretion.[28] Early decisions are made with a particular case, a particular victim or victims, in mind. Police are the first "boots on the ground" decision points, and so the first exercise of discretion. Police investigate the death or deaths with its inevitable and grisly tableau of violence and horror.[29] They compartmentalize the evidence they recover and turn their focus to a suspect or suspects. Once the case is established sufficiently, they refer it to prosecutors.

Depending on the jurisdiction, the police themselves may make a charging recommendation to the prosecutors – a plea from the streets that for all the violence they see in their daily job, this crime stands alone, is exceptional, and deserves the "ultimate" punishment. In other jurisdictions the police make no such recommendation, but in reviewing their reports, the prosecutor may find the same claims and normative judgments that this crime not only meets the legislature's definition of death eligible, but warrants capital prosecution.

---

[26] "Tennessee Is Faulted in Collapse of Bridge," *New York Times*, June 5, 1990, www.nytimes.com/1990/06/06/us/tennessee-is-faulted-in-collapse-of-bridge.html (noting that the NTSB faulted Tennessee for failing to properly repair the Hatchie River Bridge, which resulted in its collapse killing eight people).

[27] Peter Dreiger, "Reagan's Real Legacy," *The Nation*, February 2, 2011 (arguing that President Reagan's policies of deregulation and reduced social welfare programs had catastrophic effects on the poor and marginalized in the United States).

[28] In *Gregg v. Georgia*, the Court found "discretion guided" death penalty statutes to be constitutionally permissible, ending the temporary halt of the death penalty after *Furman v. Georgia*. 428 U.S 153, 195 (1976).

[29] After the Supreme Court's decision in *Kennedy v. Louisiana*, only murders may be punished by death. 554 U.S. 407, 412 (2008).

For their part, prosecutors review the case and make charging decisions. In sifting through the evidence the police have amassed, weighing each case with its lingering proof problems and its competing mitigating and aggravating factors, prosecutors ultimately decide whether or not to pursue a death penalty. The calculation, in theory at least, is somewhat unique in executive decision-making – the law requiring that the prosecutor look forward and backward. The decision imagines "this crime" on the continuum of all crimes that have been and will be committed. It is impossible and paradoxical from the outset.[30]

Before the police or prosecutors engage in such decision making, the legislature designates particular crimes as death eligible and particular "aggravating factors" as a prerequisite to establish that this crime or defendant is indeed different from all others and so deserves a different punishment.[31] While the Supreme Court has held that only murders may receive the death penalty,[32] and only certain defendants are eligible in our modern death penalty era,[33] states enjoy a significant amount of leeway to name particular aggravators as qualifying for death. These designations, like all laws, are imperfect and incomplete from the moment they are set to paper. They are, by their nature, constructed in advance of the scenarios to which they will eventually be applied as best guesses of what the future might hold. They are static as a construct and must rely on the executive branch to exercise its discretion, asking the horrible but necessary question – is this the case the law has waited for? Is it truly the worst of the worst? Will the community and the world be better for the defendant's death?

This discretion serves a critical role – it seeks to match the law's articulated purpose with the community's expectations. But like all discretionary decisions it is also fraught with risk. By its very nature it seeks to situate the considered case in the context of all the cases that have come before it and all those that will come in the future. It seeks to weigh tangible, real facts – a person or people are dead, likely in the course of suffering or witnessing another crime – and less tangible facts – the

---

[30] All this leaves one to wonder whether the fraught decision, once made, is difficult to abandon as Prof. Medwed suggests, even in the face of evidence that the decision was ultimately "wrong."

[31] See *Ring v. Arizona*, 536 U.S. 584, 589, 604, 606–07 (2002) (overturning *Walton* and requiring aggravating factors be found beyond a reasonable doubt); *Walton v. Arizona*, 497 U.S. 639, at 659 (1990) (Scalia, J., concurring) (requiring that aggravating factors be found before a death penalty can be imposed); see also *Godfrey v. Georgia*, 446 U.S. 420, 428 (1980) (requiring clear and objective standards for imposing the death penalty); *Gregg v. Georgia*, 428 U.S. 153, 189 (1976) (plurality opinion) (approving of new capital sentencing scheme because it constrained discretion by requiring a finding of aggravators). Aggravating factors can be offset by mitigating factors which sentencers must also be allowed to consider. See *Eddings v. Oklahoma*, 455 U.S. 104, 110 (1982).

[32] *Kennedy v. Louisiana*, 554 U.S. 407, 412 (2008).

[33] *Atkins v. Virginia*, 536 U.S. 304 (2002) (holding that severely developmentally delayed individuals may not be executed); *Roper v. Simmons*, 534 U.S. 551 (2005) (holding defendants may not be executed for crimes committed while a juvenile).

crime was especially heinous or cruel, the victim or victims had a "special" status (for example, they were a child or elderly or a police officer). And it seeks to weigh the community's current reaction – the shock, outrage, and fear that accompanies violent crime – with the community's more distant reaction – the local versus global, the recent memory versus the wisdom of retrospection. In each of these balances the calculus is imprecise, a reasoned estimation. The legislative, executive, and citizenry accept this imprecision in part because that is, after all, the nature of discretionary decisions, but also because the decision is made in the context of once and future review.

From the beginning, like all criminal cases, the filing of a charge does not produce a conviction. The trial judge makes a series of decisions that provide procedural protection to the defendant while seeking to ensure a fair trial and through it a just result. From restrictions on jury selection to evidentiary rulings and beyond, trial courts daily engage in a series of planned and unplanned decisions that can influence the outcome of a particular trial. In this, the prosecutor's discretion and the legislature's designation meet the first level of review of "outside" review and check. In the universe of these judicial decisions and restrictions, the jury itself weighs the evidence presented and then deliberates alone over the proper verdict and potential sentence. In the course of their deliberation, the jury brings a unique perspective, weighing the facts of the case, the law, and their own sense of the world as members of the very community where the crime allegedly occurred.[34]

Once rendered, the jury's verdict (if guilty) is reviewed by the trial judge and subject to overturn. And if the verdict is guilt, the judge then sentences the defendant – either with the benefit of jury recommendation or without – injecting still another level of review and discretion into the process. Finally, the appellate review process commences through state and federal courts. As Professors Lain and Hessick note, this process is both similar to other appellate review process and unique.[35] It is lengthy and costly. One may certainly debate the sincerity or effectiveness of this review process (as Professors Hessick and Medwed admirably do); trial judges may defer to prosecutors, appellate courts to lower courts, prosecutors even in the face of evidence of innocence may endorse previous errors – the list goes on, all raising a spectre that the appellate review process is illusory, yet its very existence offers some comfort in the face of the potential arbitrariness of discretion or legislative error or judicial failure.[36] At least from a procedural perspective, the death penalty is indeed a different type of death.

---

[34] Jenny E. Carroll, "Nullification as Law," 100 *Georgetown Law Journal* 579 (2014): 602.
[35] Lain, "Following Finality" and Hessick, "Finality and the Capital/Non-Capital Punishment Divide."
[36] Medwed, "Grand Finality" at 90 and Hessick, "Finality and the Capital/Non-Capital Divide" at 9.

The Constitution and the Penalty

Constitutionally, the death penalty enjoys a particular status as well. The Eighth Amendment, with its prohibition of cruel and unusual punishment, creates a substantive imperative around which process is developed. This imperative binds all government actors to seek to maintain "fair" standards of punishment in the face of shifting social expectations around that standard.[37] While the Eighth Amendment applies globally to all "punishments," this struggle to avoid the cruel and unusual has driven the Court's creation of procedural protections that distinguish the death penalty both in terms of State-motivated decisions and in terms of punishments.

The imposition of death as punishment by its very nature is the most cruel and the most unusual.[38] It is a punishment of no return for those upon whom it is imposed, as well as for the community on whose behalf it is imposed. As a result it suffers both heightened restrictions in terms of who may receive the penalty, but also heightened review once the punishment is handed down. It may be overturned in ways that are not available for other punishments. At least in terms of judicial review, courts seem far more willing to adopt novel judicial reasoning when it comes to overturning a death penalty than they are in undoing even a life without parole sentence.

This is not to say that the death penalty is per se in violation of the Eighth Amendment; the Court, despite its restrictions on the death penalty, has been willing to bless its implementation so long as it is not arbitrarily distributed and not cruelly executed.[39] But it is to say that it is a punishment that will receive extraordinary judicial scrutiny.

Death and Process

As a practical matter, in comparison to other State-sanctioned or -caused deaths, the death penalty lends itself to a vigorous procedural framework. By its very nature it offers a known or predictable moment of harm. A citizen sentenced to death is not left to wait and wonder when he will meet his end. Even as his case winds its way slowly through the appellate process he knows an execution date or at times many execution dates. He knows approximately how he may die and that the State will be the cause of that death.

With this certainty the State is readily able to install procedural protections around this known moment of the State's action against its citizenry. Beyond this, it is constitutionally necessary to do so. At those predictable and controllable

[37] Fredric M. Bloom, "State Courts Unbound," 93 *Cornell Law Review* 501 (2008): 545–46 (noting the Eighth Amendment's shifting standards with regard to the death penalty).

[38] *Furman* v. *Georgia*, 408 U.S. 238, 290 (1972) (Brennan, J., concurring).

[39] In *Callins* v. *Collins*, Justice Blackmun urged the abandonment of the death penalty as an irretrievably flawed system; this position, however, was not adopted by the majority and cert was denied on the case. 501 U.S. 1141, 1145 (1994).

moments of contact – whether they be expulsion from a school, termination of a right, commitment to a mental heath facility, arrest, or execution – there is a moment that can be designated and recognized in advance as the time sub-zero when the State will take an action and a harm will result to the subject of that action – the citizen.[40] To ensure that the action conforms with community expectations – be they constitutional requirements as articulated by the Court or some more amorphous concept like justice or fairness – procedure is put in place and constantly revised to achieve these illusive goals.

In contrast, less finite concepts and moments of State caused harm tend to elude formal process or to be subject to only minimal review prior to realization of the harm. Arguably every decision to create or enforce law spawns a consequence and often one that will deprive the citizenry of some liberty. Sometimes the risk is more apparent, on the surface; other times it is more opaque. The decision to arm police officers and to militarize the police is premised on the barely implicit understanding that there will be times when officers pull their guns (or use other weapons) to secure a suspect or protect themselves and others, and still other times when officers will fire their weapons and kill a citizen. Sometimes that decision to use the weapon will be a righteous one, a correct calculation of the risk posed and the available options. But other times it will not, and an innocent citizen will die because of an error in judgment.

Even more mundane decisions carry an imbedded risk of death, however distant from the decision itself. Setting a speed limit involves a calculation of the number of lives risked or saved by the chosen number. Decisions to fund or defund particular programs may, given time, result in a citizen's death.[41] Inevitably any of these decisions may err in their cost-benefit analysis. More citizens may die than expected. Likewise the State's culpability in those deaths may exceed original projections.

Still we as citizens both witness these errors and (for the most part) accept them with little promise of process or remedy when they occur. There are exceptions of course, but for the most part criminal liability for such deaths does not exist.[42] A fellow motorist may be charged with vehicular homicide even if traveling the

---

[40] For a general discussion of this proximity of harm and process, see *Zinermon v. Burch*, 494 U.S. 113 (1990).

[41] The law admittedly struggles to draw lines around such calculations that are often distant causes to a nearer harm. Should the blacksmith be charged with treason when he fails to properly attach the horse's shoe? *See* For want of a nail, the shoe was lost,/For want of a shoe, the horse was lost,/For want of a horse, the rider was lost,/For want of a rider, the message was lost,/For want of a message, the battle was lost,/For want of a battle, the war was lost,/For want of a war, the kingdom was lost,/For want of a nail, the world was lost and *Massachusetts v. EPA*, 549 U.S. 497, 546 (2007) (Roberts, C.J. dissenting) (citing for want of a nail to discuss chains of causation).

[42] Civil liability may also be limited. Section 1983 has been interpreted to provide qualified immunity to government actors. *See generally Anderson v. Creighton*, 483 U.S. 635, 640 (1987) (holding that a state actor is entitled to qualified immunity unless he or she acted unreasonably under clearly established law).

speed limit, provided there is evidence of some other negligence. But the State will not assign liability to itself for designating a speed limit that, even when followed, carries a risk of producing a death.

Some process does exist around such moments of State-"caused" death – even when the causation is a distant or meandering chain. The very calculation of the risk in the first place is a type of process – a process that may well be revisited if the death toll mounts in the face of speed-limit compliance. In the context of police use of force, an array of state agencies set guidelines and require training of officers on the appropriate use of force.[43] Government actuaries measure the probability of death for legislative and agency decisions. In this sense, even in the face of distant harm, there is still a process.

This process, however, takes place out of context. It either contemplates the harm in the abstract before any action or in the real after the actual harm. Speed limits are calculated and posted in advance – before the driver ever gets into his vehicle, travels the speed limit, and still kills another or himself because the rate set was too high. School lunch programs are defunded in the interest of balancing state budgets long before their former recipient starves. The officer trains on the appropriate use of force before he enters the field and draws his weapon.

If death results from any of these decisions, there are review processes in place. Commissions may sift through the original calculations and question their accuracy. In the case of officer-involved shootings, prosecutors may refer a case to a criminal grand jury or seek to indict by information.[44] As a result of these retrospective reviews the underlying laws or policies that created the harm may be revisited or modified – presumably in the hope of minimizing or preventing future harm.

Unlike the death penalty there is no moment of process (or not the same type of process) that springs up prior to these State-initiated deaths – no appellate court urges that a speed limit or funding was miscalculated. The Supreme Court does not stay the bullet before it leaves the officer's gun to counsel caution and to offer the insight that the object in the suspect's hand is a cellphone or a toy or a trick of the imagination. Whatever process exists for the victims of these State-initiated deaths it is more distant and does not address their particular harm or injury.

Likewise, there is no Eighth Amendment based substantive constitutional claim upon which a victim of these state actions might claim relief. Absent some evidence that defunding or a speed limit or an officer-involved shooting was punitive, the

---

[43] The Department of Justice tracks state and local police use of force guidelines. These are available at: www.nij.gov/topics/law-enforcement/officer-safety/use-of-force/pages/welcome.aspx.

[44] Recent cases involving death by police or while in police custody have garnered much attention and led to increased guidelines. Such cases include (but of course are not limited to) Eric Garner (New York), Michael Brown (Missouri), Freddie Grey (Maryland), and Sandra Bland (Texas).

Eighth Amendment remains indifferent no matter how cruel or unusual their machinations or result. Victims of police violence may have a distant claim to a Fourth Amendment violation, but even this is tenuous.

WHY NOT ENOUGH PROCESS? OR WHAT WE WILL
AND WILL NOT ACCEPT

In all this, the death penalty is indeed different. And so it is afforded a degree of process that eludes other state decisions that may produce a death. But this effort to differentiate also belies similarities. The death penalty is a State-imposed death and, just as with any State-imposed decision, it is the product of larger social forces. As recent decisions have noted, the penalty persists because it remains socially accept-able.[45] Whatever shifting interpretations of justice and the Eighth Amendment may permeate the Court's decisions, the penalty is favored by a sufficient portion of the population to allow its survival. Likewise, other State decisions that may produce death are accepted as part of a permissible risk of governance and larger social order.

Whether speaking of the death penalty or another decision that may produce death, part of this acceptability may stem from a sense of community well being. In the context of the death penalty, acceptance of the punishment may be the product of a belief that a community's interests are best served if it can impose, or least has the potential to impose, a death sentence.[46] The fact that this sentence is imposed improperly – either because its subject is in fact innocent or because of some procedural deficiency – may not undo (and as Professor Medwed argues does not undo) the belief that the death penalty both serves a valuable role and, even when administered improperly, may achieve its deterrent purpose.[47] In many ways this calculus is akin to other acceptance of risk inherent in State regulation.

We may accept that any given speed limit will result in some senseless and avoidable deaths, but we may still see a value in allowing the State to set the limit because we cannot or do not want to imagine a world where no limit exists. In such a world we fear that the death rate would be higher if citizens were left to create their own speed limits or no limits were ever set. To buy into a capital punishment system is to accept some imperfections in execution (no pun intended) because such errors either still produce a benefit (citizens feel safer, they are less likely to commit crimes

---

[45] *Kennedy v. Louisiana* spoke in terms of the social acceptance of the death penalty for particular types of crime. In *Gregg v. Georgia*, the Court spoke of evolving standards of decency which require a constant vigilance to ensure that the administration of the death penalty conforms to social expectations and standards. Prof. LaChance's piece also discusses the social tradition of the death penalty.

[46] *See* Robinson and Darley, "The Utility of Desert," 453 (describing social reasons for punishment including the death penalty).

[47] Medwed at 90.

themselves), or because the world without the punishment seems more chaotic than the world with it.

But something else is also afoot that aligns the death penalty with other deaths that are the product of State action. The death penalty is not evenly distributed across all populations or across all citizenry.[48] First, only some states impose the death penalty and the federal government, while having a death penalty, so rarely imposes it. Second, men are far more likely than women to receive such a

---

[48] There are a myriad of studies on the disproportionate application of the death penalty. Here are a few: David C. Baldus et al., *Equal Justice and the Death Penalty: A Legal and Empirical Analysis* (1990); Barry Nakell & Kenneth Hardy, *Arbitrariness of the Death Penalty* (1987); Stephen D. Arkin, "Discrimination and Arbitrariness in Capital Punishment: An Analysis of Post-Furman Murder Cases in Dade County, Florida, 1973–1976," 33 *Stanford Law Review* 75 (1980): 75–76; Arnold Barnett, "Some Distribution Patterns for the Georgia Death Sentence," 18 *U.C. Davis Law Review* 1327 (1985): 1327; Leigh B. Bienen et al., "The Reimposition of Capital Punishment in New Jersey: The Role of Prosecutorial Discretion," 41 *Rutgers Law Review* 27 (1988): 46–66; William J. Bowers, "The Pervasiveness of Arbitrariness and Discrimination under Post-Furman Capital Statutes," 74 *Journal of Criminal Law and Criminology* 1067 (1983): 1076–77; William J. Bowers & Glenn L. Pierce, "Arbitrariness and Discrimination under Post-Furman Capital Statutes," 26 *Crime and Delinquency* 563 (1980): 563; Sheldon Ekland-Olson, "Structured Discretion, Racial Bias and the Death Penalty: The First Decade after Furman in Texas," 69 *Social Science Quarterly* (1988): 853; Linda A. Foley, "Florida after the Furman Decision: The Effect of Extralegal Factors on the Processing of Capital Offense Cases," 5 *Behavioral Science and Law* (1987): 457; Linda A. Foley & Richard S. Powell, "The Discretion of Prosecutors, Judges, and Juries in Capital Cases," 7 *Criminal Justice Review* 16 (1982): 16; Samuel R. Gross & Robert Mauro, "Patterns of Death: An Analysis of Racial Disparities in Capital Sentencing and Homicide Victimization," 37 *Stanford Law Review* 27 (1984): 27; Thomas J. Keil & Gennaro F. "Vito, Race and the Death Penalty in Kentucky Murder Trials: An Analysis of Post-Gregg Outcomes," 7 *Justice Quarterly* 189(1990): 189; Thomas J. Keil & Gennaro F. Vito, "Race, Homicide Severity, and Application of the Death Penalty: A Consideration of the Barnett Scale," 27 *Criminology* 511 (1989): 511; Gary Kleck, "Racial Discrimination in Criminal Sentencing: A Critical Evaluation of the Evidence with Additional Evidence on the Death Penalty," 46 *American Sociology Review* 783 (1981): 783; Peter W. Lewis et al., "A Post-Furman Profile of Florida's Condemned - A Question of Discrimination in Terms of the Race of the Victim and a Comment on *Spenkelink v. Wainwright*," 9 *Stetson Law Review* 1(1979): 1; Elizabeth Lynch Murphy, "Application of the Death Penalty in Cook County," 73 *Illinois Bar Journal* 90 (1984): 90; Raymond Paternoster & Ann Marie Kazyaka, "The Administration of the Death Penalty in South Carolina: Experiences over the First Few Years," 39 *South Carolina Law Review* 245 (1988): 278–79; Michael L. Radelet & Glenn Pierce, "Race and Prosecutorial Discretion in Homicide Cases," 19 *Law and Society* 587 (1985): 587; Michael L. Radelet, "Racial Characteristics and the Imposition of the Death Penalty," 46 *American Sociology Review* 918 (1981): 918; Michael L. Radelet & Margaret Vandiver, "The Florida Supreme Court and Death Penalty Appeals," 74 *Journal of Criminal Law and Criminology* 913 (1983): 913; Marc Riedel, "Discrimination in the Imposition of the Death Penalty: A Comparison of the Characteristics of Offenders Sentenced Pre-Furman and Post-Furman," 49 *Temple Law Quarterly* 261(1976): 261; M. Dwayne Smith, "Patterns of Discrimination in Assessments of the Death Penalty: The Case of Louisiana," 15 *Journal of Criminal Justice* (1987): 279; Gennaro F. Vito & Thomas J. Keil, "Capital Sentencing in Kentucky: An Analysis of the Factors Influencing Decision Making in the Post-*Gregg* Period," 79 *Journal of Criminal Law and Criminology* (1988): 483; and Hans Zeisel, "Race Bias in the Administration of the Death Penalty: The Florida Experience," 95 *Harvard Law Review* 456 (1981): 456.

sentence,[49] and men of color are far more likely than white men to receive the penalty. Third those who kill white victims, particularly white female victims, are far more likely to receive the death penalty.[50] This suggests endless possibilities.

To the extent that the death penalty is meant to deter, perhaps it is less effective or persuasive in particular populations. Perhaps some jurisdictions provide better lawyers, or exercise more tempered discretion, or have less death-inclined decision makers – all affecting the overall statistics. It may also be true that the death penalty is a product of social constructs and biases that render us, as a national community, far more likely to accept some as death eligible and others simply as not.[51]

Seen through this lens, marginalized communities bear the force of the death penalty just as they bear a disproportionate force of some other governmental decisions that lead to death. While such decisions may have a ripple effect on all members of a community, for some the ripples are closer to the epicentre of impact. Poor children may not eat when school lunch programs are cut, poor women may not get prenatal or other prophylactic care when women's health care funding is reduced, and men of color are more likely to be shot by the police, suffer over-policing, be incarcerated, or receive death sentences than their white brothers or their sisters.

Certainly this is painting policy with a broad, bordering on irresponsible, brush, but maybe such is the nature of afterwords that try to broadly discern trends or truths. Decisions to impose a death penalty or to cut a school lunch program or to send armed police patrols into a neighborhood are inevitably complex and multilayered. But at their core, each involves a final calculation of what we as a community will accept and what we will not. They are talisman for our communal values and the legal infringements on such values that we will tolerate in the name of "law and order." There are moments when law exceeds acceptable levels. In the 1980's when Ronald Reagan's administration sought to reduce its budget by, among other things, declaring "ketchup" a vegetable for the purpose of meeting school lunch guidelines, citizens reacted.[52] Ultimately, in the face of public outcry, the Reagan adminis-tration withdrew the proposal.[53]

---

[49] Steven F. Shatz and Naomi Shatz, "Chivalry Is Not Dead: Murder, Gender, and the Death Penalty," 27 *Berkeley Journal of Gender Law and Justice* 64(2012): 64 and Jenny E. Carroll, "Images of Women and Capital Sentencing among Female Offenders: Exploring the Outer Limits of the Eighth Amendment and Articulated Theories of Justice," 75 *Texas Law Review* 1413 (1997): 1413.

[50] The Baldus study *supra* note 48 which was referenced in *McCleskey v. Kemp* argued that the race of the victim was the primary factor in determining the probability of a death sentence. *See* McCleskey v. Kemp, 481 U.S. 279 (1987). In *McCleskey*, the Court ultimately rejected the use of empirical data to make an equal protection claim.

[51] By extension, the *Baldus* study seems to suggest that certain victims (white women) are considered more worthy of a penalty of death.

[52] Ronald Reagan proposed the described cuts in the school lunch program as part of the Omnibus Spending Bills of 1980 and 1981. H.R. 7765 – The Omnibus Reconciliation Act of 1980, December 5, 1980; H.R. 3982, "Omnibus Reconciliation Act of 1981, August 13, 1981.

[53] Benjamin Weinraub, "Washington Talk; Briefing," *New York Times*, September 18, 2011.

The proposed Omnibus Spending Bill was consistent with Reagan's rhetoric of reducing social welfare programs in the interests of balancing the budget. In fact, prior reduction in school food programs had not met similar mainstream reaction. The effort to designate ketchup a vegetable, however, seemed to run so counter to community expectations, even among a populous that valued a conservative economic approach, that it was rejected by the citizens themselves even as formal government actors seemed poised to accept it. It is hard to say precisely what sparked this citizen reaction. Perhaps it was the absurdity of a condiment designated as a vegetable in a nation that prided itself on its abundance – certainly this was one of the prevalent narratives among those who protested the proposal. But another argument seems equally likely, though less often articulated – more people reacted to the decision because more people were affected by it. Unlike other cuts in school-provided nutrition programs, this decision affected all children who received their lunches from school cafeterias. Whether the child was rich, poor, or middle class, he or she would receive ketchup as one of two recommended vegetable servings.

In the case of ketchup-is-not-a-vegetable activism, community sentiment directly pushed change. The citizens rallied against law that failed to properly balance the benefit (a reduced budget) against the harm (children eating ketchup in lieu of actual vegetables). But community power can be imagined more broadly. Sometimes formal government actors use power in ways that, while contrary to local values, may reflect larger communal values and thereby achieve another sort of balance between local, state, and national citizenries.

When Oklahoma Governor Mary Fallin was presented a bill that would have criminalized doctor-performed abortions in her state she vetoed it.[54] In explaining her decision she stated that the law would have effectively outlawed abortions in Oklahoma. She vetoed the bill despite her own anti-abortion position and strong support for the bill among the state's citizenry. She based her decision instead on the fact that the bill was an end run around the Supreme Court's decision in *Roe v. Wade*, which remains binding precedent. She reasoned not only that the bill would likely be found unconstitutional by the Court, costing the citizens of Oklahoma valuable resources to defend the bill, but more fundamentally that the bill undermined the Rule of Law in a nation in which state governments must at times yield to national sentiment. In this, the Governor in her formal role as the state's top executive weighed the values the bill put into play: the community's apparent rejection of abortion and the need for the rule of law and to obey the national Constitution as interpreted by the nation's highest court.

These cases suggest that there are times when laws run so contrary to citizen values that the people, or some formal actor, will push back against the law. Most

[54] Erik Eckholm, "Oklahoma Governor Vetoes Bill That Would Charge Abortion Doctors," *New York Times*, May 20, 2016.

laws, however, suffer no similar pushback, because they do not run so counter to the community's most sacred values. In most instances, the citizen's relationship with the law is relatively passive. Laws are simply something that happen – either in passage, application, or interpretation – to the vast majority of us. Our involvement in any given law is usually little more than a vote for the person who may one day make, apply, or interpret the law or appoint someone else to do so. Low voter turnout and increasing trends toward disenfranchisement suggest that, for many, the involvement does not even span that far.[55]

For the most part, we as citizens accept law and discretionary decisions surrounding law as a passive act of being governed. That we protest some laws while accepting the vast majority of others suggests that most laws are within the margins of what we expect from a government that sets the boundaries in which we live our lives and potentially face our deaths. This expectation and the acceptance of law that it produces may be the product of many things – apathy, a busy schedule, the mind numbingly boring nature of policy debates, the elitism inherent in republican democracies, disenfranchisement. The list could go on, but it doesn't change the reality that for the vast majority of citizens some other matter is far more pressing than a challenge to the law. As depressing as this may seem, it does allow the representative democracy, in all its glorious imperfections, to function. And of course, even apathetic or busy citizens may protest the decisions of formal actors at times.

The persistence of the death penalty would seem to suggest that it falls within the range of what at least some jurisdictions will accept from the government, even in the face of evidence that it is improperly administered. Part of that acceptance, I suspect, has little to do with moral weighing, but is based on a belief that enough checks exist within the system such that odds favor a "fair" application of the penalty. This assumes both that there is a morally permissible application of the penalty and that even erroneous or improper application of the penalty may support a retributive function. Put another way, once you accept that the penalty is morally right or necessary, it may still survive and be consistent with social values even if it is not always perfectly administered. As others have argued, even the execution of an innocent may produce a deterrent effect.

Beyond this faith in accuracy or theoretical values promoted by the penalty, I suspect that for at least some, allegiance to this ultimate punishment stems from the fact that the penalty touches their lives in theory only. While it is the ultimate weapon that ensures order and safety (if one buys the deterrence theory), it by its very definition affects a small portion of the population – the worst of the worst. Its rarity, its complexity, and its distance from the daily existence of most citizens renders its existence palatable, particularly when coupled with the legislatively created, executively adopted, judicially reviewed and endorsed narrative that only the worst of the

---

[55] Jenny E. Carroll, "Nullification as Law," 102 *Georgetown Law Journal* 579 (2014): 602.

worst will ever receive the sentence. We as citizens accept the penalty because we accept that it will never "happen to us." It is more akin to a reduction in aid to a foreign country than to making our children eat ketchup. The State, after all, does not sentence most citizens or even their neighbors to die – that fate is reserved for the most marginalized people whom we as a collective are taught to fear and revile from an early age.[56] They are nothing like us, and so their deaths are distant events that we hear about, but rarely witness.[57]

This acceptance of the death penalty based on its "guaranteed rarity" is consistent with the implicit bias of our collective conscience. Implicit bias is an underlying thought system that allows each of us as people to draw ever narrowing circles around those who are like us and those who are not. Those who are like us, we protect, embrace, and keep from eating ketchup. Those who are not like us, we fear. Those not like us require the law's most brutal power to ensure the safety of those like us. We accept the death penalty not only because of its promise of process and review, but because we believe both that it will not happen to us and that it will only happen to people not like us that deserve the sentence. Our biases – implicit and explicit – that teach us to fear the harm that poor, black or Latino men might cause in our midst tell us we need the death penalty even with its costs and its errors in application. The death penalty will maintain that ever-precarious balance between the lawlessness of the other and the safety of ourselves. It reinforces a circular logic that it is OK to execute a disproportionate number of men of color because they pose a greater threat. We know they pose a greater threat because they commit more death eligible crimes and those who make the decisions of whether or not to seek the death penalty choose them more often.

In the end, this is what bothers me most about the claim that death is different. In this, death is not that different. The calculus that drives a death sentence is more closely aligned with the police-involved shootings or speed limits or funding decisions than might be discernable at first glance. They are all products of a construct that dictates when it is OK for the State to kill its citizenry, and when it is not. Whatever procedure surrounds the death penalty, it is designed to do what has eluded other governmental decisions that may result in a death – to stop a mistake or an injustice from occurring. That it may be imperfect in realizing that goal does not lessen the value or the burden of the attempt. Yet this leaves the lingering question: in the effort to treat death as different, have we overlooked how it is the same as other legislative decisions that produce deaths that are collectively accepted by the citizenry? Have we worked to construct a process around one machination of death while ignoring that it is part of a larger system that renders the life and death of some less remarkable than others?

[56] Cynthia Lee, "Making Race Salient: Trayvon Martin and Implicit Bias in a Not Yet Post-Racial Society," 91 *North Carolina Law Review* 1555 (2013): 1557; Jerry Kang et al., "Implicit Bias in the Courtroom," 59 *UCLA Law Review* 1124 (2012): 1124.

[57] LaChance at 123.

CONCLUSION

In these words after others' commentaries that confirm or designate the death penalty as different, I concur in part and dissent in the rest. Capital punishment is different. It claims a finality that other punishments can only come by in a roundabout way. It is also different in that it enjoys more review and more resources to ensure that this governmental decision that requires no special effort to link to the death of a citizen is applied fairly, accurately, and judiciously.

But it is also the same. It is the same as any governmental decision that relies on the compliance and acceptance of the citizenry to remain law. It is the same as any other governmental decision that produces death for the citizen. Like its fatal brethren it has managed to carve out a space in the collective imagination of at least some of the citizenry that reassures that the death was not without reason and justification. The police shoot young men of color because they were hostile, or disrespectful, or had objects in their hands. The State executes convicted men of color at a disproportionally high rate not because of the color of their skin but because of the danger of their crimes. Each of these decisions is the product of discretion, discretion fueled by our perception that such men are more dangerous than all others.

To treat death as different is to mask that it is symptomatic of larger social values and norms that play out in arenas with far less process and far less review. Until the underlying biases that fuel these community values and norms are altered, no amount of process will render decisions truly just. Just as we rallied against ketchup as a vegetable, our collective selves should rally around the position that State caused deaths, however distant from us or the decisions that sparked them, demand scrutiny, process, and equity.

Index

9 781316 609019